EARLY MAN IN AMERICA

EARLY MAN

A Study in Prehistory

A Publication of
THE TEXAS MEMORIAL MUSEUM

Illustrations by
HAL STORY

By E. H. SELLARDS

IN AMERICA

GREENWOOD PRESS, PUBLISHERS
NEW YORK

UNIVERSITY OF TEXAS PRESS
AUSTIN 12

THOMAS NELSON AND SONS LTD

Parkside Works Edinburgh 9
3 Henrietta Street London WC2
312 Flinders Street Melbourne C1
5 Parker's Buildings   Burg Street   Cape Town

Thomas Nelson and Sons (Canada) Ltd
91–93 Wellington Street West   Toronto 1

Société Française d'Editions Nelson
25 rue Henri Barbusse Paris V^e

To my wife
Anna Alford Sellards

Acknowledgments

GRATEFUL ACKNOWLEDGMENT is made to all whose writings are listed in the Bibliography and to many others who have directly or indirectly aided in this undertaking. Also acknowledgment is made by the author for permission to adapt for this book certain material which was published originally in the *Bulletin of the Geological Society of America* and in *American Antiquity*. The extent to which the author has become indebted to others in the preparation of the publication is indicated by acknowledgments in the text and by frequent references to literature.

Thanks are due also to the Bureau of Economic Geology and to J. T. Lonsdale, director, for co-operation given in geologic field studies.

A part of the cost of the publication has been generously contributed by the Humble Oil and Refining Company of Houston, Texas.

Special indebtedness is acknowledged to associates in the Texas Memorial Museum including Glen L. Evans, Grayson E. Meade, Adolph H. Witte, and artist Hal M. Story, and in the Department of Anthropology of The University of Texas, to Thomas N. Campbell and Alex D. Krieger. Others who have aided the author in excavations made in recent years are Richmond Bronaugh, Louis Griffith, Gerald V. Harris, James Meador, Charles E. Mear, Carl Moore, George Moreland, Pat Noel, Albert Potter, Benton Poyner, F. N. Rochat, Kenneth Rochat, James Vick, and John White. Special acknowledgment is made for editorial assistance to Josephine Casey and Sue James.

ELIAS HOWARD SELLARDS

Austin, Texas
June, 1952

Contents

ix

List of Illustrations

xiii

xiv

RESTORATION OF LARGE MAMMALS OF THE LATE PLEISTOCENE

xvi

EARLY MAN IN AMERICA

Introduction

ONE WHO UNDERTAKES studies in prehistory quickly finds himself facing the difficult questions of the place and time of the origin of the human race. Man has not always inhabited the earth, nor has the earth always been a place suitable for human habitation. During earliest geologic time the earth was naked and barren and would not support man or other animal or plant life. But conditions changed and the face of the earth and the waters of the sea gradually came to be populated with myriads of primitive organisms. Then through succeeding eons there followed a procession of varying plants and animals. It is as though the earth were a stage across which passed an endless succession of changing scenes and changing life. Each succeeding group and kind held the stage temporarily and disappeared to be seen no more.

We, ourselves, who are now a part of the moving scene, are privileged through records of the past to obtain glimpses of this great procession. No actual break appears in the moving panorama, but there are outstanding epochs. Among these are, in chronological order, the Azoic, with, in so far as is known, no life; the Archeozoic, the time of archaic life; the Proterozoic, the time of early life; the early Paleozoic, or ancient life, during which invertebrate animals predominated; and thereafter, in succession, the age of fishes, the age of reptiles, and the age of mammals. Into this passing scene man entered, possibly one or two million years ago. At first he was not readily distinguished from some other animals. However, in addition to standing upright or nearly so, he possessed superior intelligence. A broken stick, useless to animals about him, became in his hands a weapon of defense and offense. A stone of suitable weight and size became an aid in securing game and in warding off enemies. From the occasional use of ready-made objects, he progressed slowly until he learned to fashion tools by his own hands. He learned also to utilize such fires as may have accidentally occurred, and later to kindle flames where none previously existed; he also learned to use fire to ward off attack by animals. With the aid of fire he was able to extend his range over the earth. These simple accomplishments were momentous in the life of man. Here for the first time was an inhabitant of the earth able to defend himself with more than brute strength, to adapt objects in nature to his purpose, and to make and use tools that previously did not exist. Thus was initiated the age of man on earth. From a weakling he in time became master of all animals. To these accomplishments with advancing civilization others have been added. The inventive genius that resulted in shaping tools has extended itself to devices that enormously increase the powers of man, until there now looms the possibility of mankind being freed from the heaviest burdens of life. The way is open for a glorious future, and if man has the intellectual and spiritual capacity to do so, he may walk therein.

The place of origin of man is believed to have been in the eastern hemisphere. The time of the first migrations into the western hemisphere is a problem on which progress is being made, although much remains to be discovered. Several genera and species of fossil men are recognized in the eastern hemisphere. In the western hemisphere there is recognized only the one species *Homo sapiens*.

This publication, a chapter in prehistory, is concerned with records of early man in the western hemisphere. Of the American localities that contain records of early man some are here described in detail while others are treated more briefly or appear only in the List of Localities and Index to Literature. The localities selected for detailed description are those that seem particularly well adapted to illustrate the conditions of occurrence, manner of preservation, age of deposits, types of artifacts, and development and succession of cultural groups.

No extended discussion of fossilized human skeletal remains is given in this volume. For discussion of skeletal characteristics of early man the reader is referred to the several papers of Stewart, Hooten, Roberts, Hrdlicka, and others listed in the bibliography.

Geologic Time Divisions

The term "early man" is here used to include man of some appreciable antiquity in a geologic sense. It is not possible to limit exactly the term "early," which, in any case, is relative. The earliest human remains, found in the eastern hemisphere, are said to occur in formations as old at least as the middle Pleistocene period of geologic time, while in America the earliest human relics known are found in what appears to be the latter part of the Pleistocene. In this publication the writer will, insofar as is practicable, consider as early man all occurrences of man or relics of man of such antiquity as to be associated with species of animals or plants that are now extinct; those that occur in geologic formations which appear to be of an age equivalent to those which elsewhere contain extinct species, as in some of the river terraces; and those that, lacking both stratigraphic equivalents and diagnostic fossils, nevertheless afford evidence of having been formed under climatic conditions notably different from the present. Even with these limitations the dividing line between early man and his counterpart, late or recent man, is still indefinite, and necessarily so. Time is continuous and man's habitation of the continent, once fully established, was probably continuous. As in modern history the time divisions established are for convenience of discussion. In delimiting such epochs, however, the historian takes advantage of such major natural divisions as may exist. This principle of utilizing major breaks in continuity of events is used likewise in establishing subdivisions in geologic history. Human history and geologic history are, after all, parts of the one larger science, earth history.

In the accompanying chart the geologic time divisions are entered in order, the oldest at the bottom. The human materials found in the western hemisphere are from the three latest divisions, Wisconsin, Archaic, and Modern. The exact placing of the dividing line between the Pleistocene and the Holocene or Recent throughout America will require long continued investigation. For the purpose of this publication the Pleistocene is considered as extending until the time of disappearance of most of the large mammalian species.

5

Table of Geologic Time Divisions

Era	Period or System	Epoch or Series
Cenozoic	Holocene (Recent)	Modern Archaic
	Pleistocene	Wisconsin Sangamon Illinoian Yarmouth Kansan Aftonian Nebraskan
	Pliocene Miocene Oligocene Eocene Paleocene	Subdivisions omitted
Mesozoic	Cretaceous Jurassic Triassic	Subdivisions omitted
Paleozoic	Permian Pennsylvanian Mississippian Devonian Silurian Ordovician Cambrian	Subdivisions omitted
Proterozoic Archeozoic Azoic	Subdivisions omitted	

Age Determinations

Age determinations may be actual in years or merely relative with respect to other formations. The relative age of sedimentary formations and deposits is determined primarily and often chiefly by superposition. This obvious fact is sometimes referred to as the "law of superposition," which means simply that any given stratum or horizon normally is younger than that on which it rests. Seeming exceptions to this law arise where igneous rocks have intruded existing formations or where the formations have been folded to the extent of being overturned or overthrust. Fortunately, the investigator will not often meet with such apparent deviations from the law of superposition in determining the relative age of deposits containing human relics.

In applying the law of superposition, however, the observer must not be misled by relative elevation of strata, which may be quite a different thing from superposition. Thus a river system, entrenching itself by cutting downward, may progress by stages and in so doing form terrace deposits bordering the streams, the high terraces being older than the low terraces. Also, as a result of faulting, a given stratum may be displaced to a level above other strata of younger age. In neither instance, however, is there an exception to the law of superposition. The law of relative age by superposition, supplemented by another law—the orderly succession of faunas and floras on the earth—has enabled geologists to determine the relative age of the major divisions of the earth's sedimentary formations.

Age in years of geologic eras and other time divisions has long been a vexing problem to geologists. A great advance was made when it was discovered near the beginning of the present century that at least approximate dating in years can be obtained for some formations by a study of the disintegration of certain contained radioactive minerals.

Some age determinations in the oldest formations, the pre-Cambrian (including the three eras Azoic, Archeozoic, and Proterozoic), based on the uranium-lead ratios, are as follows: South Manitoba, Canada, 2,200 million years; Great Bear Lake, Canada, 1,400 million years; Wilberforce, Ontario, Canada, 1,050 million years; Barringer Hill, Texas, 1,040 million years; Quebec, Canada, 900 million years; and Ontario, Canada, 800 million years (Hurley, 1950, p. 142).

Uranium, thorium, and other minerals used in determining the age of the older formations have not been used in fixing the age of the late geologic formations because these minerals are not suitable for measuring the relatively short intervals of time with which it is necessary to deal in human history. However, in recent years considerable progress has been made in determining the age of the relatively recent formations by a new procedure known as the radiocarbon method. In a paper written in 1946, Libby, noting that nuclear physical data indicate that cosmic ray neutrons produce radioactive Carbon[14] from atmospheric nitrogen, concluded that "Since the age of the earth is much greater than the life of C[14], a radioactive equilibrium must exist in which the rate of disintegration of C[14] is equal to the rate of produc-

7

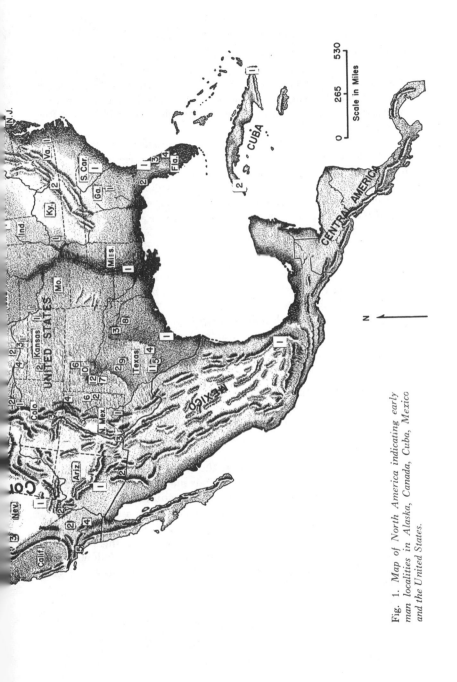

Fig. 1. Map of North America indicating early man localities in Alaska, Canada, Cuba, Mexico and the United States.

tion." He suggests also that radioactive carbon should be present in living matter. The presence of radioactive carbon in organic materials was proved by Anderson and others (1947). The rate of disintegration of radioactive carbon was determined by Reid and others in 1946, with supplementary investigations by Engelkemeir and Libby (Rev. Sci. Inst., vol. 21, 1950).

The age determinations made by this method in the Institute for Nuclear Studies of the University of Chicago to September 1, 1950, have been recently published (Arnold and Libby, 1950; Johnson and others, 1951). The probable limit of error is given for each determination. The age determinations made by this method relating directly or indirectly to early human cultures in America are included in the accounts given in this publication of the following localities: Cochise, Arizona; Lime Creek, Nebraska; Gypsum Cave and Leonard Rock Shelter, Nevada; Fort Rock Cave, Oregon; Angostura Reservoir site, South Dakota; Horner site, Wyoming; Palli Aike Cave in South America; and a determination from the Lubbock, Texas, site made and reported subsequent to September 1950 (Libby, letter of Dec. 8, 1950). These and other localities of equal or greater age in North and South America are within the range of early man or Paleo-Indian as the term is here used.

The Arnold-Libby publication contains also a considerable number of determinations of localities of later age representing modern or relatively modern Indians. These later localities of Indian habitations ranging in age from somewhat less than 6,000 years to entirely modern times are not here described or listed.

In the process of fossilization, bones undergo change in organic and mineral constituents. The rate of change varies with varying conditions. However, bones deposited at the same time at a given locality and preserved under identical conditions may reasonably be expected to undergo alteration or modification of constituents at somewhat the same rate. For this reason chemical analysis may afford a means of determining whether man and animal bones found in a given formation are approximately of the same age. Localities in this publication to which a test of this kind has been applied are the following: Los Angeles, California; Natchez, Mississippi; and Melbourne and Vero, Florida.

Conditions of Occurrence and Preservation of Early Man Records

The records relating to any given race of men or species of animals or plants usually become increasingly difficult to obtain with the passage of time. This, of course, is due to erosion and the constant shifting of materials on the face of the earth by wind and water and by disintegration and decay, which are always at work. The character of the material has much to do with its chance of preservation. Fabrics of all kinds and artifacts made of wood are preserved only under exceptional conditions, such as occur in very dry caves or shelters and to some extent in peat bogs and tar pits. Some objects, such as bones, are preserved by continued submergence in water which by excluding air prevents oxidation and promotes petrification. Of the artifacts, those made of stone are most capable of relatively permanent preservation under all conditions. Many of these were made with great care and doubtless were objects of great pride to their owners. The several kinds of projectile points have received distinctive names based on some one of the localities at which they have been found, usually a locality where they were found in numbers and in an unmixed or pure culture. Thus, the Folsom point is named from Folsom, New Mexico, and the Plainview point from Plainview, Texas.

The races or tribes who made the projectile points are mostly unknown but for convenience of reference will be referred to by the name of the projectile point or artifact complex which they produced. Thus, those who made the Folsom point are referred to as Folsom man, and those who made the Plainview point as Plainview man. It is possible, of course, that many tribes or family groups used the same kind of projectile point. Thus, the Folsom point was used throughout a considerable part of North America, just as the bow and arrow, when invented or introduced, spread widely throughout North and South America. Nevertheless, for the present, and until more information is available, this is a convenient method of referring to these early peoples. Pure unmixed localities have been found for many of the named projectile points referred to in this publication.

Some of the extremely important records relating to man which have been preserved—the implements that he made and used, and the animals and plants contemporaneous with him—have been ob-

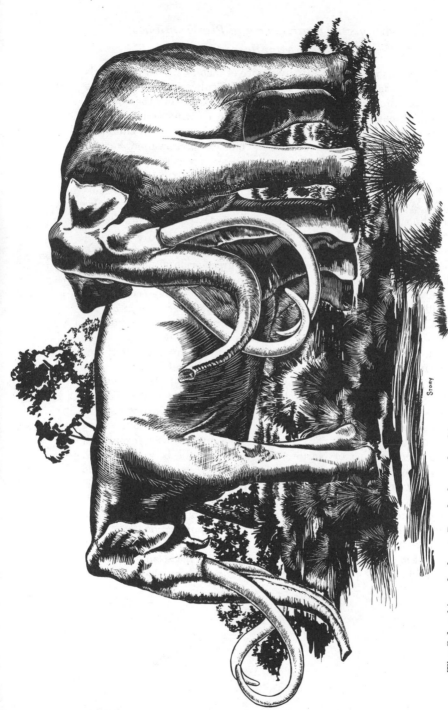

The Columbian elephant, *Parelephas columbi.*

tained from caves. In several such caves record has been found of successive cultures, indicating that the cave had long been used by man either continuously or intermittently. Such localities with super-imposed cultures are particularly helpful in determining relative and, in some instances, actual age. Some of the caves or shelters of North America in which particularly instructive records of early man have been found are the following: Ventana, Arizona; Etna, Gypsum, and Leonard Rock, Nevada; Bishop and Sandia, New Mexico; Fort Rock and Paisley, Oregon; and Kincaid, Texas. Caves located in very dry regions sometimes yield objects that would not otherwise be preserved, including such articles as cloth, fiber, skin, hair, and artifacts made of wood. Thus in Gypsum Cave in Nevada is preserved the hair of a ground sloth, of a species now extinct. This cave also contains objects made of wood. A sloth with hair and skeleton preserved has been found in New Mexico but with no associated human relics. An atlatl, the determined age of which is about 7,038 years, has been found in Leonard Rock Shelter, Nevada; and sandals, age about 9,053 years, have been found in Oregon.

In Alaska and in northern Siberia, animals, including elephants and mastodons, have been found preserved frozen in the ice. In Alaska, implements made by man are found in the frozen earth with or near bones of elephants, mastodons, and other animals, now extinct. But no human body or skeleton contemporaneous with these animals has as yet been found in the frozen earth of the far north.

Open sites, by which is meant sites not in caves or otherwise specially sheltered, are of two kinds—camp sites and hunting sites. It is difficult to say which of these has contributed most to our knowledge of early man. A camp site, especially a site long used by man, often yields much information about the people who lived at that place. In or near the later camp sites graves containing skeletons and man-made objects buried with the dead are frequently found. However, burials recognized as contemporaneous with the very early sites in America have seldom been noted, possibly because the skeletons have disintegrated and wholly disappeared or when found have not been recognized as ancient skeletons.

Hunting sites are not infrequently found representing a kill of either a few or many animals at one time, the large kills being of animals found in herds. In some instances a kill may have resulted from a stampede, as of bison. The Plainview locality, described later, is believed to represent a stampede of these animals. Early man may

13

also have found opportunity for a kill when great droughts caused weakened animals to crowd around a watering place. Tar pits at Rancho la Brea, Los Angeles, California, contain an exceptionally large and varied accumulation of animal skeletons, with only a meager representation of human remains. Animals were evidently trapped in the tar in great numbers, while man, if he inhabited the region at that time, as he probably did, escaped or was rarely trapped. One implement, an atlatl, has been found in the tar pit.

In contrast to the kills of a large number of animals at one time and place are the occurrences of animals killed singly or a few at a time around watering places. The large animals in America killed in this way include elephants, bison, probably mastodons, and possibly horses, camels, and others. Accumulation of a bone bed of appreciable thickness in this way probably represents considerable time and doubtless includes many animals that died a natural death, in addition to those killed by man. The best known localities of this kind are found in the fresh-water lakes and near the headwaters of streams in the High Plains. A small lake on the Baxter ranch in Roosevelt County, New Mexico, described later, affords an illustration of a watering place visited by man and animals through a long period of time. The accumulation of bones of animals and implements made by man are here distributed through at least three successive strata, representing intermittent accumulation over thousands of years.

In considering early man in America it is well to remember that man of 10,000 years ago of the species *Homo sapiens* was structurally much like man of today. In mental aptitude, likewise, he probably did not differ greatly from men now living under similar conditions. His skill as a hunter, if equalled, certainly has not been excelled, notwithstanding the fact that his hunting weapons were spears tipped with stone points of his own handiwork. In the delicate and artistic finish of these points he has revealed a sense of symmetry and beauty, as in his markings on shell, stone, and bone. The extent to which this is true will appear in the descriptions of cultures which follow. Of the cultures of these people there remain, of course, only objects capable of preservation. Culture in a spiritual sense can only be inferred. The term "complex" or "culture complex" may be used to apply to an entire artifact assemblage or industry of a people.

The artifacts here illustrated, except as otherwise indicated, are from the collections of the Texas Memorial Museum and were obtained in connection with excavations made by the Museum and associated departments of the University of Texas. All artifacts illustrated from the Museum collections, with one exception, were obtained *in place* in the formation and stratum to which they are assigned. The exception is Figure 44, in which Folsom points found not in place in Kincaid Shelter, Texas, are included to illustrate the beauty and finish of Folsom workmanship. For illustrations of artifacts not contained in the Texas Memorial Museum collections, credit is given to the source of the artifact or illustration. The courtesy extended by the several institutions concerned in allowing use of these borrowed illustrations is greatly appreciated.

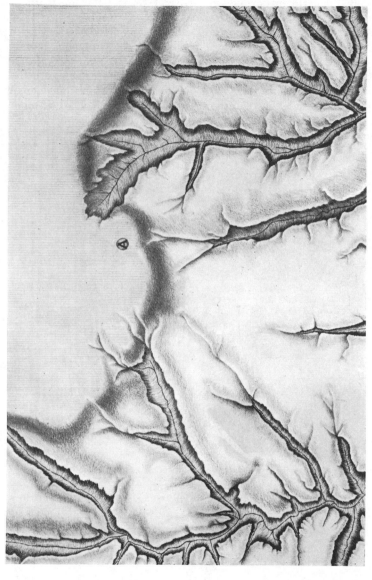

Fig. 2. *Environs of the Miami locality on the Cowan ranch, Roberts County, Texas. Locality at A.*

Hunters of the Plains

To OBTAIN a sufficient year-round food supply was a major undertaking for early man, as it is for most moderns. That which he found at hand varied greatly in kind and in quantity, being abundant in some localities and absent or nearly so in others. A great variety of plant and animal species were undoubtedly utilized, as man must necessarily adapt himself to the conditions existing in the region where he lived. Fruit, nuts, bulbs, and seeds, where abundant, formed an important part of his food; where animals were plentiful and of a kind that could be captured by man, meat became an important part of his diet. This adaptation of eating habits to prevailing conditions is well illustrated by the early man of the plains region who lived with and learned to hunt such great animals as the elephant and the bison. Indeed, among the early tribes hunting reached its maximum development in the Great Plains. Description of several sites will serve to indicate something of the life and habits of these early hunters of the plains.

THE ELEPHANT HUNTERS

Llano Complex and Llano Man

The terms Llano complex and Llano man, taken from the Llano Estacado, or Staked Plains, of Texas and New Mexico, are new and are proposed to include both a complex of artifacts found in place in association with extinct animals in the southern High Plains region of the United States and the people who made and used those artifacts. The principal localities known are Miami, Roberts County, Texas; Blackwater No. 1 locality, Roosevelt County, New Mexico; Dent, Colorado; McLean site, Taylor County, Texas; Naco, Arizona; and Angus, Nebraska. The known artifacts of the complex are bone implements, hammerstone, the projectile point known as Clovis

Fluted, and smaller, non-fluted points and scrapers. The age of Llano man is unknown, although at the Clovis locality in New Mexico the Llano culture underlies and is older than the Folsom culture.

Miami Locality, Roberts County, Texas

Early records of man tend to become obscure with the passage of time. This is well illustrated by a locality on the C. R. Cowan ranch 9 miles northwest of Miami, Roberts County, Texas. Prior to excavation, this locality presented nothing to distinguish it from any other place in the level lands of the Texas plains (Fig. 2). The fact that something unusual existed underground at this point became known when in 1933 Charles Puckett, ploughing deeper than usual on the Cowan ranch, brought bone fragments to the surface (Fig. 2). He reported this discovery to J. A. Mead, County Judge of Roberts County, who had long been interested in fossils and artifacts. The deep ploughing, it may be added, was incident to changed farming practices brought about by the great droughts of the "dust bowl" period of the 1930's. In December 1934, Judge Mead and others, excavating at the locality, obtained four elephant teeth, two leg bones, and several ribs. With the elephant bones, lying close to the ribs and about 20 inches from two of the elephant teeth, was a spear point. This discovery was reported to *Science Service* by Floyd Studer, and a brief statement appeared in *Science News Letter*, February 9, 1935. In 1937, extensive excavations made at the locality under the direction of Glen L. Evans of the University of Texas showed that this spot had been at one time a depression in the level land of the plain which held water and served as a water-hole or pond frequented by elephants (Fig. 3). Remains of several elephants ranging in age from very young to adult were found in the water-hole and with them two additional projectile points and one scraper. The scraper and all the points that have been found were made of flint. After the excavation had been completed the depression was refilled and the spot once more became a part of the Cowan wheat field.

The pond was 75 feet across. Its original depth below the present surface was 9 feet. The first fill that came into the pond was fine silt colored dark by organic matter. This kind of fill accumulated to a thickness of 7 or 7.5 feet in the deepest part of the pond, with lesser thickness at the margins.

The silt is overlaid by a loess stratum about 6 inches thick which pinches out and does not extend fully to the margins of the pond. The

18

Fig. 3. *The Miami locality when excavated to the bone bed.*

silt and the loess contain unidentifiable fragments of bones. Above the loess the fill consists of silt similar to that below.

Within this uppermost unit, above the loess stratum, is a bone bed as indicated in the section (Fig. 4). Over most of the pond the bottom of the bone bed is a few inches above the loess stratum. At the north and east the bone bed, like the loess stratum, lies at a slightly higher elevation than at the south and west.

A mechanical analysis of samples from these several strata has been made by V. E. Barnes of the Bureau of Economic Geology, the University of Texas, showing graphically (Fig. 5) the amount of the material that lodges on screens of mesh 20 to 200 and the amount that passes through the 200-mesh screen for each of the three strata in the pond fill. From these analyses it is seen that the fill in the pond above and below the loess differs from the loess chiefly in that it is darkened by organic matter and contains some aggregate consisting largely of bone fragments. The origin is probably the same as the loess—fine material carried by the wind, to which has been added organic matter and sufficient clay, washed in or carried in by animals, to introduce a small percentage of coarser mineral grains.

The dark clays contain much organic matter, while the loess is almost free of organic matter. It is probable that the pond was a watering place in or around which plants grew and to which animals came to drink and on damp days carried on their feet mud containing

19

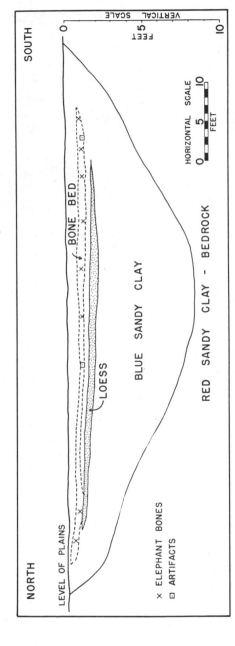

Fig. 4. *North-south section through the deposits of the Miami locality.*

sand which became incorporated with the finer silts. The loess is undoubtedly wind-deposited. It has the characteristics of loess, including numerous vertical tubelets, particles of hornblende, and other minerals. The fill in the pond differs distinctly from the underlying red sandy clay bed-rock, which has considerably larger grains and different mineral composition. The maximum depression, about 9 feet, is somewhat west of the center of the pond.

The ground plan of the Miami locality (Fig. 6) shows the location of the principal bones found in the bone bed. Not all bones originally contained in the bone bed are shown in the figure, poorly preserved and less important bones and bone fragments having been omitted. All remains recovered from the pond are elephant bones. This is unusual, for one would expect in such a pond a mixture of animal remains, including rodents, coyotes, and especially bison, deer, and antelope, all of which must have been present in this region. In con-

Fig. 5. *Graphic representation of mechanical analysis of sediments.* (I) Bone-bearing stratum; (II) loess stratum; (III) lowermost stratum marked "blue sandy clay" in Figure 4.

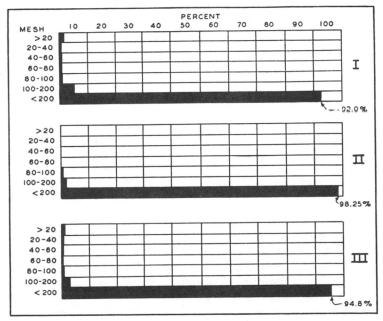

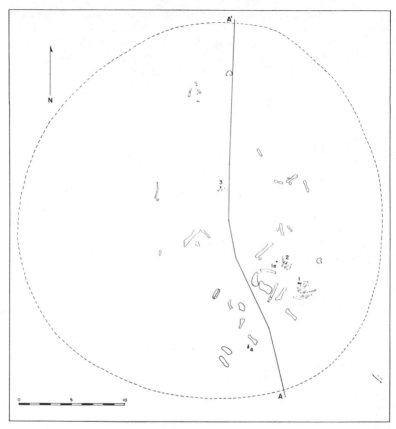

Fig. 6. *Ground plan to show location of elephant bones and of artifacts at the Miami locality.* Nos. 1, 2, and 3, projectile points; 1a, base of No. 1; 4, scraper; A-A[1], location of north-south section of Figure 4. Other entries indicate elephant bones, tusks, and teeth.

trast, there is a profusion of bones, tusks, and teeth of the Columbian elephant. The skeletons scattered in the bone bed are incomplete, and the number of individuals present must be determined chiefly by duplication of parts and by relative size and age. Three right femora of approximately mature elephants have been obtained, indicating at least three mature or nearly mature individuals. To one of these elephants belongs a considerable number of bones found in the southeastern part of the depression, including the tusk, tip and base; two well-worn teeth; parts of the skull; bones of the left foreleg, the ulna and radius; right ulna; vertebrae and ribs; a right femur; a right tibia, and some foot bones. As indicated by size, this individual was essentially mature but was not old, the epiphyses having not yet firmly fused to the limb bones. What particular bones or teeth go with the other two right femora is undetermined. A young elephant is represented by a lower jaw found in the north part of the pond. Near-by is an elephant a few years old, also represented by a lower jaw and parts of the skull. It is thus possible to recognize the presence of at least five elephants, and there may have been more.

It is difficult to determine how parts of five or more elephants came to be preserved at a common level in the pond deposits at this place. There is no indication that the elephants were trapped. The locality does not have the proportions or the appearance of a pit, and if there was a stockade around the pond, all trace of it has disappeared. The animals do not seem to have been bogged, because none of the leg bones was found in vertical position. On the contrary, all were lying horizontal. If overtaken by a storm, it would seem that the elephants would have taken refuge in canyons rather than in a depression of this kind. Drought might very possibly bring elephants in numbers to a water-hole, but if extreme drought caused the elephants to die at a vanishing water-hole, one would expect some of the other animals, particularly bison, deer, and antelope, to be associated with them. Epidemic disease would likewise bring elephants to a water-hole and might possibly affect only one species of a fauna. Although the evidence in this connection is meager, the most probable explanation of this unusual occurrence of a group of elephants in a water-hole, with associated artifacts, seems to be that disease, starvation, or drought may have caused the death of some of the elephants and that others, enfeebled by disease or otherwise, may have been killed by early man. In any case, early man sought these animals, probably utilizing their hides or possibly both hides and flesh. It is worthwhile to note that the elephant remains occur just above a loess stratum. Loess, being wind-blown, implies drought and absence of vegetation. The elephants, therefore, may have died as the result of drought causing the watering places to dry up.

The location of artifacts found associated with the elephants at the Miami locality is indicated in Figure 6. The artifacts include three projectile points and a scraper (Figs. 8 and 9). The projectile points are of the type originally referred to as Folsom-like and later named Clovis Fluted. The association of the artifacts with the elephant bones is certain; they lie definitely in the bone bed and on a level with the elephant bones. A calcium carbonate coating is found on the underside of the artifacts, and a similar incrustation is found on the underside of many of the bones.

A projectile point (1, Fig. 6) was found within 2.5 inches of an atlas vertebra of an elephant; the base, which was broken, lay nearby (1 a, Fig. 6). In Figure 7 the point and vertebra are seen in natural position. They were removed in a single block. The point, including the broken base but excluding the extreme tip, which is wanting, is 113 mm. long, 22 mm. wide at the base, and 30 mm. wide above the base. It is made from slightly mottled light chert or flint. The base is lightly fluted. The point found at this locality by Judge Mead (Fig. 8, b) is 116 mm. long, 23 mm. wide at the base, and 30 mm. wide somewhat above the base. Like the preceding, it is fluted at the base. On one side fluting extends about 29 mm. from the base. On the opposite side the termination of fluting is indefinite. It is possible to give only an approximate location of this spear point because it was removed before systematic excavation had been made. The third projectile point of this locality is much smaller (Fig. 9, a). Its total length is 76 mm.,

Fig. 7. *Spear point and elephant vertebra from the Miami locality.* The vertebra and the spear point, except the base, are in place as found. The broken base was about 3 feet from the remainder of the spear point.

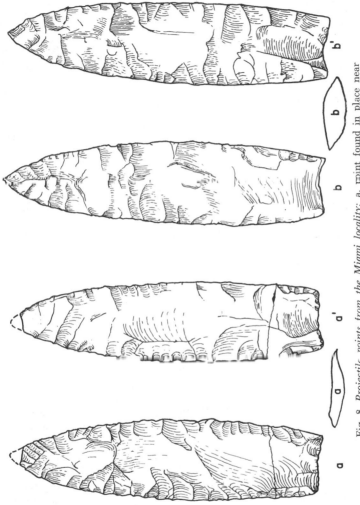

Fig. 8. *Projectile points from the Miami locality:* a, point found in place near elephant vertebra as shown in Figure 7; b, point found by Judge Mead. Tex. Mem. Mus. Acc. 976, Nos. 3 and 1. Slightly reduced.

25

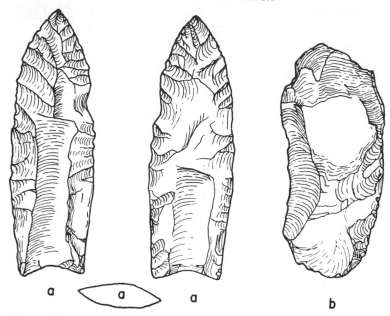

Fig. 9. *Artifacts from the Miami locality:* a, projectile point, No. 3 of Figure 6; b, scraper, No. 4 of Figure 6. Tex. Mem. Mus. Acc. 976, Nos. 2 and 4. Natural size.

width at the base 20 mm., and maximum width above the base 25 mm. This point is definitely fluted; on one side fluting extends 30 mm. and on the opposite side, 43 mm. On both sides fluting terminates in a hinge-like break.

The scraper (Fig. 9, b) was found near the left humerus of an elephant. It is 70 mm. long, 29 mm. wide, and is made from banded chert. The view seen in the illustration is of the side that was up as the scraper lay in the ground. On the underside is an incrustation of calcium carbonate.

It is thus seen that in this ancient water-hole on the plains, relics are found of men who were contemporaneous with the Columbian elephant. These men in salvaging what they could from the carcasses of several elephants lost certain of their artifacts and thus left to us a meager but nevertheless important record of their hunt at this place. How the projectile points were used is not fully known. Possibly they served to tip wooden spears thrown by hand or by the atlatl. So far as

Fig. 10. *Environs of the Blackwater locality No. 1, Roosevelt County, New Mexico. Restored as of the time of ⸺ano man.*

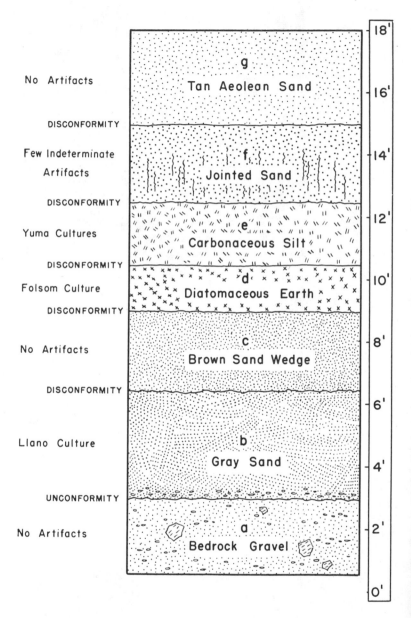

No Artifacts	**g** Tan Aeolean Sand	18' 16'
DISCONFORMITY		
Few Indeterminate Artifacts	**f** Jointed Sand	14'
DISCONFORMITY		
Yuma Cultures	**e** Carbonaceous Silt	12'
DISCONFORMITY		
Folsom Culture	**d** Diatomaceous Earth	10'
DISCONFORMITY		
No Artifacts	**c** Brown Sand Wedge	8'
DISCONFORMITY		6'
Llano Culture	**b** Gray Sand	4'
UNCONFORMITY		
No Artifacts	**a** Bedrock Gravel	2' 0'

is known, bows were not in use at this early time. The scraper was presumably used in cleaning hides.

Blackwater No. 1 Locality, Roosevelt County, New Mexico

On the Baxter ranch at the north side of Blackwater Draw in Roosevelt County, New Mexico, is a depression; originally a lake or marsh which was probably fed by seepage springs, in time it became filled by debris. This lake is a place of great importance in the human history of the plains and will be more fully described elsewhere. The geologic section of this place consists of seven units or horizons in order as follows: 1, bed-rock; 2, gray sand, the basal stratum of lake fill; 3, brown sand lens, absent in central part of the lake; 4, diatomaceous lake deposits; 5, clayey dark sand; 6, dark reddish wind blown sand; and 7, light colored surface wind blown sands. At this time it is desired to refer only to No. 2 of the section, the oldest or basal stratum of the lake fill, this being the part containing evidence of men contemporaneous with the elephant (Fig. 10). This locality became known about 1932 as the result of commercial development of gravel deposits in this region.

The first excavation for fossils and artifacts at this locality was made by E. B. Howard, J. L. Cotter, and associates during the years 1933 to 1937. The institutions chiefly concerned in the excavations made during these years were the University of Pennsylvania Museum, the Academy of Natural Sciences of Philadelphia, the Carnegie Institution of Washington, and the California Institute of Technology. The place at that time was referred to as being in the Clovis-Portales region (Howard, 1935) and has been referred to in the literature together with other localities in and near Blackwater Draw collectively as the Clovis locality or localities. For exactness of reference the original locality described by Howard is here designated as Blackwater No. 1. The locality is about 7 miles north of Portales and 14 or 15 miles southwest of Clovis. Additional excavations were made here by the Texas Memorial Museum during 1949 and 1950. In recent years the property has changed ownership several times.

―――――――

Fig. 11. *Geologic section at the Blackwater locality No. 1:* a, bed-rock; b, the basal horizon or member of lake fill consisting of gray or speckled sand with some pebbles; c, brown sand resting with erosional contact on the gray sand, absent in central area of the lake deposit; d, diatomite, clay and sand; e, dark sand and clay member; f and g, wind blown sand, variable in thickness and occurrence. Adapted from Evans (1951).

29

Fig. 12. *Section at the west side of the south quarry, Blackwater No. 1 locality:* a, bed-rock at level of the hammer and below; b, gray or speckled sand, basal horizon of the lake fill (Llano culture); brown sand absent at this place; d, diatomite horizon (Folsom culture); e, dark sand, clay horizon (later culture); f, dark colored sand. Photo by Glen L. Evans.

When the excavations were being made by Howard, Cotter, and others, the property was a part of the P. H. Hanagan ranch and later was owned by Lee Carter, then by Anderson Carter; at present it is a part of the Charles Baxter ranch.

The basal fill in this depression, here referred to as the basal stratum, consists of a gray or "speckled" sand, 5 or more feet thick in places, thinning towards the margin of the depression, the average thickness being 2 or 3 feet (Fig. 11). The most distinctive fossil of this sand stratum is the Columbian elephant, of which four more or less complete skeletons and many parts of skeletons have been found. Other fossils present but not so abundant are of horses, bison, turtles of several species, and various small mammals (Fig. 12). Artifacts were found with three of the elephant skeletons. Some of these artifacts were in such relationship to the elephant bones as to indicate that they had either been used in killing the elephants or had been lost while securing whatever parts of the elephants the people of that time were able to utilize.

The artifacts obtained by Cotter in 1936 and 1937 which were in

30

direct association with elephant bones are as follows: projectile point from 1 inch below the top of the sand underneath elephant vertebra; projectile point from 1 inch below top of sand between elephant ulna and humerus; part of blade (or possibly part of projectile point) from 3 inches below top of the sand under elephant scapula; scraper from 3 inches below top of sand between the tusks of elephant; bone artifact 6 inches below top of sand under elephant ulna; a bone artifact from 7 inches below top of sand near elephant tusk; projectile point from 1 foot or more below the top of the sand near elephant scapula; and a small point, not illustrated, from 1 foot below top of sand beneath elephant ribs (Cotter, 1937).

The additional artifacts found by the Texas Memorial Museum in the sand stratum during 1949 and 1950 were: one worked bone from 1 to 3 inches below the top of the gray sand; one projectile point from 2 inches below the top of the sand; one piece of bone marked by implements found within about 3 inches of the base of the sand stratum; one hammerstone found near the middle of the sand stratum; several split bone and worked bone artifacts; one scraper; and a chip of the size and general appearance of a core from a Clovis Fluted projectile point. The core was found resting directly on the gray sand and hence may or may not belong to the stratum in which Clovis Fluted points were found.

Artifacts obtained in place in this stratum are illustrated in Figures 13 to 18. The large points obtained from this horizon are of the Clovis Fluted type; the two smaller points obtained, although having similar chipping, are indefinitely or not at all fluted.

Artifacts from later horizons at Blackwater No. 1 locality will be described in the next chapter.

Dent, Weld County, Colorado

A locality near Dent, Weld County, Colorado, excavated in 1932 and described by Figgins (1933a) presents unusual conditions in that parts of skeletons of at least twelve elephants have been found within a small area. One was a large adult, the others being young animals or small adults. The species is probably *Parelephas columbi*. The deposits are said to be a part of the terrace of South Platte River. A large Clovis Fluted point was found at this locality on November 5, 1932, and later a smaller point of the same kind was obtained (Fig. 19). Both were associated with the elephant bones.

31

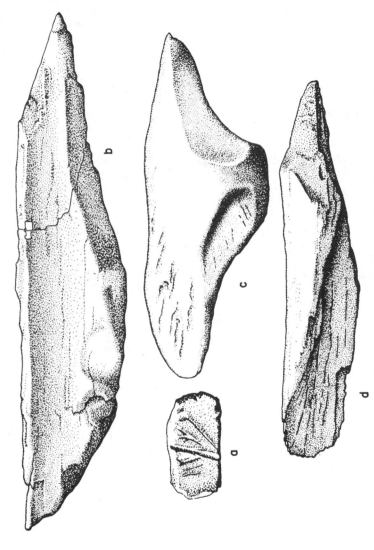

Fig. 13. *Bone artifacts from Stratum 2, Blackwater No. 1 locality:* a, bone with marking; b, c and d, implements. Tex. Mem. Mus. Acc. 937, Nos. 89, 84, 99, and 91. Slightly reduced.

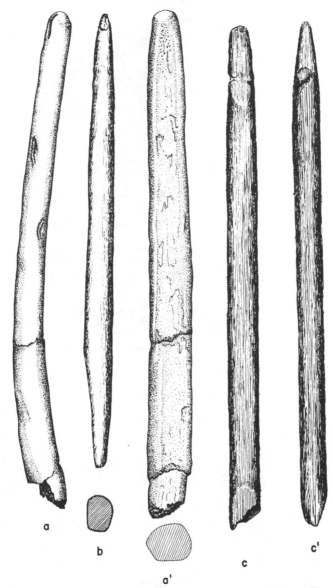

Fig. 14. *Bone artifacts from gray sand, Blackwater No. 1 locality:* a, Tex. Mem.
Mus. Acc. 937, No. 61; b, courtesy University of Pennsylvania Museum; c, courtesy
Philadelphia Academy of Natural Sciences. Seven-twelfths natural size.

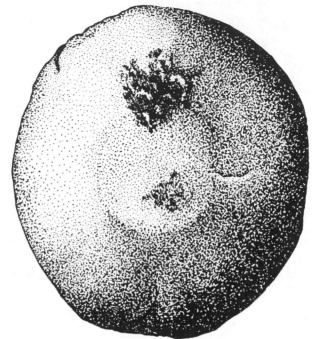

Fig. 15. *Hammerstone from the gray sand horizon, Blackwater No. 1 locality.* Side view. Tex. Mem. Mus. Acc. 937, No. 77. Natural size.

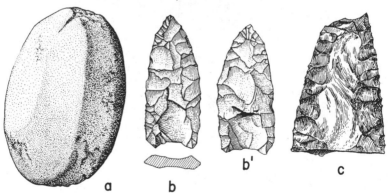

a   b   b'   c

Fig. 16. *Artifacts from gray sand horizon, Blackwater No. 1 locality:* a, hammerstone, one-half natural size; b and c, projectile points, natural size; a and b, Tex. Mem. Mus. Acc. 937, Nos. 77 and 72; c, courtesy University of Pennsylvania Museum.

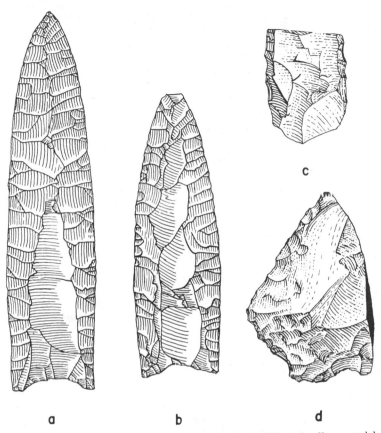

a   b   d

Fig. 17. *Artifacts from gray sand stratum, Blackwater No. 1 locality:* a and b, after Cotter, Phil. Acad. Nat. Sci. Proc., vol. 89, p. 12, 1937; c and d, Tex. Mem. Mus. Acc. 937, Nos. 51 and 76. Natural size.

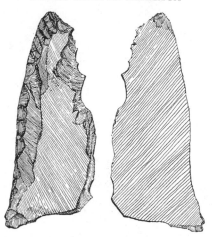

Fig. 18. *Scraper from gray sand horizon, Blackwater No. 1 locality.* Courtesy University of Pennsylvania Museum. Natural size.

McLean, Texas, and Angus, Nebraska

At a locality on the McLean farm 30 miles southwest of Abilene, Texas, an artifact was found imbedded in the earth near the lower jaw of an elephant (Bryan and Ray, 1938). The point (Fig. 20, b) is not unlike those found with the elephant at the Miami and Blackwater No. 1 localities, and if not used in hunting elephants was at least contemporaneous with the elephant near which it was found.

A projectile point reported to have been found with remains of an elephant at Angus, Nebraska (Figgins, 1931), is shown in Figure 20, a. This point, which is 71 mm. long and 29 mm. in maximum width, differs from the other points found with the elephant in at least two respects: it is fluted from base to tip, other points being less extensively fluted; and the base shows no concavity, while the others have a concave base. The formation containing the fossil elephant and artifact consists of stratified deposits of sand and gravel, with thinner layers of silt, clay, and marl, overlain by wind-blown sand to a depth of 16 feet. The elephant has been identified by Osborn (1932) as *Archidiskodon meridionalis nebrascensis*. Some doubt may exist as to the certainty of the contemporaneity of the Angus point and the elephant remains.

36

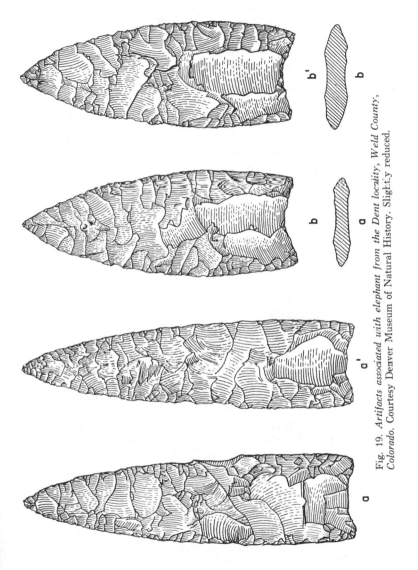

Fig. 19. *Artifacts associated with elephant from the Dent locality, Weld County, Colorado.* Courtesy Denver Museum of Natural History. Slightly reduced.

37

Naco, Arizona

Discovery of an elephant skeleton with associated Clovis Fluted points has recently been announced by Emil W. Haury and associates of the University of Arizona. The find was made near the village of Naco, on the Mexican border (Haury, letter of May 21, 1952). The elephant was not fully adult and a specific age determination has not yet been made. With or near the elephant bones were a total of eight projectile points. Of these, five were found in place among ribs of the elephant and were removed under direction of Dr. Haury; two had previously been found by Fred and Marc Navarette, father and son, of Naco; and one was picked up in an excavation that had previously been made at this locality. The points vary in size, the smallest being about 57 mm. long by 23 mm. wide, and the largest about 116 mm. by 34 mm. Dr. Haury identifies all as Clovis Fluted points. The smaller points if found alone would probably not have been identified as Clovis Fluted. However, intermediate sizes occur between the smaller and larger points. At the Blackwater No. 1 locality, as previously stated, a slightly fluted point measuring only 38 mm. by 16 mm. was found at the level and in the stratum from which Cotter obtained two moderately large Clovis Fluted points.

This discovery in Arizona is of great importance. It confirms the presence of Clovis Fluted points and elephant hunting by early man in Arizona. Here also is proof of the use of at least five points either in killing or in processing an elephant. This locality would seem to justify extensive additional excavating. It would be extremely important to secure, if possible, material suitable for radiocarbon determination. Six of the points are shown in Figure 22 A.

Geographic Distribution of Clovis Fluted Points

As may be seen from the illustrations, the artifacts found with or near the skeletons of elephants at the localities mentioned vary considerably in finish, size, and workmanship. Large more or less fluted points predominate at most localities, and yet of four complete flint points found in the basal horizon at the Blackwater No. 1 locality, two are relatively small and only moderately fluted or not at all. While the elephant predominates in this horizon, bison, horse, and other animals are also present, and the smaller points probably were used for game smaller than the elephant. The two larger complete points from this locality are shown in Figure 17. One is 110 mm.

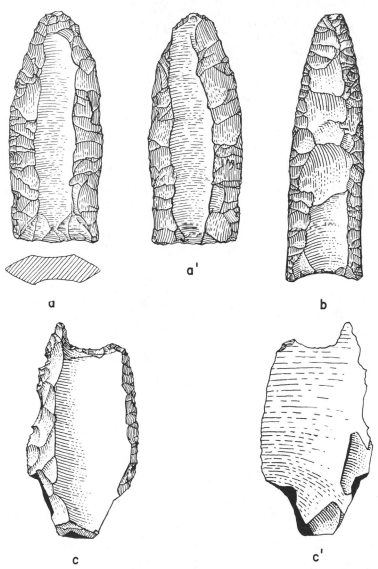

Fig. 20. *Artifacts associated with elephant:* a, Angus, Nuckolls County, Nebraska;
b, McLean, Taylor County, Texas; c, Lubbock, Texas; a, courtesy Denver Museum
of Natural History; b, courtesy Museum, Texas Technological College; c, Tex.
Mem. Mus. Acc. 892, No. 84.

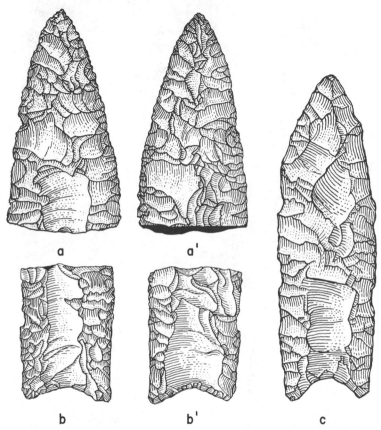

a   a'

b   b'   c

Fig. 21. *Fluted points:* a and b, after Harrington, from Borax Lake, California, courtesy Los Angeles Museum; c, after Byers, from Wisconsin, courtesy American Antiquity, vol. 7, Pl. 37. Natural size.

long by 26 mm. wide and the other 84 mm. long by 25 mm. wide; in size they compare closely with points found at the Miami locality. Of the other points found in the sand stratum either directly with or in the immediate area of elephant skeletons, one is 55 mm. long by 16 mm. in maximum width; another is 36 mm. long by 15 mm. wide. Of the two points found at Dent one is 116 mm. long by 31 mm. in maximum width; the other is 95 mm. long by 37 mm. in maximum width (Fig. 19). The point found on the McLean farm is 82 mm.

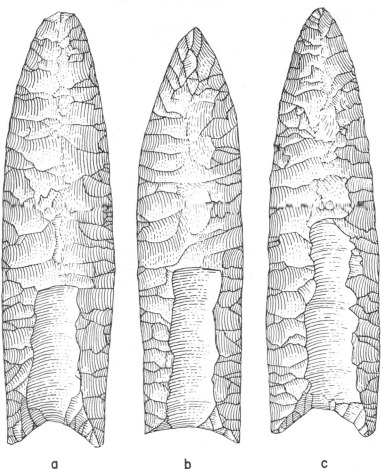

a   b   c

Fig. 22. *Fluted points from the McCary collection:* a, from Kentucky; b, from Ohio; c, from Indiana. Natural size.

long exclusive of the broken tip and is 24 mm. in maximum width, which is at the base. The point found at Angus is 71 mm. long exclusive of the somewhat battered tip and is 29 mm. in maximum width (Fig. 20, a).

Many points similar to the Clovis Fluted point have been picked up on the surface at various places in North America, indicating wide

41

geographic distribution of this type of stone projectile point. The Borax Lake locality near the Pacific Coast in California, as shown by Harrington, contains this projectile point. A point picked up on the surface near Royalton, Wisconsin, described and illustrated by Byers (1942), is very like some of those found with the elephant. The point is unequally fluted on the two sides and the fluting ends with a prominent hinge fracture similar to that of the smaller point obtained at the Miami locality (Fig. 21). Points more or less similar have been found as far east as near the Atlantic Coast and northward into Canada. The writer has had the privilege of examining in the collection of B. C. McCary, Williamsburg, Virginia, projectile points of this type from surface localities in Colorado, Illinois, Indiana, Kentucky, Mississippi, Ohio, Tennessee, and Virginia (Fig. 22). The collection contains points of this general type from several other states. However, from the states listed above were found points essentially identical in size, workmanship, and finish with Clovis Fluted points found in place and in faunal association at the Miami, Blackwater No. 1, and Dent localities. These localities are considered typical for the Clovis Fluted point. Several deeply fluted points have been described recently from Ontario, Canada (Kidd, 1951).

The Blackwater No. 1 locality was not merely a hunting site but was also a camp site. The stone projectile points are clearly those of a hunting people. In addition to stone projectile points, recent collecting has revealed the presence in the culture of a hammerstone which may also have served the purpose of a grinding stone. Of greater importance is the evidence of a split-bone industry among these people. The worked split bones were probably digging implements and may have been used to dig tuberous roots from the sand bed of the shallow water pond.

Valley of Mexico

Hunting the elephant in America was by no means confined to the United States. Elephants ranged southward into Central America and in late Pleistocene time were abundant in the Valley of Mexico. In 1952 a Department of Prehistory was organized in Mexico as a division of the National Institute of Anthropology and History. The first project undertaken by this new department was to excavate and collect the skeleton of an elephant which had been discovered in the

Fig. 22 A. *Fluted points found with elephant, Naco, Arizona.* Courtesy Department of Anthropology, University of Arizona. Natural size.

construction of an irrigation ditch in the Valley of Mexico about two years earlier. Zest was added to excavating at this locality by the fact that it is only about three kilometers from the place where the famous Tepexpan man was discovered February 1947 (De Terra, 1949). Directing the excavating was Luis Aveleyra-Arroyo de Anda. Others who participated were Manuel Maldonado Koerdell, Señora Borbolla, Arturo Romano, and Pablo Martínez del Río, Director of the National Institute of Anthropology and History.

The elephant skeleton, which lay buried in the earth to a depth of 4 to 5.5 feet, was uncovered in about one week. Then came the critical examination to find whether or not artifacts were with or near the skeleton. The first artifact found was a flint spear point lodged between the ribs of the elephant pointing inward as though thrown into the animal in an attempt to make a kill. The second artifact discovered, made of obsidian, was part of a scraper. A third artifact, also of obsidian, was perhaps a combination implement, being a scraper apparently adapted also for use as a spoke shave. A fourth artifact, made of flint, dropped out of place before being seen by those who were excavating. At this stage excavation was halted temporarily until interested persons had opportunity to see the elephant skeleton

Fig. 22 B. *Elephant skeleton found with artifacts in the Valley of Mexico.*

Fig. 22 C. *Artifacts found with elephant in the Valley of Mexico.* Courtesy National Institute of Anthropology and History of Mexico. Natural size.

with artifacts still in place as found. Among those who witnessed the artifacts in place in the earth were representatives of several governmental and educational agencies of Mexico, and, by courtesy of the Department of Prehistory, representatives from the United States, as follows: Marie Wormington from the Denver Museum of Natural History, Colorado; Alex D. Krieger, Department of Anthropology of the University of Texas; and Elias H. Sellards, University of Texas and the Texas Memorial Museum.

The elephant skeleton was not removed until later, and when the bones were taken up two additional scrapers or flake knives were found, one made of obsidian and one of flint. Both were among the elephant bones. The six artifacts found with this skeleton are illustrated in Figure 22C. The projectile point, as will be noted, is not of the Clovis Fluted type as are those found associated with the elephant in the United States.

The cause of death of this particular elephant can not now be determined. The animal apparently was not bogged down in the mud and silt of the lake of that time, as the leg bones lay horizontal and not in bogged position. The part of the skeleton found was for the most part articulated. The skull, unfortunately, had been removed and largely destroyed by the ditch digging done in 1950. The right femur lay a few feet away from the remainder of the skeleton.

The scrapers and knives proved that man salvaged what he could from the carcass, and the spear point indicates that man's efforts hastened, if they did not cause, the death of the animal. There can be no doubt as to the certainty of the association and the contemporaneity of the artifacts and the mammoth. The discovery is of great importance in archaeology and the Department of Prehistory is to be congratulated on the success of this project.

This brief statement of an important new discovery, with the accompanying illustrations, is given through the courtesy of Pablo Martínez del Río, Director of the National Institute of Anthropology and History of Mexico. A more complete account of the discovery appears in a recent publication issued by the Mexican government (Martínez del Río, 1952).

THE BISON HUNTERS

The first discovery in America of an artifact known to have been used by early man in hunting bison of a species now extinct was made by H. T. Martin and T. R. Overton in 1895 at a locality 12 miles east of Russell Springs, Kansas (Williston, 1905a). The bison bones at the locality were numerous, representing seven or eight individuals. With regard to the removal of the bones and the discovery of the artifact, Mr. Martin writes as follows:

"After we reached within a few inches of the bone layer, the surface was cleaned off perfectly level for a space of fifteen by twenty to twenty-five feet. The skeleton lay with the head pointing nearly east, and the skull separated about three feet to the southwest, so that when I commenced removing the parts after pasting, the scapula came in the second block to be removed. These sections separated from the matrix beneath freely, so that when the scapula was removed it left a nearly perfect impression in the bluish marly matrix, leaving the arrowhead plainly in view firmly embedded in the hard matrix. When the artifact was removed, it too left a perfect mold in the firm clay, so you can see that accidental intrusion in any way imaginable was absolutely impossible. The arrowhead was embedded more deeply at its base, while the point was pressed firmly against the shoulder blade. The skeleton lay on its right side and the arrowhead underneath the right scapula." (Letter of January 15, 1918.)

Unfortunately, the point found at this locality and contained in the collections of the University of Kansas was subsequently lost.

Folsom Man

Folsom Locality, Union County, New Mexico

Thirty years after Martin and Overton made their discovery at Russell Springs, Kansas, a Negro cowboy on a ranch near Folsom, Union County, New Mexico, noticed bones exposed in the banks of a small stream known as Dead Horse Gulch, a small tributary of Cimarron River. The locality was reported to the Denver Museum of Natural History by Fred J. Howarth and Carl Schwachheim of

47

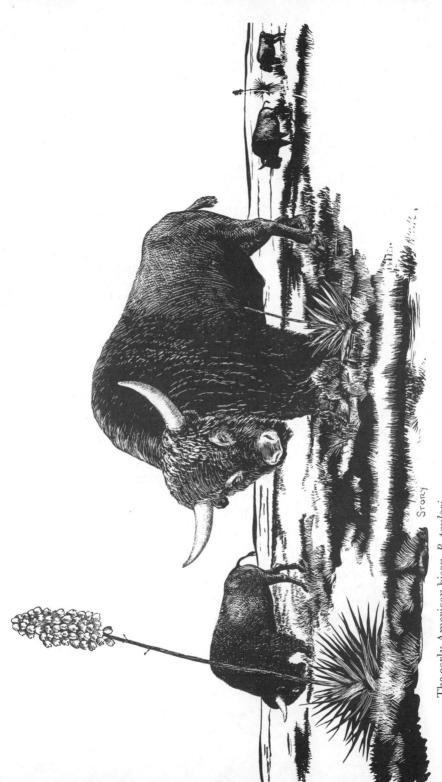

The early American bison, *B. taylori.*

Raton, New Mexico. Collections made at this locality by the Denver Museum of Natural History and the American Museum of Natural History proved this to have been a bison kill.

Nineteen projectile points were obtained, and with them bones were found, indicating that at least twenty-three bison had died at this place. Most, if not all, had evidently been killed by the men who made the projectile points. The points were appropriately named for the near-by town of Folsom, and this locality became the recognized type locality for this kind of projectile point (Wormington, 1949, p. 21). In addition to the projectile points the locality yielded only a scraper and a broken flake knife (Roberts, 1939b, p. 534). By common usage the people who made these artifacts are known as "Folsom man"; as in the case of the elephant hunters, they are known only by the artifacts and ornaments which they made and used, no human skeletal remains having been found.

The Folsom locality was studied during the years 1926 to 1928. Since that time the kind of projectile point made by Folsom man has been found from Texas to Alaska, being particularly characteristic of the great interior plains of North America. This wide distribution indicates that the points may have been used not only by the tribe that originated them but, like the bow and arrow of later time, spread widely over the interior of the continent. The region where Folsom points were most used and consequently are found in greatest abundance is the Great Plains east of the Rocky Mountains of the United States and Canada. The range of abundance of Folsom points probably coincides essentially with the range of abundance of the bison of that time. Solecki (1951) refers to Folsom points found in Alaska as indicating the time of Folsom man's migration from Siberia into North America. In this connection it should not be overlooked that these points and accompanying camp sites may indicate not a migration from Siberia but a northward spread of Folsom culture from a region of much greater abundance in central North America. This is a problem that can be solved only by future discoveries.

Lindenmeier Locality, Larimer County, Colorado

Most of the places from which relics of Folsom man have been obtained are sites in which were found only artifacts used in hunting, such as projectile points, knives, and scrapers, all made of flint. However, one camp site has been found and fully excavated by the Bureau of American Ethnology, the Denver Museum of Natural History,

49

and others. By this fortunate occurrence much has been learned of the culture of these people. The camp site referred to is in Colorado on the William Lindenmeier land north of Fort Collins, near the Wyoming State line. This site was discovered in 1924 by Judge C. C. Coffin and his son A. L. Coffin. In 1930 Prof. E. B. Renaud of the University of Denver identified the projectile points obtained from this locality as Folsom points. Major Roy G. Coffin, Professor of Geology at Colorado State College, also took an active interest in the discovery. In 1934, Dr. Frank H. H. Roberts, Jr., of the Bureau of American Ethnology, began excavations at the locality which were continued through 1936, resulting in a collection of artifacts which undoubtedly represent most of the objects made of stone and bone used by the people who lived at this place. Artifacts obtained at the camp site include scrapers, gravers, knives, blades, hammerstones, choppers, bone tools and bone discs, rubbing stones, channel flakes, and palettes to hold hematite, which was probably used as a paint for adornment and possibly for other purposes. In addition to bone and stone artifacts these people must have had objects made of wood, horn, hide, and possibly of fiber. These, however, would not be preserved in open camp sites, and we must look to future fortunate discoveries, possibly in the dry caves of the Southwest, for knowledge of such objects. Some of the artifacts found at the Lindenmeier locality are shown in Figures 23 A and B.

Fig. 23 A. *Folsom points from the Lindenmeier site, Colorado.* After Roberts, from Smithsonian Misc. Coll., vol. 94, p. 16, 1935. Natural size.

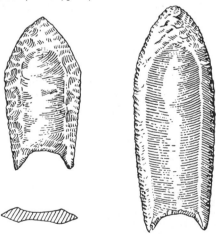

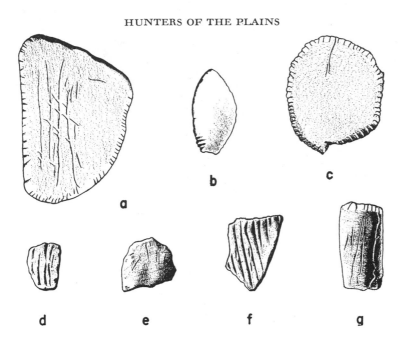

Fig. 23 B. *Bone artifacts with markings from the Lindenmeier site, Colorado.* From Smithsonian Institution Annual Rept., 1938. Natural size.

A 20 by 47 foot excavation made by Roberts at the Lindenmeier site, about 1,500 feet from the Folsom camp site, was continued to the bottom of the artifact-bearing deposits. In this excavation, bison bones were found representing nine individuals. Many of the bones were still articulated, and one animal was represented by the skull, a forequarter, most of the ribs from one side, and the vertebral column. Evidently this animal had been killed and quartered but not fully used. Thirty-four worked pieces of stone or flint were found among the bones in this excavation. These consisted of projectile points, either whole or broken, scrapers, blades, flake knives, and gravers. Several fragments of points were lying between components of articulated segments in such a way as to suggest that they had been imbedded in the flesh of the animal. If any possible doubt remained that the Folsom point was used in killing bison, such doubt was effectively removed by the discovery in this excavation of a broken Folsom point lodged in the vertebra of a bison (Roberts, 1936a, p. 14).

51

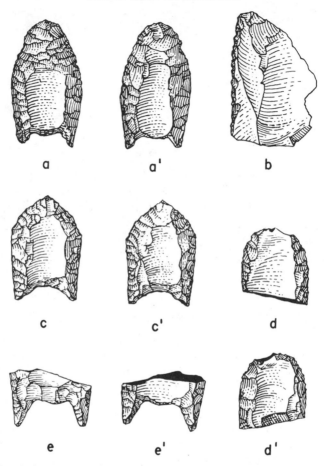

Fig. 24. *Artifacts from Folsom horizon, Lubbock locality.* Tex. Mem. Mus. Acc. 892, Nos. 76, 78, 71, 77, and 70. Natural size.

Lubbock Locality, Lubbock County, Texas

The Lubbock locality, near Lubbock, Texas, represents a filled lake in the valley of Yellow House Draw. The Texas Memorial Museum carried on excavations at this locality in 1948, 1950, and 1951. During the field season of 1948 the lake fill was found to include five recognizable depositional units or strata, but no artifacts were found in place in the deposits at that time. During 1950, in the next to the oldest stratum of lake fill, burned and charred bison bones were found. With the burnt bones were flint chips but no recognizable artifacts. In 1951 a special search was made to determine whether or not the stratum, a diatomite layer, which held the burned bison bones also contained artifacts. With aid generously contributed by the city of Lubbock in removing the approximately 15 feet of overburden, and with much patient digging, evidence of Folsom culture was found in this stratum—four projectile points and one side scraper (Fig. 24). Two of the projectile points are complete and two broken. The scraper, made from a thin flake, is worked on one side only. In the meantime a radiocarbon test had been made in the Institute for Nuclear Studies of the University of Chicago on the carbon of the charred bison bones, the resulting age determination being 9,883 ± 350 years (Libby, letter of December 8, 1950). The upper and lower boundaries of the diatomite horizon are definitely marked and there is no question but that the Folsom artifacts and the charred bones are in the same horizon in the section and are of the same age, proving that Folsom man hunted the bison at this place about 10,000 years ago.

From a gray sand stratum next underlying the diatomite, one artifact was found, a combined scraper and graver, or a scraper subsequently reworked as a graver (Fig. 20c). This older artifact may represent a culture older than Folsom, which has been found at a similar position in the section at the Clovis-Portales area in New Mexico. The conditions in New Mexico were briefly reported by the writer at the 1950 meeting of the Geological Society of America (Program, Abstracts, p. 73).

The several strata of lake deposits at the Lubbock locality vary somewhat in thickness from place to place. The geologic section, as determined and measured by Glen L. Evans, near the place where the Folsom artifacts were collected, follows. The several horizons are listed in order, No. 5 being the surface member and number 1 the basal member of the lake fill.

Section at Station D, Lubbock Reservoir Site

STRATUM

THICKNESS IN FEET

5. "Muck" layer, here essentially a thin, humus-bearing wet-meadow or cienaga soil in the upper part, with softer, weakly bedded, dark gray lenticular sands in the lower part. This represents the maximum thickness of Bed 5 at this site. *Bison bison* bones locally abundant in this member. Total thickness.. 3.0

4. Compact gray to tan calcareous sand, with a thin layer of small caliche pebbles along the base. Basal contact at this section appears as a weak disconformity. Bison bones and skulls locally present. (This is a large bison, distinctly different from the modern species.) Total thickness.... 5.4

3. Friable calcareous clay member containing numerous lime-replaced root canals of aquatic plants. Bison bones are present but comparatively rare. Total thickness.................................... 3.7

2. Diatomaceous earth consisting of a basal layer of pure white diatomite 8 inches thick, with banded and laminated gray, impure diatomaceous earth making up the remainder of the bed. The main bone bed occurs at the contact between the basal 8 inch white layer and the overlying banded or laminated material. All of the Folsom points found in place were in this bison bone bed. The fauna includes great numbers of extinct bison, species *B. taylori*. Also some coyote, antelope, muskrat, turtle, and other fossils. Thickness of the diatomite ranges from less than 2 feet near the margins to 5.5 feet in the deeper part of the old lake. Thickness at this station................................. 4.0

1. Basal sand and calcareous gravel, unconsolidated, cross-bedding evident everywhere except in local clay zones that appear in upper part of the member. Fauna includes elephant, tapir, horse, bison, fish, turtle, and fresh-water mollusks. Thickness ranges from 2 to 6 feet. Thickness at this station 4.4

Total thickness of section...... 20.5

Thickness of the part of the section overlying the Folsom points, 15.4

Folsom Horizon at Blackwater No. 1 Locality, New Mexico

The basal unit of lake fill, Stratum 2 of the Blackwater No. 1 locality, is overlain unconformably in the eastern part of the depression by a brown sand containing considerable organic material and in places quantities of bison bones. This sand, Stratum 3 of the section, is absent in the central and western parts of the depression. No artifacts have been found in the brown sand.

Stratum 4 of the Blackwater No. 1 section, 2 to 2.5 feet in thickness, is made up in places largely of diatoms. With the diatoms is considerable clay and organic material. The color of the stratum varies from dark where organic matter predominates to almost white where diatoms predominate and blue gray where much clay is present. This stratum consisting of clay, sand, and diatomaceous earth rests disconformably on the brown sand where that unit occurs, and elsewhere disconformably on the gray sand. Within this horizon, in places occupying most of it, is a bone bed made up of skeletons of hundreds of bison. Owing to imperfect preservation no really good skulls have been obtained. However, from what has been seen of the skull, and particularly because of the size of the bones of the skeleton, the bison is believed to be the species *Bison taylori*. The elephant and horse present in the underlying gray sand have not been found in Stratum 4. In addition to the bison a few bird bones have been obtained at this level. The artifacts found in stratum 4 are those of the Folsom culture. The age of this horizon has not been determined at this locality. However, burned bison bones obtained by Glen L. Evans and Grayson F. Meade of the Texas Memorial Museum staff from a similar diatomite horizon near Lubbock, Texas, provisionally correlated with this horizon on basis of sediments and vertebrate fossils, gave by radiocarbon test an age of 9,883 ± 350 years (W. F. Libby, letter of December 8, 1950).

Of the twelve artifacts listed from this horizon seven are projectile points, all of which are broken or battered by use (Fig. 25). One, No. 18, is nearly complete, lacking only the point; another, No. 12, shows approximately the basal half of a point; No. 50 is a small fragment, showing, however, the distinctive Folsom fluting on both sides. It was found some distance from the other points. No. 28 is deeply fluted on one side and imperfectly fluted on the other side. No. 57 is imperfectly fluted on both sides. No. 27 is imperfectly fluted on one side and not at all fluted on the reverse. This point is made from a banded flint of a texture that apparently was not adapted to flaking. No. 59 is a small point made from banded flint. Although unfluted, it has otherwise the outline and workmanship of a Folsom point. The battered and broken condition of these points testifies to the hard usage they received in the hunt.

The geologic section at the Blackwater No. 1 locality is given in Figure 11. The large bison found associated with artifacts of the Folsom complex at Folsom, Lubbock, Blackwater and some other localities is here listed as *Bison taylori*. This bison may be either identical with or a variety of *Bison antiquus* (Skinner and Kaisen, 1947, p. 178).

55

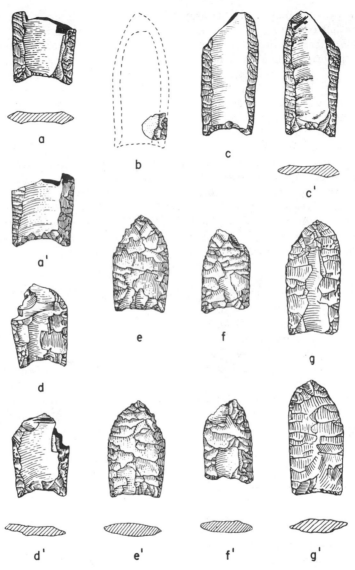

Fig. 25. *Projectile points from the Folsom horizon at the Blackwater No. 1 locality, Roosevelt County, New Mexico.* Tex. Mem. Mus. Acc. 937, Nos. 12, 50, 18, 28, 59, 57, and 27. Natural size.

56

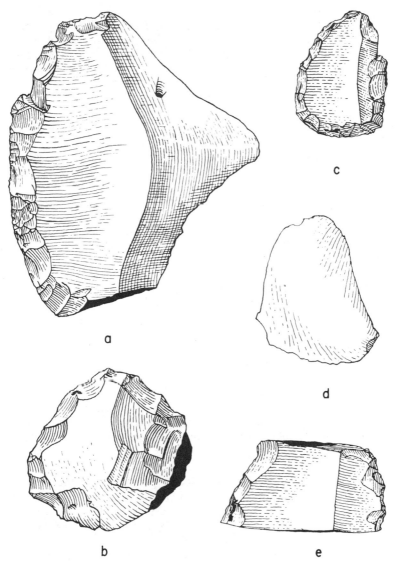

Fig. 26. *Scrapers from Folsom horizon, Blackwater No. 1 locality, New Mexico.*
Tex. Mem. Mus. Acc. 937, Nos. 30, 4, 66, 71, and 54. Natural size.

Four scrapers and one flake which may have been used as a scraper were found at this level (Fig. 26). The flake, No. 71, is thin and sharp edged and may have been used for cutting rather than as a scraper. The four scrapers are worked on one side only. The largest of the lot, No. 30, a side scraper, is from a nodule of bluish-gray flint, worked on one edge only. No. 4 is from a small nodule and is worked almost entirely around the margins. Both scrapers, No. 30 and No. 4, retain part of the original patinated surfaces of the nodules from which they came. No. 66 is a small slab of dark flint also worked almost entirely around the edges. No. 54 is part of a blade or scraper, probably a scraper as it is worked only on the side illustrated.

It is thus seen that at this locality the Folsom level overlies and is later in time than the Llano complex previously described. It is probably considerably later since, as has already been indicated, two disconformities intervene, one separating the Folsom horizon from the brown sand, and the second separating the brown sand from the gray sand which holds the Llano culture.

Lipscomb Locality, Lipscomb County, Texas

Several other localities are now known where the Folsom point has been found under conditions indicating that it was used in hunting bison of a species now extinct. In Lipscomb County, Texas, Schultz (1943) excavated a site which evidently represents a bison kill by Folsom man. The bones at this place were distributed over an area approximately 100 by 20 feet. In the part of the quarry where the bones were most concentrated Schultz reports fourteen articulated skeletons, including skulls, in an area 12 by 20 feet. "The skeletons were headed chiefly in an easterly or southerly direction and overlapped one another considerably. The skeletons of some individuals were entire, including even the caudal vertebrae" (Schultz, 1943, p. 246).

Twenty-two artifacts were found by Schultz at this locality in 1939. Of these eighteen were projectile points, and of the eighteen projectile points (whole or broken) fifteen were found *in situ* in the bone bed and three in the talus removed in excavating. The remaining artifacts include scrapers, flake knife, and one channel flake. The projectile points are of the Folsom culture.

The description of the skeletons as heading in one direction, one overlapping the other, suggests that the animals, during a storm, entered one of the many depressions of the plains where the snow

58

was of such depth as to compel them to stop, some to freeze, and others to be killed by man. Certain it is that the skeletons were in a natural depression and many of the animals, if not all, entered the depression at the same time as a herd or part of a herd.

An incident of modern bison caught by a snowstorm and falling an easy victim to hunters is related by Garretson (1938, p. 88) from Shoemaker as follows: "The buffalo were all huddled together, up to their necks in snow, in a great hollow space known as the Sink in the heart of the White Mountains, near the present town of Weiket, Union County, Pennsylvania. The animals were numb from cold and hunger, and were unable to move, so deep were they crusted in the great drift. The hunters started at once to slaughter the helpless bison. Some were shot, but most of them were killed by cutting their throats with long bear knives. Many of the tongues were saved, and that was about all, as the snow was too deep to attempt skinning them."

Hornaday (1899, p. 384) records an incident in which bison in the vicinity of Hay and Peace Rivers near Great Slave Lake, Canada, caught in an exceptionally heavy snowstorm of 1821, froze to death by the thousands, their skeletons having persisted on the plains until at least as late as 1871.

Linger and Zapata Sites, Alamosa County, Colorado

In the valley of San Luis River in Alamosa County, Colorado, west of the Sangre de Cristo Mountains, Hurst in 1941 found artifacts and skeletal remains of bison. This locality is on the Linger ranch near Monte Vista, Colorado. The conditions of occurrence were not of the best for critical collecting. In the words of Hurst (1943, pp. 251 and 252): "The site is a blowout which has almost reached the level of an old waterhole where bison had apparently been accustomed to come for water. The blowout is roughly 50 yards across. The skeletons of five bison appeared on the surface." The deposits were examined until entirely sterile sand was encountered. The maximum depth at which crumbled bone lay was 2 feet. This was true only in one place; all the rest of the material lay less than 1 foot below the surface. Nine artifacts were collected in 1941 from among the bison bones. Five of these were Folsom projectile points, the others being mostly scrapers. Several other artifacts had previously been obtained from the blow-out. There seems no doubt but that bison frequenting this water-hole were hunted by Folsom man.

More recently a similar locality, known as the Zapata site, has been reported, located about 1 mile from the Linger site. At this site one complete and one fragmentary Folsom point and some other artifacts have been found associated with fossil bison skeletons (Wormington, 1949, p. 23).

Localities affording unmistakable evidence that Folsom projectile points were used in hunting the bison have thus been found over a wide area. However, it is not to be supposed that points of this type were used for this purpose only. They doubtless were used on all game for which a point of this size was suitable. Folsom points have been found at a considerable number of localities in the great plains of the interior of the United States, from Texas north into Canada. The southernmost locality from which they have been secured is at the Kincaid Shelter near Sabinal, Uvalde County, Texas. The northernmost locality is a surface find of a point on the plains of northwest Alaska.

Plainview Man

Plainview Locality, Hale County, Texas

The Plainview locality has been described by Sellards, Evans, Meade, and Krieger (1947). The discovery of this locality came about as follows: During the summer of 1944 Glen L. Evans and Grayson E. Meade, while studying the Pleistocene geology of the Texas High Plains for the Bureau of Economic Geology of the University of Texas, discovered a fossil bone bed exposed in a pit made for road materials within the city limits of Plainview, Hale County, Texas. The pit, opened in 1933 and worked intermittently for several years, is located on the south margin of the valley of Running Water Creek, one of the headwater tributaries of the Brazos River. The road material utilized is caliche and calcareous clay from the Panhandle formation. This formation, which includes strata of Pliocene and early Pleistocene age, underlies most of the Texas High Plains and is the bed-rock on which the valley fill of Running Water Creek is resting. As the pit was being extended northward into Running Water Creek valley to obtain caliche underlying the valley fill, the bison bones were exposed. Although bison bone bed was thus uncovered and a part of it removed, the locality was not reported until it was discovered by Evans and Meade in the summer of 1944. Excavations

60

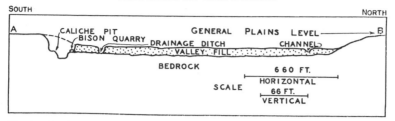

Fig. 27. *Section across the valley of Running Water Creek at the Plainview locality, Hale County, Texas.*

were carried on at this locality by the Texas Memorial Museum and the Bureau of Economic Geology of the University of Texas from June to October 1945 and during a part of November 1949. A north-south section across Running Water Creek valley is given in Figure 27.

The length of the bone bed excavated is about 70 feet. The width ranges from a maximum of 10 feet near the middle to 5 or 6 feet near the ends. The thickness ranges from a few inches near the margins to about 18 inches in the central part. The total excavated area is about 500 square feet. Many teeth, foot bones, and metapodials were well preserved in all parts of the deposit, but the larger bones were well preserved only in the thicker parts. Eight blocks of bones showing the full thickness of the bone bed were taken from the quarry in 1945. The location of three of these, marked 1, 2, and 3, is shown on the plat (Fig. 28). In November 1949 the excavation was extended eastward by about 8 feet and three additional blocks of bones were removed. Over most of its area the bone bed rested directly on caliche bedrock, but near the upstream and downstream ends it was separated from bedrock by a few inches of the valley fill. The bones evidently accumulated in a stream channel which at this place impinged on the south valley bluff.

The location of twenty-two artifacts found in place in the bone bed is shown on the plat (Fig. 28). Five other artifacts were displaced from their position in the bone bed during the process of excavation and are not shown on the plat. One additional artifact, a scraper, was found in November 1949. All artifacts illustrated are now in the collections of the Texas Memorial Museum.

The Plainview bison (Fig. 29) is much larger than the modern bison or American buffalo and is provisionally identified as *Bison taylori*. The mature skull is comparable in size to *B. taylori*, the type

61

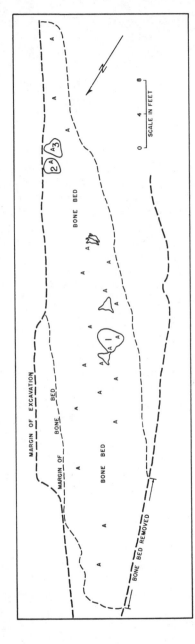

Fig. 28. *Plat of the bison quarry at the Plainview locality.* A, location of artifacts; 1, 2, and 3, location blocks of bones removed with artifacts in place.

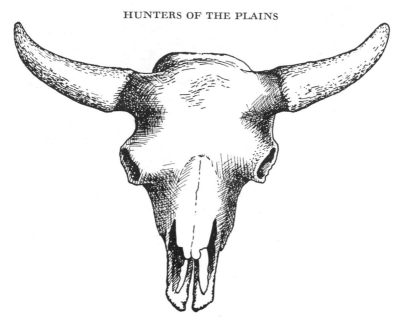

Fig. 29. *Skull of the bison found at the Plainview locality.* Approximately one-eighth natural size. Measurement of horn cores, tip to tip, 34 inches.

specimen of which is from Folsom, New Mexico (Hay and Cook, 1928).

The bone bed at the Plainview locality is a mass of closely packed bones. Skeletons and partial skeletons of approximately 100 bison were found in an area of about 500 square feet; the bone bed has an average thickness of about 1 foot. The manner of accumulation of so many bison in a limited space presents an interesting question.

The bones evidently accumulated in a shallow water-hole or pond within a former channel of Running Water Creek. That the water was shallow is indicated by the thin layer of pond sediment with broken and poorly preserved bones in the upper part. The bones accumulated either all at one time or within a short period of time, as proved by the homogeneous character of the bone bed which contains no separating layers of sediments. Had the accumulation taken place over a relatively long period of time, the bone bed would have been divided by successive layers of stream sediments since it lies in a stream channel and would have been flooded at relatively frequent intervals. The accumulation took place at least in part during the

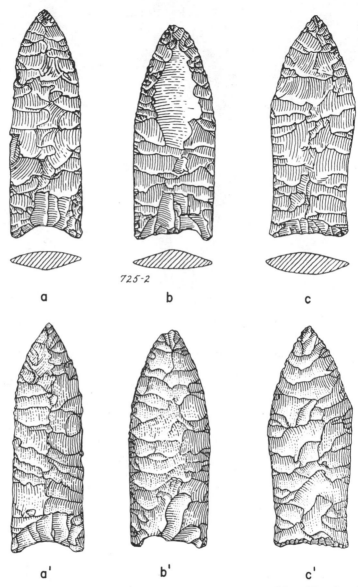

725-2

a   b   c

a'   b'   c'

Fig. 30. *Projectile points from the Plainview locality.* Tex. Mem. Mus. Acc. 725, Nos. 10, 2, and 5. Natural size.

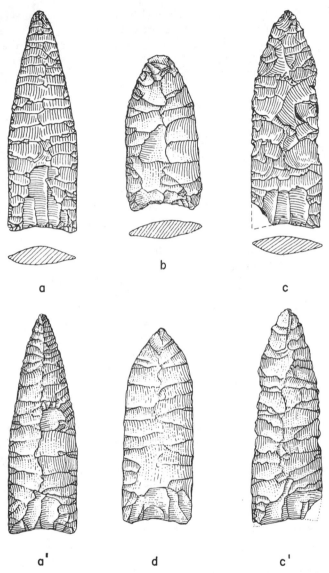

Fig. 31. *Projectile points from the Plainview locality.* Tex. Mem. Mus. Acc. 725, Nos. 4, 1, 8, and 23. Slightly reduced.

spring or early summer, as indicated by the several foetal skeletons which, judging from their size, must have been nearing the time of birth. The bison did not mire in the pond sediments, as the limb bones were found lying in a horizontal position. The associated artifacts prove that man was present at the locality and possibly had a part in killing the bison.

On the basis of these observations one may entertain several hypotheses as to the causes of the accumulation of so many skeletons. One such hypothesis is a bison stampede. Castañeda, the chronicler of Coronado's expedition (1540–1542), records an incident of a stampede of modern bison that is suggestive of what may have happened from time to time on the plains (Winship, 1896, p. 505). Speaking of one of the many great herds of bison seen on the High Plains, Castañeda says: "They came across so many animals that those who were on the advance guard killed a large number of bulls. As these fled they trampled one another in their haste until they came to a ravine. So many of the animals fell into this that they filled it up, and the rest went across on top of them. The men who were chasing them on horseback fell in among the animals without noticing where they were going. Three of the horses that fell in among the cows, all saddled and bridled, were lost sight of completely."

At the location of the bone bed the channel impinged against the valley wall, and hence there was probably a steep bluff bordering the south side of the water-hole. Stampeding bison attempting to cross the stream at this point might easily have fallen and become trampled by the remainder of the herd.

Implements found with the bones show that Plainview man was a skilled implement maker and probably a skilled hunter. The early hunters, like the modern Indians, probably were quite capable of planning and carrying out a bison stampede for their own benefit. There is no evidence to indicate whether the projectile points were shot into the bison prior to, during, or subsequent to such a stampede. However, the projectile points were in the upper half of the bone bed which may indicate that they were shot into those bison at the top of the pile which were crippled or attempting to extricate themselves. Probably only those bison at the top of the pile could have been utilized, which may account for the scrapers, as well as the projectile points, being found in the upper half of the bone bed.

An alternate hypothesis for the accumulation of so many bones in such a small area is that the bison skeletons may have accumulated

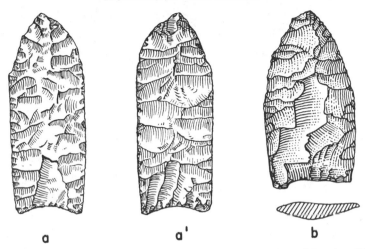

a   a'   b

Fig. 32. *Projectile points from the Plainview locality*. Tex. Mem. Mus. Acc. 725, Nos. 29 and 9. Natural size.

gradually over a period of several months or even several years. A gradual accumulation would have had to take place during a dry interval when the stream did not flow enough to carry layers of sediments into the pond. During such an interval, or even during a severe drought, scattered water-holes, such as the Plainview locality may represent, would have been regularly frequented by the bison and so would have provided an ideal stalking ground for hunters. The presence of the several dart points among the bones in the upper part of the fossil bed leads to the conclusion that man killed at least some of the bison. The slain animals, possibly individuals already weakened by natural causes or by man's darts, may have been dispatched on the spot or were severely wounded and came to the pond to die.

The artifacts found with the bison at Plainview include projectile points, scrapers, and probably knives. The unbroken projectile points and the best of the scrapers and knives found are illustrated in Figures 30, 31, 32, and 33. Several additional broken projectile points and two small scrapers were found. All of these were illustrated in the publication announcing the discovery of the locality (Sellards, Evans, Meade, and Krieger, 1947). Since Plainview man was a bison hunter his range possibly was throughout much of the plains region of North America.

67

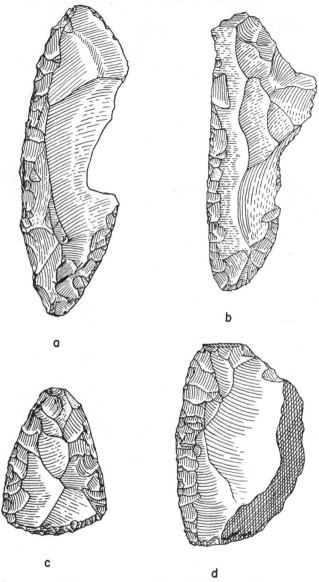

a

b

c

d

Fig. 33. *Scrapers from the Plainview locality*. Tex. Mem. Mus. Acc. 725, Nos. 17, 20, 15, and 21. Natural size.

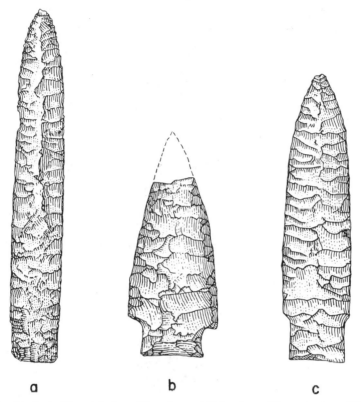

a b c

Fig. 34. *Projectile points from Wyoming and Nebraska.* a, Eden point from Finley, Wyoming; b and c, Scottsbluff points from Scottsbluff, Nebraska. From Schultz and Eiseley, Am. Anthropologist, vol. 3, Pl. 8, 1935. Natural size.

Other Plains Localities

To illustrate the development of hunting cultures it is necessary to refer to several additional localities in the Great Plains region.

Scottsbluff and Eden Points

The Scottsbluff point was described in 1932 by Barbour and Schultz from a locality in Scotts Bluff County, Nebraska. At the discovery locality, a total of eight artifacts were found all of which were closely

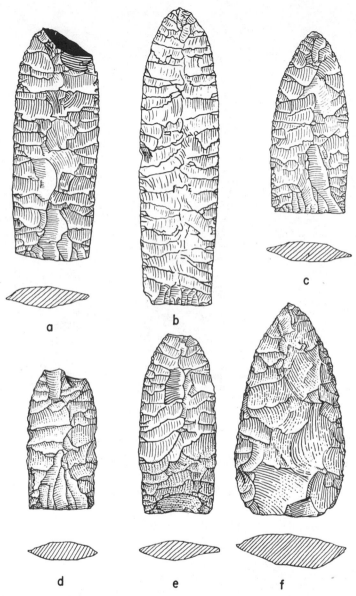

Fig. 35. *Projectile points from Stratum 5 (Portales horizon), Blackwater No. 1 locality, New Mexico.*

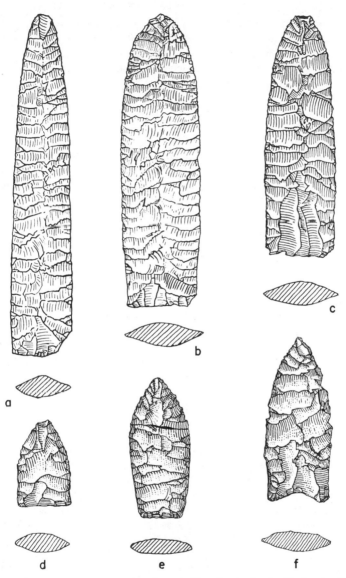

Fig. 36. *Projectile points from Stratum 5 (Portales horizon), Blackwater No. 1 locality, New Mexico.* Tex. Mem. Mus. Acc. 937, Nos. 26, 32, 22, 5, 63, and 75. Natural size.

associated with fossil bison. Of the artifacts, four are projectile points. One projectile point is complete (Fig. 34, c). Another (Fig. 34, b) lacks the tip. The other two points found lack the base. The bones and artifacts occur in stream deposits. The overlying materials, 12 feet or more in thickness, are said to be wind-blown (Schultz and Eiseley, 1935, p. 307).

Scottsbluff points are now known over a considerable part of the United States, including Wyoming, Louisiana, and Texas. Considerable variation is to be seen in the Scottsbluff points. Of the points from the type locality one is slightly constricted at the base, while the other is distinctly stemmed. A point found at the Buckner ranch locality in Bee County, Texas, although lacking the tip and part of the base, is very like the Scottsbluff points and is provisionally referred to that type.

The discovery locality of the Eden point is the Finley site in Wyoming, where these points (Fig. 34, a) were found for the first time in place in association with skeletons of bison. The locality, about 4.5 miles east of Eden, was discovered by O. M. Finley in 1940 and was excavated chiefly during 1940 and 1941. Persons and institutions participating in the excavation, in addition to Mr. Finley, were Harold J. Cook of Agate, Nebraska; Edgar B. Howard and Linton Satterthwaite, Jr., of the University of Pennsylvania; and C. Bertrand Schultz and others of the Nebraska State Museum. The fossils and artifacts were obtained from a sandy clay stratum underlying sand dune deposits (Howard, Satterthwaite, and Bache, 1941). The occurrence of the basal part of an Eden-like point in Alaska (Hibben, 1943, Pl. 15, Fig. A) apparently indicates extension of the Eden point northward to Alaska.

The Portales Complex

On earlier pages an account is given of the artifacts of horizons 2 and 4 of the Blackwater locality No. 1 on the Baxter ranch, Roosevelt County, New Mexico. Horizon 5 of this locality, which rests disconformably on stratum 4, also contains artifacts. This stratum, which has a thickness of from 1 to 3 feet, is best developed towards the west side of the south pit where it contains in its upper part a great quantity of skeletons of bison. Excavations made in this stratum have shown that with these bison bones are artifacts unlike those in either horizon 2 or horizon 4, the most marked differences being in the projectile points. Excavations made by the Texas Memorial Museum

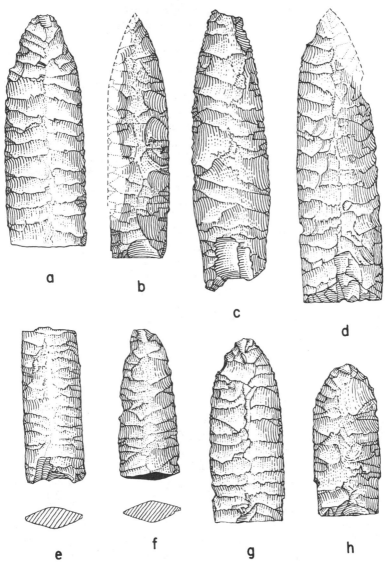

Fig. 37. *Projectile points from Stratum 5 (Portales horizon), Blackwater No. 1 locality, New Mexico.* Tex. Mem. Mus. Acc. 937, Nos. 62, 34, 16, 79, 67, 17, 33, and 80. Natural size.

in 1949 and 1950 resulted in securing twenty-three projectile points from this horizon. Of these, sixteen are complete or nearly so, the remaining seven being broken. Artifacts obtained other than points were four scrapers and some worked flakes. Considerable variation is found among the points. Three (Nos. 937–17, 937–26, and 937–67) resemble Eden points and may safely be taken as indicating a relationship in time with the Finley locality in Wyoming (Howard *et al.*, 1941). Several of the points are suggestive of the Scottsbluff point, the type locality of which is at Scottsbluff, Nebraska. However, none is as definitely constricted at the base as the points from Scottsbluff. One point (937–63) differs from all others of the lot in that it is narrowed towards the base. Another, No. 937–75, presents, as previously mentioned, some resemblance to Plainview points. This pronounced change in projectile points indicates that a new culture appeared on the High Plains during the interval represented by the disconformity between stratum 4 and stratum 5 of the Blackwater No. 1 section, as none of the points at this horizon resembles Folsom points. The culture at this level—stratum 5 of the Blackwater No. 1 locality—has been designated Portales Complex. The artifacts obtained from this level are illustrated in Figures 35, 36, 37, and 38. Among the projectile points of stratum 5 are some that resemble the San Jon point described by Roberts (1942a).

Other Sites

Collections from the Angostura Reservoir site, South Dakota, not yet fully described, include a distinctive artifact named by Hughes the Long point. A sample of burned bison bone from this locality gave an age determination by the radiocarbon method of 7,715 ± 740 years (Arnold and Libby, 1950).

The Horner site on Sage Creek in Wyoming contains many artifacts associated with bison. A sample of burned bison bone from this locality, obtained by G. L. Jepsen, gave an age determination by the radiocarbon method, average of two samples, of 6,876 ± 250 years (Arnold and Libby, 1950).

A sample submitted by C. B. Schultz from the Lime Creek site, Frontier County, Nebraska, gave an age determination, average of two tests, of 9,524 ± 450 years (Roberts, 1951, p. 21).

Another site, Medicine Creek, also in Frontier County, is uncertain as to age (Roberts, 1951, p. 21).

74

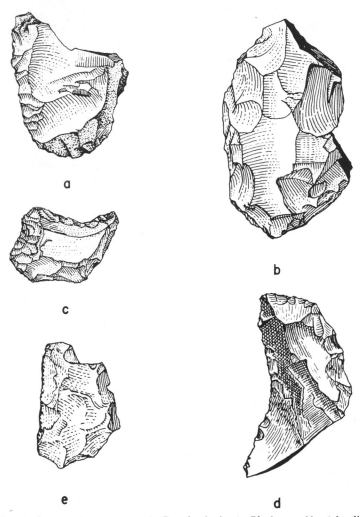

a

c

b

e

d

Fig. 38. *Scrapers from Stratum 5 (Portales horizon), Blackwater No. 1 locality, New Mexico.* Tex. Mem. Mus. Acc. 937, Nos. 64, 53, 70, 14, and 8. Natural size.

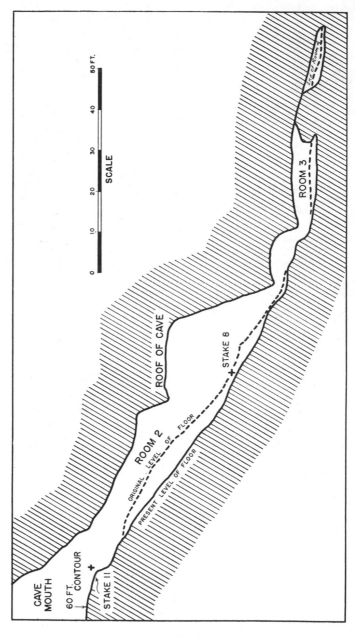

Fig. 39. *Gypsum Cave, Nevada.* From Harrington, Southwest Museum Papers, No. 8, 1933. Courtesy Los Angeles Museum.

The Cordilleran Mountain Belt

WEST OF THE PLAINS region of North America is the great Cordilleran mountain belt which, entering the continent through the Aleutian Islands and the Alaskan Peninsula, extends southward, bordering the Pacific coast through Canada and the United States and occupying most of the mountainous regions of Mexico (Fig. 1). The maximum width of this belt in the United States, from the Coast Ranges on the west to the Rocky Mountains on the east, is approximately 1,000 miles. Throughout its extent from Alaska to Mexico, it is a wonderfully complex region of mountains, mountain valleys, and plateaus. A considerable number of sites of early man lie within this region from Alaska to southern Mexico, and it is evident that while hunting cultures were developing in the Great Plains region east of the Rocky Mountains, parallel cultures, in part hunting and in part gathering, were developing in the mountain regions. Some of the sites within this area will be described briefly.

Gypsum Cave Locality, Clark County, Nevada

In the eastern foothills of the Frenchman Mountains in southeastern Nevada is a cave that has added much to our knowledge of early man. Although long known locally, the cave was not known to contain relics of early man until it was explored by the Southwest Museum of Los Angeles, chiefly during 1930. The results of the explorations have been fully presented by Harrington (1933). The name Gypsum Cave originated from the fact that gypsum (selenite) crystals are found in some abundance in parts of the cave.

The cave faces southwest, the opening being about 70 feet wide by 15 feet high. The over-all length of the cave underground is about 300 feet and its maximum width 120 feet. It is imperfectly divided into rooms. In the accompanying illustration (Fig. 39), reproduced by courtesy of the Southwest Museum, can be seen the cave mouth and rooms 1, 2, 3, and 4. Room 5 leads off from room 4, and a small room, No. 6, leads off from room 3. The feature of this cave which

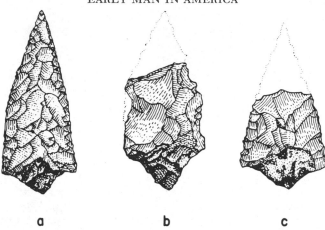

a   b   c

Fig. 40. *Gypsum points from Gypsum Cave, Nevada.* From Harrington, Southwest Museum Papers, No. 8, 1933, pp. 42 and 44. Courtesy Los Angeles Museum. Natural size.

makes it of unusual value to archeology is that it has been dry enough to preserve, through thousands of years, organic materials that would not otherwise have been permanently preserved.

Gypsum Cave had been inhabited, perhaps intermittently, through a very long period of time and contains relics of early man and of more modern Indians. Among fossil animal remains are the following species, now extinct: ground sloth, small llama-like camel, large camel, and horse. The plants well enough preserved to be identified are all of species now growing in southern Nevada. Among kinds of wood used in making atlatl darts are elder and buckthorn. The plant species obtained indicate a dry, cool climate. A new type of projectile point was found in this cave to which Harrington has applied the name Gypsum point (Fig. 40).

The organic materials found in this cave, such as sloth hair, burnt sticks, wood used in artifacts, and other organic substances, afford an exceptional opportunity to determine age by the radiocarbon method. Tests reported from the Institute for Nuclear Studies of the University of Chicago on samples obtained by Harrington, average of two samples, give 10,455 ± 340 years. These tests, however, were made not by use of the wooden artifacts of the cave but by use of sloth dung believed to be contemporaneous with the artifacts. It is to be hoped that check tests can now be made using parts of artifacts made of wood. In any case, Gypsum Cave affords a record of human habitation, probably intermittent, through a long period of time.

Leonard Rock Shelter, Pershing County, Nevada

Another important locality in Nevada is Leonard Rock Shelter on the west slope of Humbolt Mountains near Lovelock. Here Heizer (1951) obtained artifacts in the shelter deposits at different levels. One of these, the foreshaft of an atlatl, by radiocarbon test yielded an age determination of 7,038 ± 350 years. Bat guano, obtained at a somewhat lower level, gave an age determination, average of two tests, of 8,660 ± 300 years (Arnold and Libby, 1950). The artifacts of this locality have not yet been fully described.

Sulphur Springs, Arizona

An open site record of early man within the Cordilleran mountain belt is that of the Sulphur Springs stage of the Cochise culture of southeastern Arizona. Historically the Sulphur Springs region is of more than average interest. Here Professor Byron Cummings found an elephant skull and near and somewhat below it, artifacts. Bones of bison and horse were also present. According to Stock (in Sayles and Antevs, 1941, p. 64) the elephant is *Archidiskodon*. The species of bison and horse were not determined. Cummings' very important discovery was made in 1926. Later, in addition to the elephant, horse, and bison, Sayles and Antevs (1941) found in these deposits the dire wolf and the prong-horned antelope, as well as the coyote and some other living species.

The people of this region at this time had no projectile points made of stone, or at least none was found. The people were primarily gatherers of food, obtained from the native vegetation which was then luxuriant. The cultural objects obtained are essentially those of non-hunting people, consisting of hammerstones, large milling stones, small manos or handstones, and percussion-flaked tools probably used as scrapers, knives, and axes. Some use of animals as food, however, is indicated by animal bones broken presumably for the marrow, so hunting must have been carried on to a limited extent. Objects made of wood were not preserved in these deposits.

The conditions prevailing during the Sulphur Springs stage, according to Sayles and Antevs (1941), are as follows: climate more moist than at present; vegetation much more luxuriant than now, including hickory and doubtless other trees; a fauna including dire wolf, coyote,

79

The dire wolf, *Aenocyon*.

and such grazing animals as elephant, bison, horse, and antelope. Part of a skeleton found indicates a people with a long, narrow skull. Radiocarbon dates obtained from two localities, identified by Sayles and Antevs as of the Sulphur Springs stage, are 6,210 ± 450 and 7,756 ± 370 years respectively (Arnold and Libby, 1950, p. 10).

At least two, perhaps three, later stages have been recognized in the Cochise region. With these later stages all animal remains obtained are of living species, the several species which characterize the older stage having seemingly become extinct. An erosional break is said to separate the Sulphur Springs stage from the later stages. The length of time represented by this unconformity is at least in part indicated by a radiocarbon date of 4,006 ± 270 years for the next overlying culture, Chiricahua.

The elephant of this locality, identified by Stock as *Archidiskodon*, occurs, according to Sayles and Antevs, in the formation from which the carbon samples were obtained. The elephant skeletal parts were disarticulated, and therefore it should be considered whether or not they could have been moved into these deposits from an older formation.

Ventana Cave, Arizona

Ventana Cave, described by E. W. Haury and others (1950), is a shelter-like opening under volcanic rock in Ventana Mountain, a spur near the south end of the Castle Mountains, southwestern Arizona. The rock shelter opening extends along the face of the mountain in a southwest-northeast direction, the habitable part having an over-all length of about 175 feet. The opening thus faces southeast. The shelter is divided by a natural rock partition into two parts connected by one small opening. That part of the shelter to the southwest of the partition, being somewhat higher in elevation, is referred to as the upper cave, the part to the northeast of the partition being the lower cave. The opening of the lower cave extends along the mountain side about 55 feet, its depth back under the ledge of volcanic rock being about 20 feet. The upper cave is larger and has an opening extending 115 feet along the mountain side. Its extent back into the mountain varies from 25 feet near the partition on the northeast to as much as 65 feet at the southwest. In the widest part of the upper cave is a permanent spring, an unfailing attraction for human habitation.

The basal deposit in the cave is a conglomerate deposited on the original rock floor. Resting on the conglomerate is a stratum consisting

81

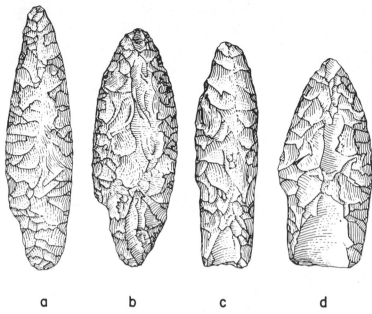

a   b   c   d

Fig. 41. *Sandia points from Sandia Cave, New Mexico.* After Hibben, from Smithsonian Misc. Coll., vol. 90, no. 23, Pl. 10, Fig. 2; Pl. 11, Fig. f; and Pl. 12, Fig. a.

chiefly of volcanic debris with some rock fallen from the roof. Above the volcanic debris and of limited distribution is a hard pinkish sand stratum. Elsewhere in the cave at about the same level as the sand is talus material washed into the cave. The four horizons, having a combined thickness of 5 or 6 feet, represent the water-deposited formations of the shelter and occur only in the upper cave. Of later age, extending over both the upper and lower caves, and having a maximum thickness of 10 feet, are deposits consisting chiefly of fine dust, animal bones, fragments of rocks, and debris resulting from human habitation. These later midden deposits form the present floor of the cave.

The basal deposit, a conglomerate, contains charcoal and what may be a scraper and a hammerstone. The extinct species found in the conglomerate layer, represented mostly by isolated teeth, are dire wolf, four-pronged antelope, horse, and tapir. The oldest identifiable culture, found in the next to the lowest horizon in the cave, clearly represents an ancient human habitation. The man-made objects found at this level, all of which are of stone, include projectile points, knives, scrapers, gravers, choppers, planes, hammerstones, and grinding stones. Of projectile points, unfortunately, only two were found at this level. One is of the size and shape of the projectile point of the Folsom culture except that it lacks fluting, the most distinctive Folsom characteristic. The other point found at this level is slightly notched at the base and is evidently of a culture quite apart from Folsom. Of a total of 88 other artifacts, 63 were scrapers of various kinds.

The pinkish sands above the volcanic debris stratum, although of limited extent, nevertheless yielded a distinctive type of projectile point which Haury has named the Ventana-Amargosa point. The associated animals at and above this level are of modern species.

From the midden deposits above the pinkish sand were obtained more than 11,000 stone artifacts. These are not only too numerous but likewise too diverse for description here. Pottery is present only in the uppermost 3 feet of the midden deposit. The upper part of the midden material is very dry. Within this part of the cave were many burials in which not only skeletons and ornaments but also wood, fiber, and textiles were preserved, affording an important record of the inhabitants of the cave in relatively recent times.

Sandia Cave, Sandoval County, New Mexico

Sandia Cave, in the Sandia Mountains of New Mexico, contains deposits in which are found artifacts and vertebrate fossils. The basal artifact-bearing deposit in the cave, a limestone breccia overlying a barren gravel horizon, contained a distinctive projectile point to which was given the name Sandia. Nineteen whole or broken Sandia points were found at this level. These may be imperfectly separated into two varieties designated *a* and *b* (Hibben, 1941). Variety *a* usually has a well-defined side notch, is rounded to the base, and lacks pronounced basal flaking; variety *b*, in addition to the side notch, usually present, is not distinctly rounded to the base, has more or less pronounced basal flaking, and has, in most instances, a slightly concave base (Fig. 41). Type *a* occurs mostly, but not entirely, at a lower level in the deposits than type *b*. Also, the two types intergrade. With the projectile points in the cave were found scrapers, flint chips, worked bone, and hearths. The fossil vertebrates found in the deposits containing the Sandia points include horse, camel, mastodon, elephant, and bison.

Some yellow ocher occurs in the deposits and above the ocher is a

83

breccia consisting largely of limestone fragments. The vertebrates found at this level are horse, camel, elephant, ground sloth, bison, and wolf. In this breccia were points similar to points obtained from above the Folsom level at Blackwater locality No. 1, New Mexico. Three such points, according to Hibben, were obtained, two having been found in place and one on the screen. One lanceolate point was also found in this breccia (Hibben, 1941, Pl. 5, Fig. 2, and Pl. 6, Fig. 2). These four points lack longitudinal grooves. In addition, four fluted or grooved points were found. Three of these, two complete or nearly so and one consisting of the base only, are typically Folsom points. The fourth, of which the base only is preserved, is also from a fluted point of some kind. A considerable number of other artifacts, including scrapers, gravers, and some bone implements, were found in the limestone breccia.

Dr. Hibben offers the hypothesis that this breccia is primarily a Folsom horizon, the non-fluted points being Folsom points which lack longitudinal grooves. This hypothesis receives support from the fact that non-fluted Folsom points are known at some other localities. However, the divergence from the fluted type is greater here than at any other known Folsom locality.

Fort Rock Cave, Oregon

In the side of a denuded cave of basaltic scoria, 1.5 miles west of the crater of an extinct volcano known as Fort Rock, are two caves, one opening to the north, the other to the south. The cave opening to the south was long inhabited by man while that opening to the north was uninhabited or nearly so. The south cave extends back into the scoria 65 feet. The entrance is about 33 feet wide. Not only did the cave face south but it had the additional protection of a wall extending beyond the cave mouth on the west side, so that it was admirably located for human habitation. The region in which this cave is located is of historical interest to geologists because Cope published on Silver Lake and Fossil Lake of this region in 1878, and in 1879 obtained fossil animal bones and obsidian artifacts from Silver Lake.

During the period of human habitation of the south cave a volcanic eruption in this part of Oregon resulted in the deposition of pumice in both north and south caves. This pumice is believed to have come not from Crater Lake, 60 miles to the southwest, but from Newberry

Fig. 42. *Bone artifact from Tequixquiac, Mexico.* From De Terra, 1949, p. 68, Fig. 13A. Courtesy, Viking Fund. Also illustrated by Aveleyra (1950, Pl. 15).

Crater in the Paulina Mountains 20 miles north. In the north cave the pumice layer is 4 feet thick.

Human habitation was of course interrupted by the volcanic eruption but not necessarily for a long period of time. Artifacts found under the pumice include sandals, basketry, wood, bone, horn, and stone objects. Only one piece of basketry was found. Wooden objects include part of a fire drill and part of an atlatl. Two bone awls and a flaking tool made from deer antlers were obtained. Stone artifacts were numerous, including stemmed and stemless projectile points, scrapers, drills, manos, and other stone and shell objects.

A remarkable feature of the cave is that more than seventy-five sandals were preserved, some very fragmentary, having been found under the pumice. All of the sandals, as well as other inflammable material under the pumice, were more or less charred. All of the sandals were made from shredded sagebrush bark. It is difficult to account for so many sandals at one place.

An age determination of the sandals was made by the radiocarbon method on samples obtained by Cressman, the average of two tests being 9,053 ± 350 years (Arnold and Libby, 1950).

Mexico

Dr. Helmut De Terra has recently described three localities in Mexico representing occurrences of early man. One of these is the Tepexpan man found about 20 miles northeast of Mexico City. The considerable part of a human skeleton found at this locality has been discussed by De Terra, Arellano, Aveleyra, Connolly, Fastlicht, Laughlin, Martínez del Río, Romero, and Stewart (1949). Arellano (1946, 1951) excavated parts of skeletons of two elephants and found evidence of man with each. Maldonado and Aveleyra (1949) have

85

recently obtained additional artifacts from the Tequixquiac locality.

De Terra reports artifacts in place in a Pleistocene formation at two localities. One of these is at San Francisco Mazapan near the pyramids at Teotihuacan about 6 miles northeast of the Tepexpan site. The other, Tequixquiac, is about 37 miles north-northwest of Mexico City. Both localities are said by De Terra to represent the Younger Becerra formation of late Pleistocene age. Among the few artifacts found in the formation is a worked bone (Fig. 42) not unlike implements found in the basal artifact-bearing horizon of Blackwater locality No. 1, New Mexico.

A considerable number of reported early man sites in Mexico, in addition to those here mentioned, are described by Aveleyra (1950). Aveleyra's publication also contains a bibliography of Mexican prehistory.

The Atlantic and Gulf Coastal Plains

THE COASTAL PLAIN belt bordering the Gulf of Mexico and the Atlantic Ocean presents an environment differing from that of the mountains or of the great interior plains. Some of the inhabitants of this region, particularly in certain parts of Mexico, southern Texas, Louisiana, the Mississippi embayment, and the South Atlantic states, must have met with particularly difficult conditions brought about by the presence of uncontrollable quantities of mosquitoes, some of which were carriers of disease. The vivid account given by Cabeza de Vaca of the almost unendurable conditions under which the American Indians of the Gulf region were living at the time of the arrival of Europeans is evidence of the unfavorable conditions under which many of the coastal tribes were living at that time. It is probable that during glacial time and directly following, living conditions in the southern Coastal Plains were better than at the time of Cabeza de Vaca. Man apparently inhabited the Coastal Plain belt at least intermittently at a time when the large mammals commonly accepted as indicating Pleistocene time were present. Historically the Atlantic Coastal Plain region has great interest, since localities in this region gave rise to some of the vigorous early arguments as to the presence of early man in America.

The Natchez Locality, Mississippi

In 1846 M. W. Dickeson announced the discovery of an interesting group of vertebrate fossils, which included a part of a human pelvis, near Natchez, Mississippi. Lyell, who examined the pelvic bone of man and other fossils, states that the human bone "appeared to be quite in the same state of preservation and was of the same black color as the other fossils." Leidy also observed that the degree of fossilization was exactly the same as that of the bones of extinct mammals which were found with it and that the bone differs in no other respect from that of the corresponding bone of recent man. The fossils reported to have occurred with the human bone (Leidy, 1889)

The native American horse, *Equus*.

are: *Mastodon americanus, Megalonyx jeffersonii, M. dissimilis, Ereptodon priscus, Mylodon harlani, Equus major,* and *Bison latifrons.* The horizon from which the bones were thought to have been derived is a clay stratum at a depth of approximately 30 feet from the surface. Wilson (1895), finding the fluorine content of the human bone found at Natchez to be somewhat greater than that of a *Mylodon* bone from the same locality, concludes that at this locality the man and the *Mylodon* are substantially of the same antiquity.

The Natchez locality was visited by the writer in 1917. If the exact location from which Dickeson originally obtained the fossils can be re-located, valuable additional discoveries might be made.

The Vero-Melbourne Localities, Florida

In 1916, human skeletal remains and artifacts were found at Vero (now Vero Beach), Florida, associated with remains of various extinct species. The locality is in the valley of a small drainage-way known as Van Valkenburg Creek. The deposits at this place consist of a pottery-bearing horizon separated from older non-pottery-bearing deposits by an unconformity. In 1923 and 1925 very similar conditions were observed in the vicinity of Melbourne, about 30 miles north of Vero. As at Vero, the uppermost deposits rested unconformably on the underlying deposits. Also the older deposits contained, according to Drs. Loomis and Gidley, remains of man and extinct animals.

Both of these localities, Vero and Melbourne, have been very fully discussed and reference to literature will be found in the List of Localities. Among the relatively recent publications on this locality will be found that by Dr. T. D. Stewart (1946) relating to the human skulls found at Vero and at Melbourne, and a paper by Irving Rouse (1950, p. 22) suggesting that the artifacts and human bones found in the deeper horizon reached their present location during the time interval represented by the unconformity which separates the two horizons. The conditions of occurrence of the artifacts and human bones at the two localities afford no evidence of burials.

Analyses of Fossil Bones from Melbourne and Vero, Florida

Heizer and Cook, of the University of California, have made analyses of mammoth, horse, and human bones from the Melbourne, Florida, locality. The constituents tested for were fluorine, carbon, nitrogen, water, calcium, and phosphorus. In a manuscript soon to

90

be published in the *American Journal of Physical Anthropology* these authors state that: "The data, so far as they go, are quite consistent and it thus appears that the human sample is of the same order of antiquity as those of the extinct mammals" (letter of April 10, 1952).

Analyses of 31 samples from the Vero deposits, made by the Black Laboratories in 1951 under direction of Dr. John M. Goggin of the University of Florida, were for fluorine content only. The non-human skeletal parts from the most recent deposits, Stratum 3, a total of 11 samples, were found to vary in fluorine from 0.70% to 1.90%, average 1.32%. The 11 samples, with fluorine content, were as follows: opossum teeth, 0.7%, jaw of same specimen, 1.1%, and jaw of another specimen, 1.06%; deer vertebra, 1.1%, deer calcaneum, 1.2%; proboscidian (two samples) limb bone, 1.25%, and tooth, 1.5%; ground sloth, 1.5%; rabbit ulna, 1.5%; extinct armadillo (*Holmesina*), 1.8%; and camel, 1.9%. Unfortunately, the usefulness of this particular series of analyses is largely lost by the fact that some of the fragmentary bones, particularly of several extinct animals, including proboscidians, ground sloth, camel, and armadillo, collected from Stratum 3, were quite certainly washed into this formation from an older horizon, Stratum 2, and are not indigenous to Stratum 3.

The non-human skeletal parts analyzed from Stratum 2, a total of 15 samples, were found to vary in fluorine from 1.01% to 2%, the average being 1.48%. The 15 samples, with fluorine content, were as follows: tapir tooth, 1.01%; extinct great wolf, ribs, two samples, 1.19% and 1.2%; mastodon tooth, 1.3%; deer bone, 1.3%; fossil horse, foot bone, 1.43%, and one other bone, 1.11%; ground sloth, 1.5%; extinct great armadillo (*Holmesina*), tooth, 1.4%, and parts of carapace, two samples, 1.5% and 1.9%; turtle, 1.7%; alligator, 1.75%; camel, 2%; and opossum, 2%.

Four samples of human skeletal parts from the Vero locality were analyzed. These, with fluorine content, were as follows: a part of ilium, 0.85%; femur, 1.26%; skull, 1.3%; and tibia, 1.3%. One bone artifact was analyzed and found to contain 1.43% fluorine. The average fluorine of the human samples from the deposits, including the bone artifact, is 1.22%. Extinct species present in Stratum 2 in which the fluorine in the bones was equal to or less than that in some of the human bones are tapir, dire wolf, horse, and mastodon. Whether or not the considerable variation in amount of fluorine in

91

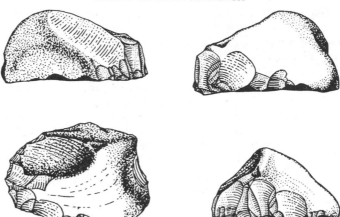

Fig. 43. *Artifact from Friesenhahn Cave, Texas.* Side, top, and end views of scraper found under skeleton of large tiger. Tex. Mem. Mus. Acc. 933, No. 2119. Natural size.

the human and animal bones is actual or is due at least in part to limitations in attainable accuracy in analytical procedure is undetermined at this time.

The writer is indebted to Dr. Herman Gunter, State Geologist of Florida, who has charge of the Vero collections, and to Dr. Goggin, who has made available the results of the analyses.

Chemical analyses of recent and fossil bones from the Vero locality, made at the writer's suggestion in 1916 in the Florida state laboratory under direction of the State chemist, were as indicated below.

	No. 1	*No. 2*	*No. 3*	*No. 4*
Specific gravity	2.0627	2.8357	2.6293	2.7505
Moisture at 100° C.	10.72	2.07	4.09	3.89
Volatile matter	19.59	8.92	8.22	10.30
Phosphoric acid, P_2O_5	27.24	32.27	30.88	32.00
Calcium oxide, CaO	39.75	46.80	45.69	48.31
Insoluble matter, silica, etc. ...	0.60	1.11	3.61	1.39
Iron and aluminum oxides...	0.13	3.71	1.85	0.76

No. 1 is a human tibia from an Indian mound and hence of relatively recent age. Nos. 2, 3, and 4 are from the deposits of the Vero locality. No. 2 is a human tibia; No. 3, femur of wolf; and No. 4, part of jaw of sloth (Sellards, 1916c, p. 133). The specific gravity was obtained from the finely powdered bone by the gravity bottle. The moisture, taken at 100° C., includes, as will be recognized, any other

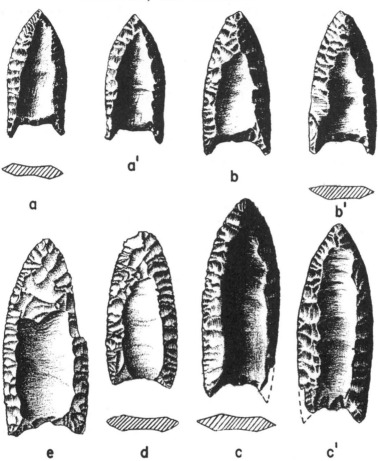

Fig. 44. *Folsom artifacts from Kincaid Shelter.* Found not in place. Locality discovered by Charles Eugene Mear and Kenneth Rochat. Tex. Mem. Mus. Acc. 926, Nos. 2, 3, and 4; Acc. 908, Nos. 2293 and 2291. Natural size.

constituents sufficiently unstable to be driven off at that temperature. Volatile matter, likewise, represents the constituents driven off when the sample is maintained at red heat in a muffle for several hours and necessarily includes carbon dioxide, organic matter, and possibly some other constituents.

The analyses, as will be seen, indicate reasonable consistency between the fossil human and animal bones in specific gravity, amount of moisture, volatile matter, phosphoric acid, and calcium oxide. On the other hand, the recent human bone differs notably in all respects from the fossil bones. The fluorine content of these samples was not determined.

Friesenhahn and Kincaid Localities, Texas

The Friesenhahn Cave located near the inner margin of the Texas Coastal Plain is unusual in that it contains a very large number of species of vertebrate fossils. The opening to this cave through which the animals entered became sealed at some time prior to the modern epoch, and this aided in the undisturbed preservation of the fossils. The cave at present may be entered through an opening in the roof. Among large mammalian species found in the cave are elephant, mastodon, horse, bison, peccary, tiger, and dire wolf. A scraper found under the skeleton of a large tiger in this cave is illustrated in Figure 43. The artifact is apparently of the age of the tiger and various other fossils, but further evidence will be sought.

Kincaid Shelter in Uvalde County, Texas, also near the Coastal Plain's inner margin, is of interest as one of the southernmost localities at which typical Folsom points are known to occur (Fig. 44). The Folsom points obtained at this locality were not in place, the cave deposits having been disturbed by previous digging.

Reference to additional localities of early man in the Atlantic and Gulf Coastal Plains and elsewhere in North and South America will be found in the List of Localities.

Some South American Localities

A DISCUSSION of South American localities of early man reported prior to 1912 will be found in a publication by Ales Hrdlicka in collaboration with W. H. Holmes, Bailey Willis, F. E. Wright, and C. N. Fenner (1912). Hrdlicka, in the 1912 publication, passes unfavorably on the early dating of all localities reported to that date. More recent investigations indicate that such condemnation was not in all instances justified.

Palli Aike Cave

From Palli Aike Cave near the Chile-Argentina boundary, Junius Bird (1938) obtained important information on the relation of early man to extinct animals in South America. The cave is in the rim of an extinct volcano, 168 feet above the surrounding plain, and faces away from the prevailing winds. It is 20 feet wide and extends into the volcanic rock 46 feet. The ceiling is 13.5 feet at the entrance and 6 feet at the back. The fill in the cave consisted of blocks of lava on the floor, overlain by 2 feet of volcanic ash and about 5 feet of fine dry dust.

Immediately above the volcanic ash, in the lower 6 inches, Junius Bird found scattered, broken, and burned bones of horse and ground sloth, and stone and bone tools in occupational debris; on the surface of the volcanic ash near the rear of the cave, he found three cremation burials. Beneath the volcanic ash were parts of seven sloth skeletons. Flakes and charcoal extended through the volcanic ash to the floor of the cave. Among the artifacts were stemmed stone points, end and side scrapers, awls, chipping and rubbing stones (Fig. 46). Burned bone of sloth and horse obtained by Bird from the oldest occupational level gave an age determination by the radiocarbon method of 8,639 ± 450 years (Arnold and Libby, 1950). Artifacts of later cultures were found at higher levels. This locality is of particular interest since it proves that man reached the southernmost part of South America more than 8,000 years ago.

Fig. 45. *Map showing a few reported early man localities in South America.* 1, Confins Cave; 2, Palli Aike Cave; 3, Punin.

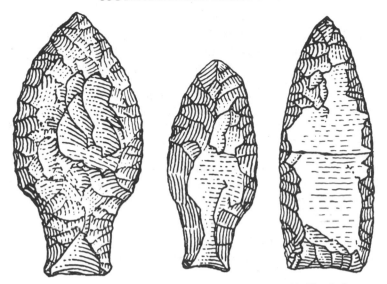

Fig. 46. *Artifacts from Palli Aike Cave.* From Bird, 1949, p. 24, Fig. 2. Courtesy, American Museum of Natural History.

Fell's Shelter

Near the Palli Aike Cave in Chile is a cave or shelter formed, according to Bird (1938), by undercutting by the Chico River. The shelter is 36 feet wide, 28 feet deep, and 11 feet from floor to ceiling. The shelter thus formed was occupied for a time during which occupational debris to a thickness of 2 to 9 inches accumulated. In this debris were four fire hearths, many bone fragments, stone and bone artifacts, and bones of horse, sloth, and guanaco. The artifacts included rubbing stones, many scrapers, stemmed projectile points, and one non-stemmed point which in outline is not unlike some relatively early points of North America. This artifact-bearing zone is believed to correlate approximately with the lower artifact-bearing horizon of Palli Aike Cave. This occupation layer was covered and sealed by sandstone caving from the roof of the shelter which formed a sterile layer 15 to 28 inches thick. Above this sterile zone was debris containing modern animals only and cultures differing from that below.

97

Confins Cave

The Danish naturalist W. P. Lund explored many caves in the Lagoa Santa region of eastern Brazil beginning as early as 1835. In these explorations he found human remains associated with extinct animal bones in several of the caves.

The Confins Cave is on the side of a limestone rock near the small village of Confins. The rock shelter in front of the cave had been long known locally because of Indian burials in it. In 1926 Dr. Pad-berg-Drenkpol of the Rio National Museum, while collecting from these Indian burials, discovered the cave, the entrance to which had been completely closed by a conglomerate of debris and fallen stones. In 1933 excavation of the cave was undertaken by the Academy of Science of Minas Geraes. The cave was then found to be 25 feet wide at the entrance, extending into the rock 65 feet, tapering in that distance to a width of about 5 feet. The fossil animals obtained were giant bear, llama, giant capybara, horse, sabre-tooth tiger, giant sloth, tapir, and mastodon. In 1935 a partial human skeleton, including the skull, was found under stalagmite at a depth in the cave debris of about 6.5 feet. The condition of the bones is reported to have been similar to that of the associated fossil animals. Inasmuch as the cave entrance had evidently been long sealed it is concluded that the man was contemporaneous with the fossil animals of the cave. No artifacts were found with the skeleton (Walter and others, 1937).

Markings on Stone and Bone

EARLY MAN IN AMERICA, as in Europe, marked or carved on bones and on rocks. Such markings are diverse; some, as the fine chipping on projectile points, are obviously an expression of a sense of beauty and symmetry. The markings on bone are not so readily accounted for and conceivably could have had some specific purpose not readily discernible.

Of the Llano culture there is known as yet only one marked bone (Fig. 13, a). However, several marked bones were obtained and illustrated by Roberts from the Lindenmeier-Folsom locality (Fig. 23). Possibly some or all of these marked bones made by Folsom man were used as ornaments. The making of ornaments implies attainment of some degree of leisure in the life of the people, some relief, however temporary, in the ever-pressing search for the daily supply of food. The people who followed the great bison herds and those who established villages probably are the ones who found time to think of something more than absolute necessities. Markings on a proboscidian tusk from the Vero locality, Florida, were described by the writer in 1916. These markings show a unity of form and regularity of spacing which seem to indicate human intelligence in their making. But the purpose of the marking is unknown.

Markings on stone, in one instance that has come to light, took the form of an attempt to reproduce the human likeness, apparently a beginning of sculpturing. No other artifacts were found with the stones, so the culture with which they are associated cannot be determined at this time.

The discovery of these stones came about as follows: In 1929 the Texas Clay Products Company, through I. Morgado and associates, had contracted for gravel from a pit on Judge Bishop's farm about 5 miles west of Malakoff, Texas. To get the deeper gravel, a hoist was installed and the gravel, which was loaded by hand labor in the pit, was hoisted to the surface. When the pit had been worked to a clay parting at a depth of about 16 feet, further downward working was

99

considered undesirable. However, in order to get better working space, a hole near the hoist was dug somewhat deeper. In making this hole, the workmen encountered a rounded boulder-like rock. After it was turned over and rolled out of the hole, Mr. Morgado observed markings on it which, when cleaned out, were found to be cuts representing the face of a man.

The stone was sent to the office of the Texas Clay Products Company at Malakoff. It is a calcareous, more or less ferruginous, sandstone concretion. The concretions in and under the gravel are more or less decayed, some of them to a depth of 2 or 3 inches. Decay in these rocks includes removal by solution of the calcareous cement and oxidation and hydration of the iron, so that the stone becomes crumbly and disintegrates. Like some of the other rocks of this locality, the carved stone disintegrated on exposure to the air to such an extent that its preservation required treatment to re-cement the crumbling sands. The stone was treated with a solution of gum arabic on January 4, 1930, and no subsequent disintegration has been apparent. When hoisted from the pit, the stone rolled against the truck and as a result of the jar lost a piece from the uncarved side which was not recovered. The break indicates that the stone is affected by decay to the depth broken and probably to some extent throughout. The stone as now preserved weighs 98.375 pounds (Fig. 47).

This stone lay, as indicated by the depression in the ground, with its longer axis north-south and with the larger end to the south. The larger end rested on bedrock, and under the smaller end were a few inches of coarse gravel. Clinging to the uncarved side is some clay and gravel of the nature of the clay-gravel parting to which the pit was worked. In view of the rate at which the stone oxidizes and crumbles when exposed to the air, it could have been preserved only by lying at or near water level at the bottom of the gravel deposit.

The pit in which the stone was found contains typical stream-deposited gravel which varies in size in successive layers. In general, the coarsest gravel is toward the bottom, although, as previously noted, near the bottom is a thin gravel and clay layer which has more or less of an iron-cemented incrustation. The gravel is, in places, intensely cross-bedded, this being particularly true in the finer materials. Within 3 or 4 feet of the surface the gravel grades into red sandy material of the nature of loamy sub-soil, and at the surface to soil. The stone is elongate or egg shaped, being about 16 inches long and 13 or 14 inches in greatest width. From that part of

Fig. 47. *Carved stone from Henderson County, Texas.* Found in place by I. Morgado. Tex. Mem. Mus. Acc. 1100. Approximately two-sevenths natural size.

the concretion which represents the face, from the ears to the chin, a portion of the original rock may have been removed, narrowing the stone downwards, thus more nearly resembling a face. Underneath the chin a roughly circular opening approximately 50 mm. in diameter and 25 to 30 mm. deep has been excavated. The concretion, like some others of the formation, was probably originally egg shaped. If so, the pointed end has been truncated to make a flat under-side to the chin, probably to make the object sit upright more readily. Behind the eyes the stone differs in color from the face, being ochre-yellow, while the face is more nearly ash-gray with some admixture of yellow. This difference in color represents not a difference in composition of the rock but rather a difference in the degree of oxidation, the gray being the less well-oxidized part; the outer more oxidized part was removed at the time the sculpturing was done.

The prominent features of the face—eyes, nose, mouth, chin and ears—are plainly carved on the stone. The excavation for the right eye is about 53 mm. long by 20 wide by 10 deep. That for the left eye is about 50 mm. long by 25 wide and scarcely as deep as that for the right eye. The eyebrows are represented by lines which are not entirely alike, that of the right eye being more carefully carved. The markings for the left eye are somewhat better preserved and less dulled by oxidation than are those of the right eye. The nose, which is low and broad, is brought out in relief by slight excavation at either side. The excavation for the mouth is 120 mm. from side to side, 35 mm. across at the widest part, and 8 or 10 mm. in depth. The mouth opening is not symmetrical, the right half being larger, deeper, and seemingly more nicely finished than the left half. Teeth are represented at the lower side of the mouth cavity by sloping excavations made, apparently, with a boring implement. Six such bore-holes seem to represent lower teeth. Three smaller bore-holes may have been intended to represent upper teeth, although the resemblance is less perfect. The ears are carved in relief. The left is the better preserved and projects as much as 8 mm. from the head. As carved, the ear is 70 mm. long by 35 wide. The chin is set off by a lightly excavated line seemingly representing a "double chin." The purpose of the excavation under the chin remains unexplained, unless it were possibly to allow a support to be inserted to hold the head upright. On the left side of the face are several lines which are more or less parallel across the cheeks. In the upper part of the face these lines have lost distinction through oxidation but are better preserved on the cheek.

Above the left eye is a cut 40 mm. long and 4 or 5 mm. deep. Near it is a circular bore-hole 15 or 20 mm. across and about 10 mm. deep. The rock could not have been very firmly cemented when these markings were made, as indicated particularly by the cut. There are no markings on that part of the stone representing the back of the head.

A second carved stone was found in 1935, in a new pit opened on the Bishop farm about 1,000 feet west of pit No. 1. The new find, which was similar in many respects to that previously obtained, was made by the operator, Mr. Joe Gunnels. Pit No. 2 had been opened and some gravel removed in 1933. No additional gravel was taken from the pit until July 1935. In September, Mr. Gunnels cut a trench in the bottom of the pit in order to determine the thickness of the gravel deposit, using a team and scraper to move the sand and gravel. Near the bottom of the gravel deposit, the scraper hit the carved stone, scratching off the outer, oxidized surface over an area 4 by 5.5 inches. The scar made by the scraper is on the top of the head, and Mr. Gunnels says the stone was sitting upright. This statement is further supported by the conditions of preservation. A deposit of calcium carbonate is seen on the carving at the right side of the chin. A similar deposit is present on the right side of the face and partially covers the cut surface at the back of the head. Since the stone lay near ground-water level, the fluctuation of which would involve alternate wetting and drying, and since the coating forms on rocks and other objects in the earth subjected to alternate moist and dry conditions, it would appear that the stone sat upright, tilted slightly towards the right side. The coating also is indisputable evidence that the carving was done prior to the time when the stone was included in the terrace deposits.

The second carved stone is somewhat smaller than the first one found. Its weight is 63.25 pounds. Like No. 1, it is shaped from one of the concretionary boulders found at this locality. This rock, like the larger stone, tended to disintegrate on exposure to the air and was treated by a solution made by dissolving celluloid in acetone. This treatment was not entirely satisfactory, and the rock was subsequently immersed in a solution of gum arabic which penetrates the pore space, effectively cements the grains, and, by excluding the air, prevents further disintegration. Stone No. 2 is likewise somewhat egg shaped. It is about 15 inches long and 12 inches wide and had received little remodeling. The mouth is represented by a carved line, there being no attempt to show teeth. The cut for the right eye is approxi-

103

mately 100 mm. long by 25 mm. wide and for the left, 90 mm. long by 25 mm. wide. Each eye slit is directed obliquely forward and downward. An eyebrow is definitely represented on the left eye, less definitely so on the right eye. Between the eyes is an unexplained deep excavation. The ears are but slightly represented, the left being more prominent. The deepest excavation on the rock was a notch in the back side of the head which was cut to a depth of about 3 inches. Because of this notch, the finished object, when viewed from the side, closely resembles a skull. However, it seems more probable that the notch was made so that the stone could lean against some object, thus making a support for the head. It is probable that stone No. 2 when in use was held in position by a band passing entirely around the head and under the chin. This is suggested by a slight trench or depression best seen on the right side.

A third carved stone was found November 1939 in pit No. 1 at a depth of 22 feet. The stone is of irregular shape, about 20 inches long, and weighs 135 pounds. It was photographed before being moved from its place in the earth. It lay near the base of the deposit, there being only a thin layer of gravel and sand intervening between it and bedrock. This carved rock is a sandstone boulder, which has more or less disintegrated at the surface. The carving consists of a cut near one end, which could have been intended to represent the mouth, back of which are some irregularly placed cuts which may have been intended to define the nose. A deep median cut back of these seems to have no meaning unless it is the mouth of another face on the same stone. The right eye of this face is represented by a deep excavation. On the opposite side, a large piece has been broken from the stone so that the left eye, if formerly present, is not preserved. Possibly these deep cuts consisting of eyes and mouth represented a face and, when it was disfigured by a piece breaking from the left side, a second face was made in front of it. So crude are the markings that the second face could represent that of an animal other than man.

All of the carving on this particular stone may possibly have been made in sharpening or polishing instruments. Some of the unexplained cuts on No. 2 may be due to the same cause. It seems possible, indeed, that cuts used in sharpening or polishing instruments may have suggested human features and thus led to fashioning the concretions into images of human heads. The instruments with which the cuts were made have not been found. If of hard wood, they would not have been preserved. Whatever may have led early man to make these carvings, the conditions of occurrence prove that they were made prior to the time when the stones were imbedded in the accumulating deposits of ancient Trinity River.

Origin of American Cultures

IN DISCUSSING CULTURES it becomes important to consider their probable origin. One possibility is that the early cultures found in the western hemisphere, or most of them, were developed elsewhere and were brought to America from the eastern hemisphere. The alternative view is that some or most of the American early man cultures are indigenous, having originated in various parts of the American continents, and that the various cultures did not necessarily orginate in the same region. It seems probable that many cultures originated in the western hemisphere. The duration of each culture would vary depending upon its suitability to changing conditions under which the races using the culture lived. The spread of any particular culture, likewise, would depend upon its suitability to the needs of the races of people who came in contact with it. Under this view the several early cultures are not necessarily successional. More than one culture may have been in process of development at one time and, spreading across the continent, have overlapped other cultures.

The characteristics of the country in which early man lived—its physiographic features, mountainous or level; its climate, whether wet or dry, hot or cold; its plant and animal life—all of these undoubtedly influenced early man as they now influence modern man. The cultures that developed in the Cordilleran mountain belt cannot be expected to agree with those that developed on the adjoining Great Plains. This is especially true of the more specialized cultures. The projectile point developed by Folsom man, for instance, specially designed as it was for the bison hunt, is not likely to be found in abundance much beyond the range of the bison herds of the great interior plains, while the projectile point which has come to be known as Clovis Fluted and which seems to have been used primarily in the elephant hunt, may reasonably be expected to be found throughout most of the continent, the range of the elephant being continent-wide. Early man living in a region where the available food is largely or in part seeds and fruits, and where the game is varied, would be likely to develop a culture very different from that of tribes which specialized in hunting some particular animal or animals. Considerations of this kind should be kept in mind in studying the succession of cultures.

The first men to reach the American continents doubtless possessed some cultural objects. On the other hand, migration into a new region and living under changed conditions promote and encourage development of new cultures. When Folsom culture was discovered and found to be extensively developed in America, some scientists were inclined to regard this as a culture introduced into America, probably from Asia. It was also assumed by some that Folsom was the oldest American culture. But Sandia points first found in Sandia Cave, New Mexico, are believed by Hibben (1937) to be older than Folsom points found at a higher level at that locality. Also at the present time fluted points are known to occur in the Clovis-Portales region of New Mexico at a horizon underlying and hence older than the Folsom culture of that locality. For this reason it now seems much more reasonable to regard the Folsom points as an outgrowth and refinement of previously existing fluted points, their region of maximum development being the great interior plains of the United States and Canada, which was also the region of maximum development of the bison herds.

If the Folsom point is indigenous to America, having developed from the Clovis Fluted point, the problem of origin is not solved but is only moved backwards in time, and we have still the question of place of origin of the Clovis Fluted points. This earlier culture flourished at a time when proboscidians were an important and wide spread element of the fauna of the American plains region. However, the makers of the Clovis Fluted points did not come to America with the proboscidians, at least not with the first proboscidians, since both mastodons and elephants were long-time inhabitants of the continent. It might be argued that this culture, for which the writer has proposed the name Llano culture, came to America with some relatively late migration of one of the elephant species. This, however, would be purely hypothetical, and we must look for additional evidence to determine the place of its origin. It may well be that this culture likewise is indigenous to America, and that we are to expect still earlier cultures. Also, if it is true that Folsom points were developed from Clovis Fluted points as a special adaptation to bison hunting on the plains, it does not necessarily follow that the Clovis Fluted

107

projectile point did not continue in use for an undetermined length of time elsewhere on the continent.

Cultures later than Llano and Folsom are found in the southern High Plains under conditions that seem to indicate that they appeared on the plains within the time interval that separates Folsom from the next later horizon. A period of severe drought would result in disappearance from the plains of both animals and man. A return to the plains of herds of bison might then bring in a new culture. Such possibly is the history of the region and the explanation of the seemingly abrupt change from the Folsom complex to the several later types of projectile points.

Large Mammals of the Late Pleistocene

IT IS NOT POSSIBLE at the present time to list with certainty all animal species now extinct which were associated with early man. The character of the deposits and the conditions of deposition require consideration. Among the more difficult deposits to be interpreted with certainty are those deposited by running water as stream and river terraces, where owing to stream action there is a possibility of mixing of fossils. Much more reliable are the deposits of lakes and ponds, where currents are largely absent and deposition proceeds continuously or with such interruptions as arise from climatic or other conditions. The condition of the bones is important. In stream-laid deposits fossils that are fragmentary may be secondary. On the other hand, an articulated skeleton can not be secondarily deposited unless introduced by human agency. A fossilized skeleton can not be moved by stream action and redeposited without becoming disarticulated. Some skulls of animals likewise are too fragile to withstand redeposition.

Although it will be many years before a listing can be made of all animal species now extinct which were contemporaneous with early man, several species can be so listed with assurance at the present time and others with varying degrees of certainty. Mention is here made of certain of these extinct species. The several localities here referred to are more fully described elsewhere in this publication.

Elephant

Of the several North American elephants, *Parelephas columbi* was the most abundant and is the species of elephant most frequently reported associated with early man. The definite association of this species with artifacts has been established by Howard (1933) and by Cotter (1937a) in the Clovis-Portales region, New Mexico, and by Sellards, Evans, and Mead in 1938 at the Miami locality in Roberts County, Texas. In the coastal plains a similar association is reported by Gidley and Loomis at Melbourne, Florida, and by Sellards and

109

others at Vero, Florida; by Sellards and Evans in Bee County, Texas; and by Ray and Bryan near Abilene, Texas. The association at Dent, Colorado, and at the McLean site in Texas, previously described, is probably with this species.

At Sulphur Springs, Arizona, and at Los Angeles, California, artifacts have been found which were said to be in the same stratum as parts of the skeleton of the imperial elephant, genus *Archidiskodon*. At Angus, Nebraska, an artifact was reportedly found immediately with the skeleton of the imperial elephant. At Potter Creek Cave, California, bone artifacts have been obtained from cave deposits which contain an elephant identified as *Elephas primigenius*.

Mastodon

The American mastodon, closely related to the elephant, has been reported as occurring associated with human relics at a few localities, including Vero and Melbourne, Florida; Sandia Cave, New Mexico; Potter Creek Cave, California; Natchez, Mississippi; and Cromwell, Indiana. The reported find of a mastodon skeleton in Ecuador associated with spear points, potsherds, and a fireplace (Osborn, 1936) remains unclarified. Mastodon and elephant remains both occur in the frozen muck of Alaska. Artifacts also occur in these deposits, but the evidence of contemporaneity is not conclusive. The mastodon skeleton discovered in 1840 in Benton County, Missouri, by Albert Koch was placed in the British Museum, and the artifacts in the Royal Museum of the University of Berlin (Montagu and Peterson, 1944, pp. 413–414). Gross (1951) has recently suggested that this skeleton may be much older than the human relics found at the same place. He offers the same suggestion for the skeleton in Ecuador.

American Horse

Several species of fossil horse, genus *Equus*, have been found in association with human relics in North and South America. Among localities that may be consulted for evidence of this association are Burnet Cave, Blackwater locality No. 1 (lowest artifact horizon), Conkling Cavern, and Sandia Cave, New Mexico; Beeville and Lone Wolf Creek, Texas; Sulphur Springs, Arizona; Potter Creek Cave, California; Melbourne and Vero, Florida; Natchez, Mississippi; and in South America, Fell's Shelter and Palli Aike Cave. No hunting site revealing mass killing of horses has been found in America. The horse native to America became extinct, the modern horse of North and

South America having been introduced by Europeans in the sixteenth century.

Bison

The bison was probably more closely and persistently associated with and hunted by early man than any other of the large mammals, an association that began many thousands of years ago and continued, with changing species of bison, until late in the nineteenth century. Four centuries ago when the first Europeans, led by Coronado, crossed the southern High Plains of the New Mexico-Texas region, the Indians of that time were found living with and following the bison. Every member of the Coronado expedition who crossed the plains and gave an eye-witness account of the expedition marvelled at the immense herds of "cows" then on the plains and several commented at length on the Indian hunters who, with their women, children, dogs, and belongings, traveled with the herds. Among many accounts, that given by one of the friars who accompanied the expedition will serve to show the impression made on the Europeans by the bison and the Indian hunters of the plains of that time (Winship, 1896, pp. 570–571):

Four days from this village [now Pecos, New Mexico] they came to a country as level as the sea, and in these plains there was such a multitude of cows that they are numberless. These cows are like those of Castile, and somewhat larger, as they have a little hump on the withers, and they are more reddish, approaching black; their hair, more than a span long, hangs down around their horns and ears and chin, and along the neck and shoulders like manes, and down from the knees; all the rest is a very fine wool, like merino; they have very good, tender meat, and much fat. Having proceeded many days through these plains, they came to a settlement of about 200 inhabited houses. The houses were made of the skins of the cows, tanned white, like pavilions or army tents. The maintenance or sustenance of these Indians comes entirely from the cows, because they neither sow nor reap corn. With the skins they make their houses, with the skins they clothe and shoe themselves, of the skins they make rope, and also of the wool; from the sinews they make thread, with which they sew their clothes and also their houses; from the bones they make awls; the dung serves them for wood, because there is nothing else in that country; the stomachs serve them for pitchers and vessels from which they drink; they live on the flesh; they sometimes eat it half roasted and warmed over the dung, at other times raw; seizing it with their fingers, they pull it out with one hand and with a flint knife in the other they cut off mouthfuls, and thus swallow it half chewed; they eat the fat raw, without warming it; they drink the blood just as it leaves the cows, and at other times after it has run out, cold and raw; they have no other means of livelihood. These people have dogs like those in this country, except that they are somewhat larger, and they load these dogs like beasts of burden, and make saddles for them like our pack saddles, and they fasten them with their leather thongs, and these make their backs sore on

111

The American camel, *Camelops*.

the withers like pack animals. When they go hunting, they load these with their necessities, and when they move—for these Indians are not settled in one place, since they travel wherever the cows move, to support themselves—these dogs carry their houses, and they have the sticks of their houses dragging along tied on to the pack-saddles, besides the load which they carry on top, and the load may be, according to the dog, from 35 to 50 pounds.

Four centuries ago there was, as this account indicates, an established economy on the interior plains based on the bison. Certain of the Indian tribes were professional hunters. They lived with the herds during the summer and repaired to villages on or off of the plains at the end of the hunting season to dispose of hides and to find shelter for the winter. It is reasonably certain that the Paleo-Indian of 10,000 years ago lived and hunted on the plains much as did these later Indians, except that so far as known the early men had no dogs, hence no travois, and did not use the bow and arrow but probably hunted with spear and atlatl. Certain it is that they developed specialized spear points, and that the style and make of points and methods of hafting changed from time to time. Among points found with and unmistakably used in hunting bison are the Folsom, Plainview, Scottsbluff, Eden, and various other points. The bison most hunted by the earlier Paleo-Indians have been variously described as *Bison taylori*, *Bison antiquus*, and *Bison occidentalis*.

Among localities where early man was associated with fossil bison are the following: Sulphur Springs, Arizona; Johnson, Lindenmeier, and San Luis Valley, Colorado; Russell Springs, Kansas; Bridgeport, Crawford, Cumro, and Scottsbluff, Nebraska; Burnet Cave, Clovis-Portales area, Folsom, and San Jon, New Mexico; Colorado City, Lipscomb, Plainview, and Lubbock, Texas; and Agate Basin, Finley, and Horner sites, Wyoming.

Camel

Camels, like horses, lived in America in earlier geologic times but had become extinct before the arrival of modern Europeans. Like horses, camels also were reintroduced, but unlike horses, the introduced camels failed to survive.

Fossil camel remains, chiefly but not entirely of the genus *Camelops*, have been found with human relics at several localities in North America. At Las Vegas, Nevada, a single obsidian flake showing human workmanship was found and collected in place by Mr. Finley Hunter. Associated fossils included camel (genus *Camelops*), horse, and bison (Simpson, 1933). In Smith Creek Cave, Nevada, Harring-

113

ton found charcoal and split and burned bones. In the same deposits were bones of *Camelops*, horse, and other mammals (Harrington, 1934). A species of camel was found in Kincaid Shelter, Texas, in deposits containing artifacts and other evidence of human habitation, and in the Sulphur Springs horizon, Sulphur Springs, Arizona. Other localities where camels were associated with human relics are Gypsum Cave, Nevada; Burnet Cave, Conkling Cavern, and Sandia Cave, New Mexico; and Vero and Melbourne, Florida. Unlike the bison, no hunting sites with mass killing of camels are known. Probably camels did not become so abundant or form such great herds as did the bison.

Sloth

Several species of sloth have been found associated with human remains in such a way as to indicate contemporaneity. One of the early reported discoveries in America of man associated with extinct animals was by Lund at Lagoa Santa in Brazil. In caves on the shore of Lake Sumidouro in the province of Minas Geraes, Lund from 1835 to 1846 found what he believed to be evidence of human habitation contemporaneous with the ground sloth and other animals now extinct. In Gypsum Cave, Nevada, sloth, genus *Nothrotherium*, occurs abundantly either with or near artifacts (Harrington, 1933). A similar association is recorded for Conkling Cavern, New Mexico (Conkling, 1932). The sloth, genus *Megalonyx*, was found in Potter Creek Cave, California, where artifacts were also obtained; also in the Melbourne bone bed at Melbourne and Vero, Florida. In Cuba, Harrington found the sloth *Megalocnus* associated with human materials at two localities (1921). In South America, Bird found remains of sloth, genus not identified, with human skeletal remains and artifacts (1938). The sloth has also been found in Confins and other caves of the Brazilian highlands associated with human remains (Walter and others, 1937).

Other Species

Several other species of large mammals are reported to have been found in America with human relics under conditions that may indicate contemporaneity. Among these finds are the following: the North American tapir found at Vero and Melbourne, Florida; the dire wolf found in the Sulphur Springs horizon of the Cochise culture, Arizona, and at Vero and Melbourne, Florida; the saber tooth at Vero, Florida, and at the Friesenhahn Cave, Texas; and a peccary of a species now extinct found at Melbourne, Florida, at Potter Creek Cave, California, at Russell Springs, Kansas, and at Blackwater No. 1 locality, New Mexico. At the Friesenhahn Cave locality in addition to the saber tooth tiger there is found also the much larger cat, *Dinobastis*.

Time of Extinction of Large Mammals

Only limited data based on the radiocarbon determinations have accumulated as yet on the time of extinction of the large mammals. In South America at the Palli Aike Cave horse and sloth, species not determined, were in existence about 8,639 years ago. How much later the horse and sloth may have survived is not known. However, no horse or sloth remains were found in the later deposits of the cave. The testing of sloth dung found in Gypsum Cave, Nevada, proves that the sloth, genus *Nothrotherium*, was in existence in this region as late as 10,455 years ago. Two species of camel and two of horse were apparently contemporaneous with the sloth. It is not possible to say at this time how much later these animals lived in the region.

The time of extinction of the proboscidians is not known. The elephant is said to be present in the Sulphur Springs stage of the Cochise section in Arizona, but whether in the later as well as in the earlier part of the Sulphur Springs stage has apparently not been made clear. That the proboscidians persisted until the time of Folsom man or later is probably indicated by a tusk found by Roberts at the Lindenmeier site in the foothills of the Rocky Mountains.

In this connection it may be noted that elephant at the Lubbock locality, although present in the basal horizon of the section, has not been found in the later horizon from which the bison bones, age 9,883 ± 350 years, were obtained. Also, at the Blackwater locality No. 1 in New Mexico, the elephant, although abundant in the basal horizon of lake fill, is absent from the overlying Folsom horizon. It would seem, therefore, that on the southern High Plains the elephant became limited in numbers and in distribution prior to about 10,000 years ago.

In November 1949 the skeleton of a mastodon was found 11 miles northwest of West Jefferson, near the village of Plumwood, Madison County, Ohio. The skeleton, collected by the Ohio State Museum, lay on and partly in a stratum of limy clay or marl. This marl in turn rests on glacial till. Overlying the marl is a layer of black muck or peaty material about 2 feet in thickness. Pieces of wood found in the

115

marl immediately beneath the skeleton and in the muck deposit surrounding it were submitted to the Harrison M. Randall Laboratory of Physics at the University of Michigan. The samples tested by the radiocarbon method gave an age determination of 8,400 ± 400 years (Thomas, 1952). This sample, coming in part from the marl and in part from the muck, does not afford an exact age determination for the mastodon skeleton, but serves as an indication that the mastodon may have been living in this region as recently as 8,000 or 9,000 years ago.

For the extinct bison species, *Bison taylori*, only one age determination has as yet been made, this being from burnt bones from the Lubbock locality. The determination obtained was 9,883 ± 350 years. This is the bison commonly found associated with Folsom man. Age determination of a bison, species not determined, has been made from the Horner site in Wyoming. This determination, made also from burned bones, revealed an age of about 6,876 years. It is reasonable to expect that much additional information will be obtained as to the range in time of the bison species associated with man. The date of origin of the modern species, *Bison bison*, has not yet been satisfactorily determined.

From the evidence now at hand one may infer that on the southern High Plains as the bison greatly increased in number, the elephant, horse, and camel decreased. This inference is supported by the observation that at localities affording evidence of great bison herds other species of large mammals, such as elephant, mastodon, camel, and horse, are scarce or wanting. Various species of bison had long been present on the plains. However, it seems probable that when the great herds of bison such as were associated with Folsom man became established, most other large grazing animals were driven through biological competition from the plains but continued in the mountains and probably in the Coastal Plains.

Age Determinations of Certain Culture Complexes

As INDICATED in the preceding pages some information based on radiocarbon determinations now exists 'for the age of certain of the early cultures of the plains and mountains. However, for the Llano culture, no suitable material for carbon dating has been obtained, and this culture remains undated except that it is known by its stratigraphic position to be older than Folsom. The Clovis Fluted projectile points, as previously explained, are found beyond the limits of the plains and the culture which produced them may have been continent-wide or nearly so.

For the Folsom culture one date is now available, 9,883 ± 350 years, obtained at the Lubbock, Texas, locality. How long the Folsom culture persisted and the time of its origin will not be known until additional tests from various localities can be obtained.

The Frontier culture described by Holder and Wike (1949) is likewise dated by carbon samples from Frontier County, southern Nebraska, where specimens obtained by Schultz yielded an age determination of 9,524 ± 450 years. It is to be hoped that more information may become available on the localities from which these samples were obtained.

A sample of burned bison bones collected by Hughes from the Angostura Reservoir, South Dakota, and submitted by Roberts, gives the age of a culture horizon at that locality as 7,715 ± 740 years. From the Horner site in Wyoming a sample of burned bison bones obtained by Jepsen dates a culture horizon not yet fully described as 6,876 ± 250 years ago.

Samples from Gypsum Cave, Nevada, obtained by Harrington, indicate an age of 10,455 ± 340 years. The material used in the test was sloth dung. Human habitation in the cave according to Harrington was contemporaneous, or essentially so, with the sloth.

Fiber sandals obtained by Cressman from the Fort Rock Cave, Oregon, gave an age determination of 9,053 ± 350 years. The use of

117

sandals to protect the feet is of especial interest as indicating appreciable civilization at this early date.

The next of the mountain cultures of which age determination has been made is that of Leonard Rock Shelter, Nevada, described by Heizer, where guano from a horizon said to contain wooden artifacts gave an age determination of 8,660 ± 300 years. An atlatl foreshaft in the same shelter at a higher level in the deposits gave a determination of 7,038 ± 350 years. The associated artifacts of this shelter have not been fully described.

Samples obtained by Sayles and Antevs from the Sulphur Springs stage in Arizona gave for one sample age 7,756 ± 370 years and for another, presumably higher in the section, 6,210 ± 250 years. These samples although in the same formation were not immediately with artifacts.

From South America but one age determination is available and that from burned horse and sloth bones obtained by Bird from Palli Aike Cave in Chile near the Atlantic Coast and also near the southern terminus of the Cordilleran mountain belt. The age of the bones which are associated with artifacts was determined as 8,639 ± 450 years, indicating that man at this early date had reached the southernmost part of America.

It is thus seen that man in America had established cultures in the mountain regions and on the plains as early as about 10,000 years ago. Still earlier cultures probably will be found and their age determined. Whether cultures were established first on the plains or in the mountains cannot be determined from the evidence now at hand.

118

List of Localities and Index to Literature

AN INDEX to early man localities in America with citation of literature for the years 1839–1939 was published by the writer in 1940. A second publication issued in 1947 continued the listing through 1945. The present publication combines and continues the previous lists through 1951. The bibliographies which accompanied the two earlier publications have likewise been combined and continued through 1951. This being primarily a finding list, most localities reported as containing relics of early man are included. Exceptions are a few North American localities reported prior to 1890 and South American localities reported prior to 1912. Probably some localities and certainly many publications that should have been included have been overlooked. Citation of literature is given for each locality.

Included in this volume are maps of North and South America on which the location is given of as many of the early man localities as is practicable. The approximate location of certain localities of North America is given in Figure 1, of South America in Figure 45.

NORTH AMERICA

Canada

Manitoba

Lac du Bonnet: About 50 miles northeast of Winnipeg.
Publication: Leechman (1950, p. 157).
An implement made from a proboscidian bone was found near the surface of the ground within the area of ancient Lake Agassiz.

Ontario

London: Localities near London.
Publications: Figgins (1934, p. 4); Kidd (1951).

Surface finds by W. J. Patterson indicate occurrence of points resembling Clovis Fluted. One of the points, illustrated by Figgins (Pl. 1, Fig. 6), is almost as deeply fluted as is the Angus point of Nebraska.

Saskatchewan

Mortlach: Several localities in the vicinity of Mortlach. About 100 miles from the south and 170 from the west boundaries of Saskatchewan. Map entry, Canada 1.

Publications: Howard (1939a); Roberts (1939a, p. 108).

Folsom, Eden, and Scottsbluff points and other artifacts found in blowouts. Fossil bison are abundant.

Mexico

Mexico City: Three localities near Mexico City. Map entry, Mexico 1.

Publications: Aveleyra (1950); De Terra, Romero, and Stewart (1949). Additional comments, pages 42 and 85.

United States

Alaska

Chinitna Bay: Locality at the west and southwest side of Chinitna Bay at the north side of Cook Inlet. Map entry, Alaska 1.

Publication: Hibben (1943).

The artifacts occur in a humus-stained stratum which overlies blue clay and is itself overlain by muck and peat deposits.

Fairbanks: Various localities in the Tanana and Yukon river valleys, in the interior plateau region about 380 miles from the Arctic Ocean, and 100 to 200 miles from the east boundary of Alaska. Artifacts found in frozen muck deposits. Map entry, Alaska 2.

Publications: Chaney and Mason (1936); Hibben (1943, p. 254; 1944); Rainey (1939; 1940, p. 299).

Among artifacts obtained from the muck deposits illustrated by Rainey (1940, p. 306) is a bone point about 11 inches long, very similar, as noted by Rainey, to those found with elephant remains in the Clovis-Portales area, New Mexico. The elephant is found with numerous other extinct species in the muck deposits, but the conditions of occurrence are such that it is not possible to determine the contemporaneity of the artifacts and fossils.

Iyatayet: On the west side of Cape Denbigh, Alaska.

Publications: Giddings (1949; 1950; 1951).

The Denbigh flint complex, consisting of the earlier artifacts found at this locality, includes burins similar to those found in Europe and spalls incident to making these instruments; scrapers, a graver, and a fluted point; a well-worked point with oblique parallel flaking; a point much like the Eden; a point said to resemble the Plainview; and numerous delicately worked blades. A complete report on the artifacts and the geologic section has not yet been issued.

Utukok River: On Utukok River, about 100 miles south of Wainwright, 70 miles southeast of Point Lay and 180 miles, more or less, southwest of Barrow. In the plateau region north of Brooks Mountains. Map entry, Alaska 3.

Publication: Thompson (1948).

A fluted point found on the surface.

Arizona

Ventana Cave: Near the west side of the Papago Indian Reservation, about 55 miles from south and 185 from east state lines and 155 miles from southwest corner of state. Map entry, Arizona 1.

Publications: Haury (1943; 1950). Additional comments, page 81.

Sulphur Springs: Type locality of Sulphur Springs stage of Cochise culture at Double Adobe School, 12 miles northwest of Douglas, Arizona, 11 miles from south and 39 from east state lines. Several other similar sites were found in this draw. Map entry, Arizona 2.

Publications: Antevs (1937b, pp. 129–132; 1937c, p. 335); Cummings (1927; 1928); Sayles and Antevs (1941). Additional comments, page 79.

Naco: Near the Mexican border and about 55 miles from the east state line, 7 or 8 miles south-southwest of Bisbee.

Clovis Fluted points with parts of the skeleton of an elephant at a locality near Naco, Arizona. Additional comments, page 38.

California

Angeles Mesa: In the western part of the city of Los Angeles, 3 miles south and somewhat east of the Rancho La Brea locality.

121

Publications: Hay (1927b, p. 175); Merriam (1924); Stock (1924). Human remains, including parts of the skeletons of at least six individuals, were found in excavating at depths of 19 and 23 feet. An awl-like object and a quartzite boulder contained in the deposits are believed to have been used by man. A camel bone and a horse bone were found at a near-by locality in deposits that may or may not be a continuation of the deposits containing the human bones.

Borax Lake: At southeast margin of Borax Lake, a small, nearly extinct lake just east of Clear Lake near Lakeport, 220 miles, more or less, from north and 127 miles from east state lines and about 60 miles from the Pacific Coast at the east margin of the coast ranges. Map entry, California 1.

Publications: Antevs (1939a); Harrington (1939a; 1939b; 1942; 1945; 1946; 1948).

Artifacts found at this locality include Borax Lake (type locality), Clovis Fluted, and Pinto projectile points, laurel-leaf points or blades, scrapers, and other objects. The artifacts are found at the surface and from one to several feet underground. No extinct species have been reported from this locality.

Lake Mohave: Principal localities at and near Soda Lake and Silver Lake in San Bernardino County, in the Mohave Desert about 200 miles east and 55 north of Los Angeles. Sixty miles northeast of Barstow and within 50 miles of the California-Nevada state line. Map entry, California 2.

Publications: Amsden (1937); Antevs (1937a; 1937b, pp. 126–129); Barbieri (1937); Bode (1937); Campbell (1936, p. 297); Campbell and Campbell (1937); Free (1916).

Artifacts including Lake Mohave (type locality), Silver Lake (type locality), various other points, knives, and scrapers, all found at or near the surface.

Los Angeles: On Rancho Cienga O'Paso de la Tijera in the banks of a storm drain constructed in 1936 from Los Angeles to the coast.

Publications: Bowden and Lopatin (1936); Hrdlicka (1937c, pp. 99–100); Lopatin (1939).

Human bones, including part of a skull, were found at a depth of 13 feet from the surface. In the same deposit, about 1,000 feet from the locality yielding the human bones and apparently in the same stratum, proboscidian remains were found, identified as *Archidiskodon imperator*. The deposits are stratified, consisting of black soil, 7

122

feet, underlain by peat, 2 feet; black clay, 2 feet; yellow clay, 1 foot; gravel containing bones, 2 feet. Professors Heizer and Cook of the University of California have made analyses of elephant and human bones at this locality and conclude that the data seem unequivocal in demonstrating an equal age for the human and elephant providing the chemical methods of bone analysis are acceptable (letter of May 10, 1952).

Lower Klamath Lake: On the California-Oregon state boundary line in Siskiyou County, west of Tule Lake and approximately 80 miles from the east California state line and about 137 miles from the Pacific Coast. Map entry, California 3.

Publications: Antevs (1940); Cressman (1940a); Cressman and others (1942).

The contemporaneity of artifacts with the fossils at the localities designated as the "Narrows" and the "Cove" has not yet been established, but some of the artifacts appear to have been derived from a thin stratum that also contains the fossil bones. The species recognized are camel, horse, and a proboscidian. Various artifacts were obtained in addition to those apparently associated with the fossil animals.

Pinto Basin: In Riverside County, east of the San Bernardino Mountains, 90 miles from the Mexican border, 65 miles west of the Colorado River, and about 35 miles northeast of the north margin of the Salton Sea. Map entry, California 4.

Publications: Amsden (1935a); Campbell and Campbell (1935); Campbell (1936, p. 296); Schart (1935); Wormington (1949, pp. 78–83).

Artifacts and bones of extinct animals, including horse and camel, have been obtained. Actual association of the extinct animals and the artifacts has not yet been established. The artifacts include Pinto points (type locality), leaf-shaped and various other points, scrapers, and other objects, all being found on the surface.

Potter Creek Cave: On Potter Creek, Shasta County, near Baird.

Publications: Cope (1879; 1891); Howard (1936b, p. 407); Matthew and Gidley (1906); Merriam (1906, pp. 223–225); Putnam (1906, pp. 230–234); Sinclair (1904); Sinclair and Furlong (1904, pp. 412–413).

Sinclair is of the opinion that the fauna of this cave is of "later Quaternary age." Among many pieces of splintered bone, two found

The North American ground sloth, *Mylodon*.

interbedded with the cave fauna represent the work of man, in the opinion of Putnam, Matthew, and Gidley. The extinct vertebrate species listed by Sinclair (1904, pp. 17–18) are the following: *Arctotherium simun, Ursus, Felis, Canis indianensis* Leidy, *Taxidea* (?), *Spilogale, Teonoma, Thomomys, Aplodontia major, Platygonus* (?), *Euceratherium collinum, Bison,* camelid, *Megalonyx wheatleyi, Megalonyx jeffersonii, Megalonyx, Mastodon americanus, Elephas primigenius, Equus occidentalis,* and *Equus pacificus.*

Rancho la Brea: In Hancock Park in the western part of the city of Los Angeles, about 128 miles from the south state line. Map entry, California 5.

Publications: Boule (1923, p. 408); Hay (1927b, p. 182); Hrdlicka (1918, pp. 17–22); Merriam (1914); Stock (1930a, p. 28); Woodward (1937).

Many extinct vertebrates have been obtained from the asphalt pits of Rancho la Brea. In pit 10, human bones were found at a depth of from 6 to 9 feet. According to Merriam, the associated fauna is of later age than that of some other pits and is either early Recent or very late Pleistocene. Woodward (1937) reports discovery of an atlatl and some other artifacts from pit 66–67.

Samwell Cave: On east side of McCloud River, about 16 miles above its mouth in Shasta County.

Publications: Furlong (1904); Merriam (1906); Putnam (1906).

A piece of chipped lava was found in association with extinct animals. Furlong considers the chipped lava as probably included at the same time as the animal remains.

Colorado

Dent: In Weld County on west side of Platte River, on the Union Pacific Railway, approximately midway between La Salle and Gowanda, about 47 miles from north and 150 miles from east state lines. Map entry, Colorado 1.

Publications: Figgins (1933a); Howard (1935, p. 148); Roberts (1937b, p. 160); Strong (1935, p. 223); Wormington (1949, p. 38). Additional comments, page 31.

Johnson: Eighteen miles northwest of Fort Collins, in the foothills of the Rocky Mountains, 12 or 15 miles southwest of the Lindenmeier locality.

125

Publications: Roberts (1939b, p. 541); Wormington (1949, pp. 32–33).

This locality, discovered by T. Russell Johnson in 1935 and excavated in 1936 by the Colorado Museum of Natural History, contains Folsom points, scrapers, and work-shop debris. The artifacts are much like those found at the Lindenmeier site.

Lindenmeier: Twenty-eight miles approximately due north of Fort Collins, within 1.5 or 2 miles of the Colorado-Wyoming state line, and about 158 miles from the east state line, just east of the Front Range, elevation above 6,000 feet. Map entry, Colorado 2.

Publications: Kirk Bryan (1937a, pp. 143–152; 1941a); Bryan and Ray (1940); Cassell (1941); Coffin (1937); Figgins (1935c); Howard (1936b, p. 408; 1937a, p. 111); Renaud (1932a); Richards (1936, p. 370); Roberts (1935a; 1935b; 1936a; 1936b; 1937b, pp. 158–160; 1938; 1939b; 1940b; 1945a); Strong (1935, pp. 223–224); Wormington (1949, pp. 18–21). Additional comments, page 49.

Linger and Zapata Sites: In San Luis Valley, west of the Sangre de Cristo Mountains, about 26 miles northeast of Alamosa, about 50 miles from the south and 195 from the east state lines. The Zapata site is about 2 miles from the base of Sangre de Cristo Mountains. Map entry, Colorado 3.

Publications: Hurst (1937; 1941; 1943); Wormington (1949, p. 23).

Fossil bison bones and artifacts were found on and near the surface. The bone bed extends to a maximum depth of 2 feet but mostly to only a foot or less. The artifacts are at least partly of the Folsom complex. The bison, identified from metacarpal bones, is regarded by Granger and by Simpson as possibly *Bison taylori*. At the Zapata site, which is similar to the Linger site, artifacts are reported associated with fossil bison. The Zapata site has been excavated by F. C. V. Worman.

Yuma County: Various localities on the uplands and stream divides.

Publications: Cook (1931a, pp. 102–103); Figgins (1934; 1935b); Renaud (1932b).

Artifacts and bones of elephants and two species of bison were found. Cook is of the opinion that some of the elephant bones and some bison bones show markings made by implements prior to fossilization. Of the two bison, one, according to Cook, is *Bison taylori*. The

126

other is a smaller species. The species of elephant is not given. The artifacts were not in place.

Florida

Anderson: Adjacent to South Indian Field, Brevard County, about 11 miles west-southwest of Melbourne.
Publications: Edwards Ms. (1951); Rouse (1951).
Artifacts obtained from a pre-pottery horizon.

Flagler Beach: On the Florida east coast, 90 miles from the north state line. Map entry, Florida 1.
Publication: Connery (1932).
Artifacts are reported to have been found at a depth of about 2.5 feet from the surface. It is said that one of the artifacts lay near or between the jaws of an elephant. The level of the bones is below ground-water level. The deposits consist of sandy layers with much organic material. The unconsolidated nature of the deposits would seem to create doubt as to the contemporaneity of the artifact and fossil.

Itchtucknee Spring: In Columbia County, 7 miles west and 15 south of Lake City, about 43 miles from north state line and 85 miles from the Atlantic Coast. Ten miles west and 10.5 north of High Springs; 8 miles northeast of the mouth of Santa Fe River. Map entry, Florida 2.
Publication: Jenks and Simpson (1941).
Artifacts and fossils at this locality are found in the bed of Itchtucknee River about 1 mile from its source in Itchtucknee Spring. The artifacts include three beveled bone points not unlike those found at the Blackwater locality No. 1 in New Mexico. The fossil bones found in the stream bed at the same place include elephant, mastodon, camel, sloth, tapir, bison, and beaver. Contemporaneity of the artifacts and the extinct animals is not proven.

Melbourne: Three localities have been described near Melbourne, as follows: 1.5 miles southwest of Melbourne; 2 miles west of Indian River, on east bank of drainage canal; and 1 mile west of golf course on south bank of drainage canal. Melbourne is about 11 miles east and 50 north of the northern margin of Lake Okeechobee and about 30 miles north of Vero Beach.
Publications: Cooke (1926; 1928; 1945); Cooke and Mossom

127

(1929, pp. 218–220); Gidley (1926a; 1926b; 1926c; 1927; 1929a; 1929b; 1930; 1931); Gidley and Loomis (1926); Goddard (1926); Hay (1927b, p. 274); Howard (1935, p. 142); Hrdlicka (1937c, pp. 95–98); Leverett (1931); Loomis (1924; 1926); McCown (1941); Romer (1933, p. 78); Simpson (1929); Stewart (1946). Additional comments, page 90.

New Smyrna: On the Florida east coast, 125 miles from the north state line. Map entry, Florida 3.

Publication: Gidley (1929b, p. 20).

Gidley found artifacts in "undisturbed natural association" with bones of extinct animals. No additional information on the locality seems to have been published.

Suwannee River: In Gilchrist County at the entrance of the Santa Fe River, 45 miles from the Gulf Coast, about 50 miles from the north state line and 95 from the Atlantic Coast.

Publications: Goggin (1950); Simpson (1948).

At this locality, underlying a pottery-bearing zone is a pre-pottery zone containing artifacts. No associated vertebrate fossils have been found.

Vero: In the valley of Van Valkenburg Creek, one-half mile north of Vero Beach. Map entry, Florida 4.

Publications: Balch (1917, pp. 481–482); Berry (1917); Boule (1923, pp. 409–411); Chamberlin (1917a; 1917b); Cooke (1926; 1928; 1945); Cooke and Mossom (1929, pp. 220–224); Gidley (1930); Hay (1917a; 1917b; 1917c; 1918a; 1918b; 1918c; 1919a, pp. 108–109; 1923; 1926; 1927a; 1927b, p. 275; 1928c); Holmes (1918a; 1918b); Howard (1935, pp. 140–142); Hrdlicka (1917; 1918, pp. 23–65; 1919; 1937c, p. 95); Keith (1929, pp. 467–468); Leverett (1931); MacCurdy (1917a; 1917b); McCown (1941); Merriam (1935; 1936, pp. 1316); Nelson (1918b); Romer (1933, p. 78); Sellards (1916a; 1916b; 1916c; 1917a; 1917b; 1917c; 1917d; 1918; 1919; 1937; 1940a; 1947); Simpson (1929; 1930a); Shufeldt (1917); Sterns (1918; 1919); Stewart (1946); Vaughan (1917); Wickham (1919); Wieland (1918); Wilder (1924, pp. 288–289). Additional comments, page 90.

Georgia

Macon: Various sites in the Ockmulgee drainage basin near Macon, about 90 miles from west and 145 from south state lines. Map entry, Georgia 1.

128

Publications: Cotter (1937b, p. 28); Kelly (1938); Haag (1942, p. 217); Roberts (1940b, pp. 56, 62).

The artifacts, of which large collections have been made, include a fluted point, scrapers, knives, drills, and perforators. No vertebrate fossils are reported.

Indiana

Cromwell: About 25 miles from north and 42 from east state lines. Map entry, Indiana 1.

Publications: Burmaster (1932); Harrington (1933, p. 180).

A mastodon skeleton was found resting on clay and protruding upwards through overlying peat. An artifact was found on the clay 20 feet or less from the mastodon. Another artifact was found in the peat deposit. Charcoal was found on the clay and under the skeleton.

Iowa

Muscatine: On the Mississippi River about 75 miles south and 18 west of the southwest corner of Wisconsin. Map entry, Iowa 1.

Publications: Shimek (1917, p. 98); Witter (1892).

Two artifacts and parts of a tooth of an elephant were found in loess deposits at depths of 12 and 25 feet. The species of elephant is not given.

Kansas

Lansing: On the Concannon farm, right bank of the Missouri River, 5 miles southeast of Leavenworth, and about 60 miles from the northwest corner of the state. Map entry, Kansas 1.

Publications: Boule (1923, p. 407); Calvin (1902); Chamberlin (1902); Holmes (1902a; 1919, p. 71); Hrdlicka (1907, pp. 47–53); Keith (1929, pp. 468–469); Salisbury (1902); Shimek (1903); Todd (1903); Upham (1902a; 1902b; 1902c); Williston (1902b; 1903; 1905b); Winchell (1902; 1903; 1917, p. 134).

Human remains were found in loess at a depth of 20 feet. T. C. Chamberlin, Salisbury, and Calvin consider it possible that the loess in which the skeleton rests is a secondary deposit. Winchell, Williston, and Upham regard the deposition as original.

Russell Springs: In Logan County, on Twelve Mile Creek, a tributary to Smoky Hill River, 12 miles east of Russell Springs, about 70 miles from north and 86 from west state lines. Map entry, Kansas 2.

Publications: Boule (1923, pp. 400–401); Lucas (1899); McClung

129

(1908); Martin (1902; 1918); Renaud (1928, p. 31); Romer (1933, p. 79); Schultz and Eiseley (1935, p. 312); Stewart (1897); Williston (1897; 1898; 1902a; 1905a). Additional comments, page 47.

Kentucky

Parrish: Locality in Hopkins County, western Kentucky. Map entry, Kentucky 1.

Publication: Haag (1942, p. 217).

A point from this locality, resembling the Clovis Fluted type, is illustrated by Roberts (1939, Pl. 15, upper right). A point from Hickman County, Kentucky, resembling Clovis Fluted is illustrated in Figure 22, a.

Louisiana

Central and Northern Louisiana: Surface sites in several parishes—Bienville, Webster, and others.

Publication: Webb (1948, p. 230).

Some of the points obtained are suggestive of Scottsbluff points.

Massachusetts

Worcester County: In Northborough, 22 miles north and 8 east of the northeast corner of Connecticut. Map entry, Massachusetts 1.

Publication: Putnam (1885).

Parts of skull and teeth of a mastodon were found at the bottom of peat deposits. About 18 feet from the mastodon skull occurred a human skull and jaws which likewise rested on the underlying deposits at the base of the peat deposits.

Minnesota

Browns Valley: Near Fertile in glacial Lake Warren, which is in the southern outlet of glacial Lake Agassiz.

Publications: Jenks (1934); McCown (1941); Wormington (1949, pp. 142–143).

Artifacts and a human skeleton were found, representing a burial.

Pelican Rapids: On state highway No. 30, 3 miles north of Pelican Rapids, about 33 miles from west and 165 from north state lines, and 212 miles from the south state line. Map entry, Minnesota 1.

Publications: Antevs (1935, p. 305; 1937d; 1938a); Bryan (1935); Bryan and MacClintock (1938); Hrdlicka (1937c, pp. 101–104);

Jenks (1932a; 1933; 1935, pp. 5–7; 1936; 1938); Kay and Leighton (1938); McCown (1941); Sardeson (1938); Thiel (1936); Wormington (1949, pp. 137–141).

A human skeleton and some artifacts were found in lake deposits at a depth of 12 feet. In the opinion of Jenks, Bryan, Kay, Leighton, and MacClintock, the human materials are of the age of the lake deposits; Antevs, Sardeson, and Hrdlicka believe the human remains to be of later age than these deposits. No extinct animals were found.

Sauk Valley: In gravel pit on the Daniel W. Frazer property, near Lake Guerney, Todd County, 6 miles north and 3.5 west of Sauk Centre.

Publications: Bryan, Retzek, and McCann (1938); Jenks and Wilford (1938); McCown (1941).

Human skeletal remains were found in a gravel deposit at a depth of from 2 to 4 feet. No associated fossils were reported.

Saint Croix River: Several localities in the valley of Saint Croix River.

Publication: Eddy and Jenks (1935).

Artifacts reported in association with extinct bison.

Mississippi

Natchez: In east bluff of the Mississippi River, a few miles from Natchez, about 40 miles from the south state line. Map entry, Mississippi 1.

Publications: Dickeson (1846); Howard (1936b, p. 394; 1936g, p. 1327); Hrdlicka (1907, pp. 16–19); Keith (1929, pp. 465–467), Leidy (1889, p. 9); Lyell (1849; 1863, pp. 200–205); Schmidt (1872); Usher (1854, p. 349); Winchell (1917, p. 133). Additional comments, page 87.

Missouri

Benton County: On Pomme de Terre River.

Publications: Dana (1875, p. 337); Howard (1935, p. 143); Koch (1839a; 1843; 1857, p. 63); Montagu (1942); Montagu and Peterson (1944).

Koch reports mastodon bones found at a depth of 20 feet with which were associated "several stone arrowheads." One of the artifacts was found underneath the femur of the mastodon "so that it could not have been brought thither after the deposit of the bones."

131

Gasconade County: From a spring in the valley of Bourbeuse River. Publications: Dana (1875, pp. 338–339); Harrington (1933, p. 177); Howard (1935, p. 143; 1936b, p. 394); Koch (1839a; 1839b; 1857); McGee (1888); Montagu (1942); Montagu and Peterson (1944).

Koch reports having found fossil bones at a depth of about 8 or 9 feet in alluvial deposits. With the bones was evidence of fire as well as "several arrowheads, a stone spearhead, and some stone axes." Some of the bones, according to Koch, had been burned. These and other collections made by Koch were kept for a time in a museum in St. Louis. According to John Francis McDermott (letter of July 31, 1939), Koch sold his museum in 1841 and upon leaving St. Louis took his collections with him, some of which were disposed of in Europe.

Nebo Hill: In Clay County, near Kansas City. Map entry, Missouri 1.

Publication: Shippee (1948).

Collections of the Nebo Hill complex have been made from four sites in old fields on the loess bluffs of the Missouri River, near Kansas City, Missouri. No associated fossils have been found.

Montana

MacHaffie: Five miles southeast of Helena, about 100 miles from west and 140 from south state lines.

At this locality Richard G. Forbis reports artifacts at three successive horizons. The oldest of the three horizons contains Folsom projectile points. The middle horizon contains artifacts said to resemble those from the Lime Creek site Ft-41, Nebraska (Forbis, letter of May 19, 1952). Some of the projectile points resemble also those from Stratum 3 of the Blackwater No. 1 locality, New Mexico. The third horizon, according to Forbis, contains artifacts of relatively recent date.

Nebraska

Angus: Near Angus, Nuckolls County, about 20 miles from south and 140 from east state lines. Map entry, Nebraska 1.

Publications: Bell and Van Royen (1934a, pp. 58–60); Figgins (1931); Harrington (1933, p. 180); Strong (1932a, p. 152; 1932b; 1935, p. 221); Wormington (1949, p. 37). Additional comments, page 36.

Bridgeport: Near Dalton, Morrill County.

Publication: Renaud (1934, pp. 12–19).

Artifacts are found in association with *Castoroides ohioensis* and *Bison antiquus taylori* (C. B. Schultz, personal communication).

Crawford: In headwater drainage of White River, near Crawford.

Publication: MacClintock, Barbour, Schultz, and Lugn (1936).

Artifacts and fire pits have been found in the valley of Sand Creek at varying depths up to about 25 feet. The artifacts and fire pits underlie and antedate varved deposits.

Cumro: Locality in South Loup Valley, Custer County, 7 miles southwest of Cumro and about 72 miles from the south state line and 128 miles east of the northeast corner of Colorado. Map entry, Nebraska 2.

Publications. Antevs (1935, p. 304); Bell and Van Royan (1934a, pp. 53–56); Schultz (1932, pp. 271–273); Strong (1932b, p. 2; 1935, p. 220).

An artifact was found in association with a bison skeleton in loess deposits at a depth of 16 feet. The bison skull was wanting, but the species was thought to be *Bison occidentalis* or a closely related species.

Grand Island: On south bank of Platte River, 8 miles southwest of Grand Island, Hall County, 53 miles from south and 185 from west state lines. Map entry, Nebraska 3.

Publications: Barbour and Schultz (1932a); Bell and Van Royen (1934a, pp. 56–58); Meserve and Barbour (1932); Schultz (1932, pp. 271–282); Strong (1932b; 1935, p. 221).

Two artifacts have been found in association with a bison originally identified as *Bison occidentalis,* now regarded as *Bison antiquus taylori* (Schultz, letter of June 24, 1939). The fossils are found in a dark silt stratum. The depth of the bone bed is about 4 feet.

Lime Creek: Locality Ft-41 on Lime Creek, a tributary of Medicine Creek, Frontier County, southwestern Nebraska. Map entry 3.

Publications: Schultz and Frankforter (1948); Schultz, Lueninghoener, and Frankforter (1948). Additional comments, page 74.

Medicine Creek: Locality Ft-50 (Allen site) on Medicine Creek, a tributary of Republican River, Frontier County, southwestern Nebraska, about 45 miles from south and 80 from west state lines.

Publications: Holder and Wike (1949); Schultz and Frankforter

133

(1948); Schultz, Lueninghoener, and Frankforter (1948). Additional comments, page 74.

Omaha: In a railway cut 2.5 miles southeast of Omaha.

Publications: Aughey (1876, p. 254); Hay (1918a; 1929a, p. 95).

Aughey obtained a large flint arrowhead from the loess deposits at a depth of 20 feet. The artifact was 13 inches below and a little to one side of the lumbar vertebra of a proboscidian.

Scottsbluff: In north bank of Spring Creek near Signal Butte, Scotts Bluff County (Sec. 11, T. 21 N., R. 57 W.), 16 miles west and 3 south of Scottsbluff, about 55 miles from the south state line and within 2 or 3 miles of the west state line. Map entry, Nebraska 5.

Publications: Barbour and Schultz (1932b; 1936a, pp. 434–442); Bell (1932); Bell and Van Royen (1934a, pp. 60–62); Figgins (1934); Howard (1935, pp. 147–148); Lugn (1934, p. 353; 1935, pp. 183–188); Romer (1933); Schultz (1934); Schultz and Eiseley (1935; 1936a); Strong (1935, p. 221). Additional comments, page 69.

Signal Butte: Locality on a mesa near Scottsbluff in western Nebraska, near the Wyoming border.

Publications: Amsden (1937, p. 94); Strong (1932a, p. 155; 1933; 1935); Wormington (1949, pp. 111–114).

The uppermost deposits at this locality contain pottery; at greater depth are projectile points, awls, scrapers, blades, and hearths.

Nevada

Etna Cave: A small cave near Etna, about 6 miles south of Caliente, 25 miles from the east state line, and 173 miles north of the southeast corner of the state. Map entry, Nevada 1.

Publications: Roberts (1944); Wheeler (1942).

Four levels containing evidence of man are said to have been found in Etna Cave near Caliente, Nevada. The two uppermost are identified as Pueblo and Basketmaker; the third somewhat resembles the Gypsum Cave culture; and the fourth contains a broken projectile point. In this basal stratum was found also a small piece of slate rock with markings regarded by Wheeler as engravings made by man. Fossils of this basal horizon are camel, ground sloth, and a small horse.

Gypsum Cave: In the foothills of Frenchman Mountains about 16 miles east of Las Vegas, 80 miles north of the southeast corner of the state, and 42 miles from the west state line. Map entry, Nevada 2.

Publications: Amsden (1931); Antevs (1935, p. 309); Harrington (1930; 1933; 1934c); Howard (1935, p. 146; 1936b, p. 406); Romer (1933, p. 81); Stock (1931); Wormington (1949, pp. 75–78). Additional comments, page 77.

Lake Lahontan: Locality on Walker River in the southern part of Lake Lahontan basin, discovered October 6, 1882; announced, Russell, 1885. Map entry, Nevada 3.

Publications: Antevs (1935, p. 304); Gilbert (1889); Harrington (1933, p. 178); Hay (1929a, p. 95); Holmes (1919, p. 68); McGee (1887; 1888, p. 23; 1889b); Powell (1893, pp. 324–325); Russell (1885, pp. 246–247); Wright (1890, p. 558).

McGee (1889b, p. 304) states that the obsidian implement found by him was projecting point outward from the later clay deposits of Lake Lahontan. It was found in the vertical bluff at a depth of 25 feet from the surface. The fossils of this later Pleistocene lake epoch are listed by Hay as elephant, horse, bison, and camel.

Las Vegas: In the drainage area of Las Vegas River about 10 miles north-northwest of Las Vegas.

Publications: Harrington (1934a); Simpson (1933).

Simpson reports "highly suggestive if not absolutely conclusive" evidence of the existence of man with the fauna of Pleistocene type. Pieces of charcoal and a flake were found with the following fossils: *Thomomys(?) perpallidus, Equus pacificus, Equus* sp., *Camelops hesternus, Odocoileus* sp., and *Bison* sp. Later Harrington found in a nearby locality additional charcoal inclusions, also split and burnt animal bones and one elephant molar, probably *Parelephas columbi.* The maximum depth of the charcoal in the deposits is 14 feet.

Leonard Rock: A rock shelter on the west slope of Humbolt Mountains, 10 miles south of Lovelock, Pershing County, about 75 miles from west and 135 from north state lines. Map entry, Nevada 4.

Publications: Arnold and Libby (1950); Heizer (1938). Additional comments, page 79.

Smith Creek Cave: In a cave near Baker, White Pine County.

Publication: Harrington (1934b).

The cave deposits at this place contain charcoal and split and burned bones, presumably indicating human agency. The associated fossils are camel (*Camelops*), horse (two species), and other undetermined bones.

135

New Jersey

Trenton: In gravel deposits on bluff of Delaware River, 2 miles south of Trenton. Map entry, New Jersey 1.

Publications: Abbott (1872; 1873; 1877; 1881, pp. 471–551; 1883; 1889); Balch (1917, pp. 474–477); Boule (1923, p. 402); Cresson (1892); Goddard (1927, p. 264); Hay (1919b; 1929a, p. 95); Haynes (1883); Hollick (1898); Holmes (1893a; 1898; 1919, p. 76); Howard (1936b, p. 394); Hrdlicka (1907, pp. 35–47); Keith (1929, pp. 461–465); Knapp (1898); Kümmel (1898); Lewis (1880; 1881); McGee (1889a); Mercer (1898); Powell (1893); Putnam (1898); Richards (1939); Russell (1899); Salisbury (1898); Shaler (1880; 1889; 1893); Smith (1910); Spier (1916; 1918); Volk (1911); Wilder (1924, pp. 286–288); Wilson (1898); Wissler (1916, p. 236); G. F. Wright (1883; 1888a, p. 427; 1890, p. 509; 1892, pp. 242–249; 1893, pp. 29–32; 1898; 1911).

Artifacts have been reported at this locality from the surface, from a 2-foot yellow sand-clay stratum just beneath the soil, and from the underlying deposits known as the Trenton gravel. Those from the sand-clay horizon are said to be of no great antiquity. Among fossils reported from the Trenton gravel is a fragment of a human mandible found at a depth of 16 feet, also a parietal bone and femur. Mastodon and bison are reported in these deposits (Abbott, 1881, p. 482). The first artifact was found by Abbott in September 1872 in the gravel at a depth of 16 feet (Abbott, 1873, p. 206).

New Mexico

Burnet Cave: About 26 miles west of Carlsbad on south fork of Rocky Arroyo on eastern side of Guadalupe Mountains (Sec. 35, R. 21 E., T. 22 S.), Eddy County, about 97 miles from the east and 25 miles from the south state lines. Map entry, New Mexico 1.

Publications: Howard (1930; 1931; 1932; 1933, p. 524; 1935, pp. 62–79; 1936b, p. 406; 1936f; 1936g, pp. 1327–1329; 1937a, p. 112); Howard and Antevs (1934); Merriam (1936, p. 1316); Roberts (1937b, pp. 157–158); Schultz and Howard (1936); Woodward (1935, p. 406).

In Burnet Cave a fluted point was found at a depth of approximately 5.5 feet, hearths at varying depths, and animal bones to a maximum depth of 8.5 feet. Among extinct animals in the cave deposits were camel, horse, musk ox, bison, four-horned antelope, and cave bear. The fluted point was found associated with musk ox, bison,

136

and charcoal. The uppermost 3 feet or so of the cave deposits contained Basketmaker material.

Cimarron: On south bank of Cimarron River, 8 miles east of Folsom and about 42 miles from east and 8 from north state lines.

Publications: Figgins (1935a); Hooton (1937); Hrdlicka (1937c, pp. 98–99); Roberts (1937a); Shapiro (1937); Woodbury (1937).

A human skull and parts of a skeleton were found in stream deposits 13.5 feet below the surface. The human remains were described by Figgins (1935a) as a new species, *Homo novus mundus.* Most others who have examined the skull consider it to represent the modern species of man. No associated vertebrate fossils have been reported.

Clovis-Portales: Several localities in or near Blackwater Draw. Principal locality Blackwater No. 1, on Baxter (formerly Carter) ranch, about 16 miles from east and 145 from south state lines. Map entry, New Mexico 2.

Publications: Antevs (1935, p. 309; 1936b; 1949, pp. 185–190); Frank Bryan (1938); Chaney (1935); Cotter (1937a; 1938); Howard (1933, p. 524; 1935, p. 79; 1936a, p. 333; 1936b, p. 407; 1936c; 1936d; 1936f; 1936g, pp. 1329–1333; 1936h; 1937a, p. 111; 1939b); Price (1944); Richards (1936); Roberts (1937b, p. 157); Sellards (1940a); Stock and Bode (1937); Woodward (1935, p. 406); Wormington (1949), pp. 40–45). Additional comments, page 29.

Conkling Cavern: Fourteen and a half miles southeast of Las Cruces, about 20 miles from south and 135 from west state lines. Map entry, New Mexico 3.

Publications: W. A. Bryan (1929); Conkling (1932); Howard (1935, p. 146; 1936a, p. 332; 1936b, p. 405); Romer (1933, p. 80).

Human remains were found in this cave at depths of 12, 21, and 52 feet. Remains of extinct animals were found at 10, 12, and 52 feet (R. P. Conkling, letter of August 17, 1939). The extinct animals were in some instances in immediate association with the human skeletal remains. No artifacts were found. Among extinct animals obtained from this cave were *Nothrotherium, Camelops,* and *Equus.*

Estancia Valley: On top of the north terrace of ancient Estancia Valley Lake, 5 miles north of Moriarty, about 130 miles from north and 170 from east state lines.

Publication: Hurt (1942).

At this locality artifacts have been exposed by wind erosion. Two Folsom points of the very small, or pygmy, variety were found here.

137

Other points have been found on the surface in this region. No associated fossil vertebrates have been found.

Folsom: In an ancient small stream valley cut by a modern arroyo, 28 miles southeast of Raton, New Mexico, and about 45 miles from east and 5 miles from north state lines. Map entry, New Mexico 4.

Publications: Amsden (1931); Antevs (1935, p. 309); Brown (1928; 1929; 1932); Kirk Bryan (1929; 1937a, pp. 140–143); Cassell (1941); Cook (1927a, pp. 243–244; 1928b; 1931a, p. 102); Figgins (1927, pp. 232–234); Hay and Cook (1930); Howard (1935, p. 145; 1936b, p. 407; 1936f; 1937b, p. 331); Renaud (1928, p. 43); Roberts (1937b, pp. 153–157); Romer (1933, p. 79); Wormington (1949). Additional comments, page 47.

Hermit Cave: Locality in the Guadalupe Mountains.

Publication: Schultz (1943).

Remains of dire wolf and a proboscidian were found in this cave. Associated with the fossils were charcoal, burned wood, and split bones. Some of the split bones were partly burned.

Sandia Mountain: On east side of Las Huertas Canyon, in the northern part of Sandia Mountains, about 120 miles from north and 160 from west state lines. Map entry, New Mexico 5.

Publications: Bliss (1940a; 1940b); Brand (1940); Bryan (1941a; 1941b); Hibben (1937; 1940; 1941a; 1941b; 1944). Additional comments, page 83.

San Jon: Near the west rim of the Llano Estacado, 10.5 miles south of San Jon, about 15 miles from east and 130 from north state lines. Map entry, New Mexico 6.

Publication: Roberts (1942a).

One type of projectile point, named San Jon by Roberts, found at this locality is associated with a large fossil bison. Other projectile points were found in other horizons which are unlike the San Jon point and are believed to be of later age.

North Dakota

Arvilla: Locality in a gravel pit near Arvilla, Grand Forks County, about 20 miles from east and 75 from north state lines. Map entry, North Dakota 1.

Publication: Jenks (1935, pp. 11–14).

Artifacts said to have been made of ivory were obtained from burials.

138

Ohio

Loveland: Locality in a gravel pit in valley of Little Miami River near Loveland.

Publications: Holmes (1893b, pp. 148–153); Leverett (1893, pp. 188–189); Wright (1888a; 1888b, pp. 258–259; 1890, p. 532; 1892, p. 250; 1893, p. 33).

An artifact is reported to have been found by Dr. Metz in a river terrace deposit at a depth of 20 or 25 feet. Mastodon bones were found in close proximity (Wright, 1892). The gravel deposits, according to Leverett, are of the age of the associated late glacial moraines of this region.

Oregon

Fort Rock Cave: At Fort Rock, Lake County, 60 miles northeast of Crater Lake, about 95 miles from south and 200 from east state lines. Map entry, Oregon 1.

Publications: Arnold and Libby (1950); Cressman and Williams (1940). Additional comments, page 84.

Fossil Lake: Thirty miles east of Fort Rock and about 180 miles from east and 80 from south state lines.

Publications: Cope (1878; 1889, pp. 970–982; 1895, p. 599); Howard (1935, p. 144; 1936b).

Artifacts at this locality are said to be "mixed with" bones of extinct animals. The extinct mammals listed are elephant, horse, camel, and sloth. Contemporaneity of the artifacts and fossils, in the opinion of Cope, is not proven.

Kirt School: In Willamette Valley (Sec. 5, T. 14 S., R. 3 W.), on a ranch formerly owned by James Templeton, 1.5 miles northeast of Kirt School.

Publication: Cressman (1947, p. 177).

The artifacts were obtained from a drainage ditch.

Klamath Lake: See Lower Klamath Lake, California.

Lebanon: Locality, a spring near Lebanon.

Publication: Cressman and Laughlin (1941).

A tooth and parts of the skeleton of an elephant were found at this locality. Near one of the bones was a stone apparently worked by man.

Odell Lake: In T. 23 S., R. 6.5 E., Willamette meridian in the Cascade Mountains.

139

The great tiger, *Dinobastis.*

Publication: Cressman (1948, pp. 57–58).

A camp site east of the Cascade Mountains divide. The relationship of the artifacts is said to be with the Lower Klamath Lake locality.

Paisley Cave: Five miles northwest of Paisley, about 58 miles from south and 180 miles from east state lines. Map entry, Oregon 2.

Publications: Cressman (1939; 1940a, p. 195; 1940b, p. 301; 1941, p. 175); Cressman and Williams (1940); Cressman and others (1942).

This locality affords, according to the authors, definite record of early man in association with extinct animals. The human materials include worked basalt chips. The extinct animals found are camel and horse.

Silver Lake: Twenty miles south of Fort Rock and about 175 miles from south and 195 from west state lines.

Publications: Cope (1889); Howard (1935, p. 144; 1936b, p. 394).

Cope found camel, horse, and sloth in a lake bed. Obsidian implements were found also but may not be contemporaneous with the fossils.

Wikiup Dam: A site on Deschutes River. About 108 miles from south and 118 from west state lines. Map entry, Oregon 3.

Publication: Cressman (1937).

At this locality two knives or side scrapers were removed by shovel from the side of a pit at a depth of 5 feet. The overlying strata consisted of thin humus soil, followed in order by pumice, 30 inches; yellow soil and scattered pebbles, 15 inches; yellow sandy soil and gravel, 15 inches; partially cemented sand, 4 to 6 inches. The artifacts were found lying on this hardened layer. No fossils are reported from the excavation.

Other Oregon caves containing human materials, described by Cressman and others, are Catlow Cave No. 1; Paisley Cave No. 2; and Roaring Spring Cave.

South Carolina

West Columbia: On the west side of Congaree River at the public road crossing between Columbia and West Columbia, 80 miles south and 16 west of jog in state line east of Catawba River. Map entry, South Carolina 1.

Publications: Roberts (1939b); Wauchope (1939).

141

Among many points collected at and near the surface, a few suggest Clovis Fluted.

South Dakota

Angostura Reservoir: On the Long farm in the basin of the Angostura Reservoir on Horsehead Creek, a tributary of Cheyenne River in Fall River County, 35 miles from west and 20 from south state lines. Map entry, South Dakota 1.

Publications: Arnold and Libby (1950); Hughes (1949). Additional comments, page 74.

Texas

Abilene: Various localities on Clear Fork of Brazos River and on Elm Creek, a tributary to Clear Fork.

Publications: Leighton (1936); C. N. Ray (1929; 1938; 1940a; 1940b; 1943a; 1943b; 1945); Roberts (1945b); Sayles (1936); Stewart (1945). An additional bibliography on these sites will be found in the Bulletin of the Texas Archeological and Paleontological Society.

Artifacts are found in alluvial deposits at varying depths up to about 30 feet. Burials made as the valleys were being filled by alluvial deposits are not uncommon.

Bee County: On Buckner ranch, on the right bank of Blanco Creek, about 12 miles east of Beeville, 50 miles north and 20 west of Corpus Christi. Map entry, Texas 1.

Publications: Kirk Bryan (1941a); T. N. Campbell (1940); Evans (1940); Sellards (1940a; 1940b).

Several artifacts have been found to a maximum depth of 16 feet in stream-terrace deposits. Charcoal, burnt rock, and hearths are likewise present. There is a possibility that this locality may contain some artifacts such as the Scottsbluff projectile point carried into this terrace formation by stream wash from an older deposit. Otherwise the Scottsbluff point and some Yuma-like points are here contemporaneous with stemmed points. Fossils that appear to be primary in the formation include *Parelephas columbi* (Falconer), *Mastodon americanus* (Kerr), *Equus*, bison, and glyptodon.

Colorado City: On Lone Wolf Creek near east city limits, about 40 miles north and 130 east of the southeast corner of New Mexico. Map entry, Texas 2.

Publications: Cook (1925; 1926, pp. 335–336; 1927a, pp. 240–243); Figgins (1927, pp. 229–231; 1935b, p. 4); Goddard (1926);

142

LOCALITIES AND LITERATURE

Hay (1927b, p. 288); Hay and Cook (1930); Renaud (1928, p. 33); Romer (1933, p. 79); Wormington (1949, p. 70).

Three artifacts were found associated with the skeleton of a bison subsequently described as *Bison figginsi* by Hay and Cook. The artifacts and fossils occur in valley fill. The fossils occur a little above present low-water level. In addition to the bison skeleton, Cook (1927a, p. 241) obtained at a slightly lower level teeth of horse, camel, and elephant.

Dallas: In Lagow sand pit in city limits of Dallas. Map entry, Texas 3.

Publications: Lull (1921); Shuler (1923).

Human bones were found in a gravel pit at a depth of 5 feet. The gravel deposits are part of a stream terrace, the top of which is about 50 feet above the flood plain of Trinity River. The overlying strata are reported to have been undisturbed. The degree of fossilization of the human bones is said to be about the same as that of the associated animal bones. The species identified from the sand pit are as follows: *Smilodon fatalis, Odocoileus* sp., *Tetrameryx shuleri,* n. gen. and sp., *Bison alleni, Camelops huerfanensis dallasi,* n. subsp., camel, gen. and sp. indet., *Equus* cf. *E. fraternus, Elephas columbi.*

Friesenhahn Cave: Near Bulverde about 21 miles north of San Antonio. Map entry, Texas 4. Additional comments, page 94.

Kincaid Shelter: On Sabinal River, 4 miles north of Sabinal, Uvalde County. Map entry, Texas 5. Additional comments, page 94.

Lipscomb: Eleven miles southwest of Lipscomb, about 25 miles from east and 27 from north state lines. Map entry, Texas 6.

Publications: Barbour and Schultz (1941); Schultz (1943).

Folsom artifacts are found at this locality in association with fossil bison. Additional comments, page 58.

Lubbock: On U. S. highway No. 84, 5 miles northwest of county courthouse, about 70 miles from west and 200 from north state lines. Map entry, Texas 7.

Publication: Sellards (1940a, p. 403). Additional comments, page 52.

Malakoff: On the Bishop farm, 3 miles north of Trinidad, on the east side of Trinity River, 57 miles southeast of Dallas and about 120 from east state line. Map entry, Texas 8.

143

Publications: Sellards (1930; 1941). Additional comments, page 99.

McLean: On a small stream, tributary to Mulberry Creek, 30 miles southwest of Abilene and near the west line of Taylor County, about 35 miles north and 190 east of the southeast corner of New Mexico. Map entry, Texas 9.

Publications: Bryan and Ray (1938, pp. 263–268); C. N. Ray (1942); Ray and Bryan (1938, pp. 257–258). Additional comments, page 36.

Miami: Nine miles northwest of Miami, 43 miles from east and 50 from north state lines. Map entry, Texas 10.

Publications: Sellards (1938); Studer (1935). Additional comments, page 18.

Montell Shelter: In Uvalde County near the Edwards County line, about 35 miles northwest of Uvalde. Map entry, Texas 11.

This shelter and cave, excavated by the Texas Memorial Museum in 1947, contains artifacts and a few extinct mammals.

Plainview: In a pit for road material, within the city limits of Plainview, about 55 miles from west and 155 from north state lines. Map entry, Texas 12.

Publications: Sellards (1945); Sellards, Evans, Meade, and Krieger (1947). Additional comments, page 60.

Virginia

Williamson site: On the Williamson farm about 5 miles east of Dinwiddie in the southern part of the state. A workshop site from which fluted projectile points and other artifacts have been obtained on the surface. Map entry, Virginia 1.

Publications: McCary (1947; 1951).

Saltville: In the immediate vicinity of Saltville, Smythe County, southwestern Virginia. Map entry, Virginia 2.

Publication: Pickle (1946).

The artifacts at this locality were found on the surface. Mastodon bones have been found also, but the actual association of artifacts and bones has not been determined.

Wisconsin

Royalton: In Waupaca County, 135 miles from south and 65 from east state lines. Map entry, Wisconsin 1.

144

Publication: Byers (1942).

Clovis Fluted point said to have been found on the surface near Royalton.

Wyoming

Agate Basin: In Niobrara County, approximately midway between Newcastle and Lusk, about 9 miles from east and 120 from north state lines. Map entry, Wyoming 1.

Publication: Roberts (1943b).

This locality, reported by Roberts, is said to represent a bison kill. The associated points, of which thirty-two were found in place in the deposits, appear to Roberts to represent a cultural unit. The species of bison at the locality has not been fully determined, and the artifacts have not been fully described.

Finley: In Sweetwater County, 4.5 miles east of Eden, about 75 miles from south and 90 miles from west state lines. Map entry, Wyoming 2.

Publications: Hack (1943); Howard (1943b); Howard, Satterthwaite, and Bache (1941); Moss (1951).

The artifacts were obtained from a stratum of sandy clay underlying dune sand. With the artifacts are bones of *Bison*, sp. indet. Invertebrates from the bone bed are of existing species. This is the type locality of Howard's Eden point. Scottsbluff points are present; also some other blades or points. Hack regards the culture layer as probably post-glacial in age.

Horner site: On Sage Creek, a tributary of Shoshone River, 3 miles east and 2 north of Cody, about 33 miles from north and 100 from west state lines. Map entry, Wyoming 3.

Publications: Arnold and Libby (1950); G. L. Jepsen (personal communication).

Artifacts associated with bison. Additional comments, page 74.

SOUTH AMERICA

Argentina

Gruta de Candonga: Locality, a cave in the province of Cordoba.
Publications: Bryan (1945); Castelanos (1943).

Four horizons are recognized in this cave; the two uppermost are

145

pottery-bearing. In the next underlying stratum, pottery is wanting. The recognizable fossils found at this level include *Mylodon* and fresh-water shells of species living in this region. The fourth or lowermost stratum was found to contain bone points, scrapers, remains of extinct animals, part of the skull of a child, burnt animal bones, and a hearth. The basal stratum is said to be separated from the overlying materials by an erosional unconformity.

Chile

Fell's Cave or Shelter: Near the Chile-Argentina boundary about 20 miles west of Palli Aike Cave, north of Magellan Strait and about 65 miles from the Atlantic Coast.
Publication: Bird (1938). Additional comments, page 97.

Palli Aike Cave: Near the Chile-Argentina boundary, about 18 miles from the north margin of Magellan Strait and some 45 miles from the Atlantic Coast. Map entry, South America 2. Additional comments, page 95.

Ecuador

Punin: Near Riobamba in the Ecuadoran highlands. Map entry, South America 3.
Publication: Anthony (1925).
A fossil human skull was found in volcanic ash beds in 1923. Like many other early American human skulls it is dolichocephalic. In these deposits were found also numerous fossil vertebrates including deer, horse, camel, sloth, and mastodon.

Brazil

Confins Cave: In the Lagoa Santa region of Rio dos Velhas valley, 5 miles from Pedro Leopaldo, State of Minas Geraes, in the highlands of eastern Brazil, about 300 miles west and north of Rio de Janeiro. Map entry, South America 1.
Publication: Walter, Cathoud, and Mattos (1937). Additional comments, page 98.

General Considerations

Progress of a Century

THE GATHERING OF INFORMATION on early man is beset with difficulties. Knowledge of this subject in America has accumulated slowly during a few years more than a century. Among early discoveries in South America were those by Lund in the Lagoa Santa region of eastern Brazil beginning about 1835, and in North America by Koch in Missouri in 1838 and 1839, and by Dickeson in Mississippi reported in 1846. Among other early contributors to this subject were Sir Charles Lyell (1849 and 1863), C. C. Abbott (1872 and later), F. W. Putnam (1885 and later), and G. K. Gilbert (1887 and 1889).

Until about 1890 no great opposition to the idea of early man in America seems to have developed. A good summary of the prevailing opinion of that time is given in a paper by W. J. McGee published in *Popular Science Monthly*, November 1888. In this paper, after discussing acceptable finds and others considered doubtful, he concludes that regardless of how the doubtful cases may be weighted, "the testimony is cumulative, parts of it are unimpeachable, and the proof of the existence of glacial man seems conclusive." However, during the last decade of the nineteenth century and approximately the first quarter of the twentieth century, most vigorous opposition was made by a few leading American scientists to assigning any appreciable antiquity to finds of human relics in North or South America. Notwithstanding these divergent views, finds continued to be reported. At present geologists and anthropologists probably without exception concede some considerable antiquity to man's habitation of the western hemisphere. To most scientists, McGee's conclusions of 1888 now seem reasonable.

Outstanding discoveries relating to the prehistory of man in America have been made during the past quarter of a century. The Folsom locality, discovered in 1926, was the first purely hunting site to be fully excavated. This locality not only afforded convincing evidence

147

The North American tapir, *Tapirus weillsi*.

that man was of some considerable geologic antiquity in America, but also gave a great impetus to the study of this subject. By subsequent discoveries Folsom man is known to have ranged over a considerable part of North America, including all or almost all of the great interior plains region. A Folsom camp site, the Lindenmeier locality in Colorado, has fortunately afforded a considerable extension of knowledge of the flint and bone utility and artistic objects made by these people. Very recently another locality, Lubbock, Texas, has afforded charred bison bones in the same stratum as artifacts made by Folsom man, and from the charcoal of the charred bones the approximate age in years of Folsom man has been determined.

When first discovered Folsom was assumed by some to be an introduced culture brought to America by migrants from the eastern hemisphere. This conclusion at the present time seems improbable. The Folsom culture has all the aspects of a culture indigenous to the great interior plains region of North America, a culture specially adapted to bison hunting.

Folsom culture was looked upon for a time after its discovery as the oldest American culture. This, however, is now definitely known to be incorrect. The Sandia locality in New Mexico, discovered in 1936, was found to contain projectile points and other artifacts in cave deposits at a level underlying the level of occurrence of Folsom points in the same cave. These Sandia points are, as indicated by their stratigraphic position, older than the Folsom culture. Another culture, Llano, is dated as yet only by its occurrence in the Blackwater No. 1 locality, New Mexico, at a level stratigraphically below Folsom culture. This culture, described elsewhere in this publication, is not only older than Folsom but is more widely distributed, occurring over much of the North American continent, and may be ancestral as well as antecedent to Folsom culture. Materials for the more exact age determination for the Llano culture have not as yet been found.

The Portales culture, later than Folsom at least in the southern High Plains region, as indicated by Blackwater No. 1 locality and probably also by the Lubbock locality, contains several types of projectile points, including the Eden, and others not named or not identified. The deposit holding this culture is separated from the stratum containing the Folsom culture by a disconformity. The time interval represented by the disconformity has not yet been determined.

The excellent results afforded by excavations of the past quarter-century, plus the radiocarbon dating of the past few years, have made

149

possible the approximate age determination of artifacts in America from the past ten or more millenniums. Artifacts believed to be more than 10,000 years old have been obtained from the basal stratum of lake fill at Blackwater No. 1 locality, New Mexico, from the oldest stratum at Sandia, New Mexico, and from Gypsum Cave, Nevada. Artifacts of approximately 10,000 years ago are those from the next to the basal stratum of lake fill at the Lubbock locality, Texas. Artifacts of the succeeding four millenniums are from the following localities, arranged as nearly as practicable in order of age: more than 9,000 years old, Lime Creek, Nebraska, and Fort Rock Cave, Oregon; more than 8,000 years old, Palli Aike Cave, South America, and Medicine Creek, Nebraska; more than 7,000 years old, Angostura, South Dakota, Sulphur Springs, Arizona, and Leonard Rock Shelter, Nevada; more than 6,000 years old, Horner, Wyoming. Many datings are now on record for localities less than 6,000 years old.

Formerly it was postulated by some that a large interval of time may have separated ancient man, or Paleo-Indian, from modern Indian. The records now available, however, do not support such hypotheses but make it appear probable that man, once established on the continent, persisted to the present time, although possibly not continuously at any one locality. He was undoubtedly influenced in choosing his place of habitation by climatic cycles and by the impact of other groups or tribes.

It is not known when man first reached the western hemisphere. By the record of Palli Aike Cave it is known that he had reached the extreme southern tip of South America more than 8,000 years ago. By the Llano culture it is known that he had become widely distributed in North America more than 10,000 years ago. The dating of his earliest occupation of the two continents must await future research.

Looking Forward

Discoveries of the future, like these of the past, will require extensive excavating. A brief summary of the amount of excavating required to obtain the information given on three of the localities described in this publication will help to make plain how rare and precious are these early records. The localities referred to are Plainview and Lubbock, Texas, and Blackwater No. 1, New Mexico. These are hunting sites in which fossil remains of animals are found associated with artifacts. Camp sites in the open or in caves would possibly on the average yield a more prolific return in artifacts than hunting sites. However, both are needed to complete the record and some of the hunting sites are, in a sense, also camp sites.

The Plainview locality was discovered as the result of excavations made for road materials, and by a rare coincidence the overburden, consisting of about 12 feet of earth, had been removed from a considerable part of the bone bed at the time the discovery was made. Time and effort ordinarily required in removing overburden was thus in some considerable degree reduced. A crew of skilled workers of four to six men, excavating at the locality from June 22 to October 24, 1945, a total of about 496 man-days, recovered twenty-six artifacts. The first artifact was found near the end of the second week of excavation, and thus represented 40 or 50 man-days of searching, indicating how long the initial discovery at a relatively prolific locality may be delayed. The principal new information resulting from the Plainview excavation was the recognition of a new early man culture complex characterized by the Plainview projectile point.

At the Blackwater locality No. 1 a Texas Memorial Museum party excavated in the summer and fall of 1949 and again in the spring and summer of 1950. The lake fill was found to include three distinct and separate artifact-bearing horizons. A total of forty-three flint artifacts were found, distributed through the deposits as follows: three in the oldest artifact-bearing horizon, which is of pre-Folsom age; one at the contact between horizons; ten in the second artifact-bearing horizon, which is of Folsom age; and twenty-nine in the third artifact-bearing horizon, which is later than Folsom. In addition, eighteen or more bone artifacts were obtained, all except one or two being from the oldest artifact-bearing horizon. The excavations made at this locality required a total of about 524 man-days. The principal results of the excavations were to determine fully the succession of strata in the lake deposits, to prove the occurrence here of a cultural complex older than Folsom, and to show the position of Eden and some other types of projectile points as later than the Folsom culture.

The Lubbock locality was discovered as a result of dredging carried on by the city of Lubbock in the valley of Yellow House Draw. Excavation by the Texas Memorial Museum at this locality during 1948, 1950, and 1951 amounted to a total of about 529 man-days. The geologic section of the lake fill was found to consist of five successive

151

strata. Six artifacts were found in place, one in the gray sand which forms the basal stratum of the lake fill, and five in the next to the basal stratum, which is a diatomite stratum. The results as measured in number of artifacts obtained seem meager. However, as measured by new information on early man, the results were outstanding. Charred bison bones were found in stratum 2, the diatomite horizon. From the charred bones the age of the diatomite layer was determined by the radiocarbon method as about, or a little less than, 10,000 years. During the careful, extensive excavation of the 1951 season this same stratum was found to contain Folsom points. Thus was obtained the important new information afforded by this locality, an approximate determination of the age in years of Folsom man.

These localities are mentioned as instances of present day search for early man records. Many other localities in North and South America could be cited illustrating further the work of anthropologists and geologists engaged in early man research.

The future, it is hoped, will witness a greatly extended and more successful search for early man. Localities of greatest usefulness are those that are plainly stratified with successive horizons of human materials lying in the undisturbed order of deposition. When such localities are found no narrow limits should be placed on the amount of excavation to be done. It can be safely assumed that where animals congregated in numbers, man, if he inhabited the continent at that time, was also present. Any locality that affords late Quaternary stratified deposits is likely hunting ground for early man relics.

Changing climate is an important factor in the history of man and one to which much attention has been given in the past and will continue to be given in the future. In the Blackwater No. 1 locality, New Mexico, three depositional units, each containing a separate culture complex, are separated by plainly marked disconformities. These disconformities, as elsewhere explained, appear to represent interruption in deposition and may have been caused by intervals of dry climate when the depression held little or no water. Under these conditions wind and possibly some water produced erosion in the lake bed, resulting in the disconformities observed in the deposits. If this is true the Blackwater locality records at least three wet and three dry intervals of time. The cultural records preserved are those of the wet intervals. The time interval represented by disconformity must be considerable, since the cultural complexes of the depositional units differ widely from each other. Future investigations will almost certainly add much to these observations. The three cultural complexes found in orderly succession at this locality are the Llano, Folsom, and Portales. There is as yet no evidence as to the length of time represented by these disconformities. However, information on the age in years of each of these cultural complexes will undoubtedly continue to accumulate and thus afford ultimately an approximate determination of the time interval represented by the disconformities.

An extremely important problem of the future will be fully to correlate the cultures of the Cordilleran mountain belt in age and geologic position with those of the great interior plains of North America. These cultures fortunately overlap considerably in geographic distribution, thus affording the possibility of direct correlation in some instances. The Appalachian mountain region and the Atlantic Gulf Coastal Plains likewise present the problem of correlation with the other regions. Aid to correlation is afforded to some extent by the overlap between regions in the range of animal and plant species. To use this method of correlation, however, will require increased refinements in our knowledge of the time of extinction of animal and plant species. The disappearance of a given species from a region does not prove complete extinction. Thus the Columbian elephant hunted by Llano man appears, on the basis of present records, to have become rare or possibly to have disappeared from the southern High Plains prior to the advent of Folsom man. This, however, by no means proves the extinction or disappearance of this species elsewhere on the North American continent. On the contrary, the species may very possibly have continued to exist for a time elsewhere in the Cordilleran mountain belt, in the Coastal Plains region, or even in the northern interior plains. A more difficult problem is that of correlation of early cultures between North and South America, which, it is hoped, may ultimately be accomplished. Climatic changes, if world-wide in extent, will aid, when more fully understood, in intercontinental and world correlations of epochs of human prehistory, and will supplement data from radiocarbon dating.

Much new information is to be expected on fossil human skeletal remains in North and South America. The inclusion of human skeletons or parts of skeletons in the accumulating sediments of the past obviously occurred rarely, in comparison with other animals. This is no doubt due in part to the concerted action by men to protect each other and to the habit which probably originated early of burying, cremating, or otherwise caring for the bodies of the dead. Neverthe-

153

less, during the long habitation of the earth by man, humans from time to time became entombed as did other animals under conditions that resulted in preservation of the skeletons. From the cave deposits of the mountain regions and from the hunting sites of the plains, further extended explorations may be expected to recover much more human skeletal material than has heretofore been obtained.

The radiocarbon method of determining age, even though approximate, is a wonderful new aid to the study of prehistory. Each excavation now made has a double objective, to secure human relics and to obtain materials of animal or plant origin suitable for radiocarbon testing. Correlations heretofore made on a basis of fauna, flora, stratigraphy, or climate may now, if materials are available, be checked on a basis of direct age determination. The lapse of time represented by an interruption or break in sedimentation, heretofore the most difficult problem facing the geologist, becomes approximately determinable, provided only that available testing materials can be obtained from immediately above and immediately below the unconformity or disconformity. Of greater promise of service to science is the fact that widely separated localities and cultures may be directly compared in age. In this way lies the hope of world-wide age correlations of human prehistory.

From what source and under what conditions outstanding new information on early man may come in the future is, of course, unknown. Undoubtedly, the deposits of caves, burials, middens, campsites, lakes, streams, wind, and waves will, as in the past, add their quota to the sum total of human knowledge. Likewise also, as in the past, some hasty and even faulty observations will be recorded, subsequently to be corrected by those who made the observations or by others. Men devoted to this science must bear in mind that ancient human relics occur sparingly and are to be obtained in adequate quantity for safe conclusions only by diligent, patient, long-continued search. At no time has the science of human prehistory held so much promise of rapid progress as at present.

Bibliography

Early Man in America
1839–1952

Abbott, C. C. (1872) *The stone age in New Jersey*, Am. Nat., vol. 6, pp. 144–160, 199–229.

———— (1873) *Occurrence of implements in the river drift at Trenton, N.J.*, Am. Nat., vol. 7, no. 4, pp. 204–209.

———— (1877) *On the discovery of supposed paleolithic implements in the glacial drift in the valley of the Delaware near Trenton, N.J.*, Peabody Mus. Am. Arch. and Ethnol., Rept., vol. 2, pp. 30–43.

———— (1881) *In* Bates, George A. (1881), pp. 471–551.

———— (1883) *An historical sketch of the discoveries of paleolithic implements in the valley of the Delaware River*, Boston Soc. Nat. Hist., Pr., vol. 21, pp. 124–132.

———— (1888) *On the antiquity of man in the valley of the Delaware*, Boston Soc. Nat. Hist., Pr., vol. 23, pp. 424–426.

———— (1889) *Evidences of the antiquity of man in eastern North America*, Am. Assoc. Adv. Sci., Pr., vol. 37, pp. 293–315.

Adams, Robert McCormick (1940) *Diagnostic flint points*, Am. Antiquity, vol. 6, pp. 72–75.

Agassiz, Louis (1854) *In* Nott, J. C., and Glidden, G. R. (1854), pp. 352–353.

Albritton, Claude C., Jr. (1941) *See* Huffington, Roy M., and Albritton, Claude C., Jr. (1941).

Albritton, Claude C., Jr., and Bryan, Kirk (1939) *Quaternary stratigraphy in the Davis Mountains, Trans-Pecos Texas*, Geol. Soc. Am., Bull., vol. 50, pp. 1423–1474.

Albritton, Claude C., Jr., and Pattillo, L. Gray, Jr. (1940) *A human skeleton found near Carrollton, Texas, geology of the site*, Field and Lab., vol. 8, pp. 59–62.

Allen, J. A. (1875) *The American bison, living and extinct*, Geol. Survey Kentucky, Mem., vol. 1; also (1875) Mus. Comp. Zool., Harvard College, vol. 14.

Allison, Ira S. (1946) *Early man in Oregon: Pluvial lakes and pumice*, Sci. Mo., vol. 62, pp. 63–65.

Amsden, C. A. (1931) *Man-hunting*, The Masterkey, vol. 5, no. 2, pp. 37–47.

———— (1935a) *The Pinto Basin artifacts*, Southwest Mus. Papers, no. 9, pp. 33–51.

———— (1935b) *America's earliest man*, The Masterkey, vol. 9, no. 6, pp. 173–177. Reprinted in Southwest Mus. Leaflets, no. 4.

———— (1937) *The Lake Mohave artifacts, in* Campbell, E. W. C., and others (1937), pp. 51–97.

———— (1944) *America's earliest man*, The Masterkey, vol. 18, no. 1, pp. 5–12. Also issued as Southwest Mus. Leaflets, no. 4, 2d ed.

Anderson, E. C., and others (1947) *Radiocarbon from cosmic radiation*, Sci., n.s., vol. 105, pp. 576–577.

Andrews, Roy Chapman (1945) *Meet your ancestors*, New York, Viking Press.

Antevs, Ernst (1931) *Late-glacial correlations and ice recession in Manitoba*, Geol. Survey Canada, Mem. 168, pp. 1–70.

———— (1934) *See* Howard, E. B., and Antevs, Ernst (1934).

———— (1935) *The spread of aboriginal man to North America*, Geog. Rev., vol. 25, no. 2, pp. 302–309.

———— (1936a) *Dating records of early man in the Southwest*, Am. Nat., vol. 70, pp. 331–336.

———— (1936b) *The occurrence of flints and extinct animals in pluvial deposits near Clovis, New Mexico*, Part 2, *Age of the Clovis lake clays*, Acad. Nat. Sci. Philadelphia, Pr., vol. 87, pp. 304–312.

———— (1937a) *Age of the Lake Mohave culture, in* Campbell, E. W. C., and others (1937), pp. 45–49.

———— (1937b) *Climate and early man in North America, in Early man*, Philadelphia, J. B. Lippincott Co., pp. 125–132.

———— (1937c) *Studies on the climate in relation to early man in the Southwest*, Carnegie Inst. Washington, Year Book, no. 36, p. 335.

———— (1937d) *The age of the "Minnesota Man,"* Carnegie Inst. Washington, Year Book, no. 36, pp. 335–338.

———— (1938a) *Was "Minnesota Girl" buried in a gully?*, Jour. Geol., vol. 46, no. 3, pp. 293–295.

———— (1938b) *Studies on the climate in relation to early man in the Southwest*, Carnegie Inst. Washington, Year Book, no. 37, p. 348.

156

BIBLIOGRAPHY

——— (1939a) *In* Harrington, M. R. (1939b), p. 209.

——— (1939b) *Studies on the past climate in relation to man in the Southwest*, Carnegie Inst. Washington, Year Book, no. 38, pp. 317–319.

——— (1940) *Age of artifacts below peat beds in Lower Klamath Lake, California*, Carnegie Inst. Washington, Year Book, no. 39, pp. 307–309.

——— (1941a) *Age of the Cochise culture stages*, Medallion Papers, no. 29, pp. 31–56.

——— (1941b) *See* Sayles, E. B., and Antevs, Ernst (1941).

——— (1944) *Regarding J. C. Jones' date for Lake Lahontan*, Am. Antiquity, vol. 10, p. 211.

——— (1945) *Correlation of Wisconsin glacial maxima*, Am. Jour. Sci., vol. 243-A, pp. 1–39.

——— (1948) *The Great Basin, with emphasis on glacial and post-glacial times; climatic changes and pre-white man*, Univ. Utah Bull., vol. 33, no. 20, pp. 168–191.

——— (1949a) *In* Wormington, H. M. (1949), pp. 185–192.

——— (1949b) *See* Martin, Paul S., Rinaldo, John B., and Antevs, Ernst (1949).

Anthony, H. E. (1925) *In* Sullivan, L. R., and Hellman, Milo (1925).

——— (1937) *Animals of America*, Garden City Pub. Co., New York.

Arellano, Alberto R. V. (1946a) *Datos geológicos sobre la antigüedad del hombre en la cuenca de Méjico*, Memo. Seg. Cong. Mex. Ciencias Sociales, vol. 5, pp. 213–219.

——— (1946b) *El elefante fósil de Tepexpam y el hombre primitivo*, Rev. Mex. Estudios Antropol., vol. 8, pp. 89–94.

——— (1951) *The Becerra formation (latest Pleistocene) of Central America*, 18th Intern. Geol. Cong., Rept., Part 11, pp. 55–62.

Arellano, Alberto R. V., and Muller, Florencia (1948) *La cueva encantada de Chimalacatlan, Morelos*, Soc. Mex. Geografía y Estadística, Bull., vol. 66, no. 3, pp. 483–491.

Arnold, J. R., and Libby, W. F. (1950) *Radiocarbon dates*, Univ. Chicago, Inst. for Nuclear Stud.

Aughey, Samuel (1876) *The superficial deposits of Nebraska: Life of the loess age, in* U.S. Geog. Survey Terr. (Hayden) 8th Ann. Rept., pp. 241–269.

Aveleyra-Arroyo de Anda, Luis (1948) *El hombre de Tamazulapan*, Memo. Acad. Mex. Historia, vol 7, no. 3.

────── (1949a) *Sobre dos notables puntas de proyectil de la Cuenca de México*, El México Antiguo, vol. 7, pp. 514–521.

────── (1949b) *See* Maldonado Koerdell, Manuel, and Aveleyra-Arroyo de Anda, Luis (1949).

────── (1950) *Prehistoria de México*, Ediciones Mexicanas, 167 pages.

Babbitt, F. E. (1883) *Vestiges of glacial man in Minnesota*, Am. Assoc. Adv. Sci., vol. 32, pp. 385–390.

────── (1884) *Vestiges of glacial man in Minnesota*, Am. Nat., vol. 18, pp. 594–605, 697–708.

Bache, Charles (1941) *See* Howard, Edgar B., Satterthwaite, Linton, Jr., and Bache, Charles (1941).

Balch, E. S. (1917) *Early man in America*, Am. Philos. Soc., Pr., vol. 56, no. 6, pp. 473–483.

Barbieri, J. A. (1937) *Technique of the implements from Lake Mohave*, *in* Campbell, E. W. C., and others (1937).

Barbour, E. H. (1907a) *Evidence of man in the loess of Nebraska*, Sci., n.s., vol. 25, no. 629, pp. 110–112.

────── (1907b) *Ancient inhabitants of Nebraska*, Records of the Past, vol. 6, pp. 40–46.

────── (1907c) *Evidence of loess man in Nebraska*, Nebraska Geol. Survey, vol. 2, no. 6, pp. 331–348.

────── (1907d) *Prehistoric man in Nebraska*, Putnam's Monthly, vol. 1, p. 413–415; also *idem, A postscript*, pp. 502–503.

────── (1907e) *In* Hrdlicka, Ales (1907), pp. 73–74.

────── (1932) *See* Meserve, F. G., and Barbour, E. H. (1932).

────── (1936) *See* MacClintock, Paul, and others (1936).

Barbour, E. H., and Schultz, C. B. (1932a) *The mounted skeleton of Bison occidentalis and associated dart-points*, Nebraska State Mus., Bull., vol. 1, no. 32, pp. 263–270.

────── (1932b) *The Scottsbluff bison quarry and its artifacts*, Nebraska State Mus., Bull., vol. 1, no. 34, pp. 283–286.

────── (1936a) *Palaeontologic and geologic consideration of early man in Nebraska with notice of a new bone bed in the early Pleistocene of Morrill County, Nebraska*, Nebraska State Mus., Bull., vol. 1, no. 45, pp. 431–450.

────── (1936b) *Did glacial man inhabit Nebraska?*, Nebraska Alumnus, May, 2 pages.

────── (1937) *Pleistocene and post-glacial mammals of Nebraska*, *in* Early man, Philadelphia, J. B. Lippincott Co., pp. 185–192.

—————— (1941) *A new fossil bovid from Nebraska with notice of a new bison quarry in Texas*, Nebraska State Mus., Bull., vol. 2, no. 7, pp. 63–68.

Barbour, E. H., and Ward, H. B. (1906a) *Preliminary report on the primitive man of Nebraska*, Nebraska Geol. Survey, vol. 2, no. 5, pp. 319–327.

—————— (1906b) *Discovery of an early type of man in Nebraska*, Sci., n.s., vol. 24, no. 620, pp. 628–629.

Barcena, Mariano (1885) *Notice of some human remains found near the city of Mexico*, Am. Nat., vol. 19, pp. 739–744.

—————— (1886a) *The fossil man of Peñon, Mexico*, Am. Nat., vol. 20, pp. 633–635.

—————— (1886b) *Nuevos datos acerca de la antigüedad del hombre, en el Valle de Méjico*, La Naturaleza, vol. 7, pp. 265–270.

Barcena, Mariano, and Castillo, Antonio del (1886) *Noticia acerca del hallazgo de restos humanos prehistoricos en el Valle de Méjico*, La Naturaleza, vol. 7, pp. 257–264.

Bartlett, Katherine (1943) *A primitive stone industry of the Little Colorado Valley, Arizona*, Am. Antiquity, vol. 8, pp. 266–268. (Reprinted with some changes from The Plateau, Mus. Northern Arizona, vol. 14, no. 3, [Jan., 1942].)

Bates, George A. (1881) *Primitive industry*, Salem, Mass.

Becker, G. F. (1891) *Antiquities from under Tuolumne Table Mountain in California*, Geol. Soc. Am., Bull., vol. 2, pp. 189–198.

Bell, E. H. (1932) *New evidence unearthed that man lived in ice age America*, Sci. Serv. Res. Ann., no. 140.

Bell, E. H., and Van Royen, William (1933) *Some considerations regarding the possible age of an ancient site in western Nebraska*, Sci. Serv. Res. Ann., no. 181.

—————— (1934a) *An Evaluation of recent Nebraska findings sometimes attributed to the Pleistocene*, Wisconsin Arch., n.s., vol. 13, no. 3, pp. 49–70.

—————— (1934b) *Studies relating to the antiquity of man in America*, Carnegie Inst. Washington, Year Book, no. 33, pp. 303–305.

Bennett, Wendell C., and Bird, Junius B. (1949) *Andean culture history*, Am. Mus. Nat. Hist., Handbook Series, no. 15.

Berry, E. W. (1917) *The fossil plants from Vero, Florida*, Jour. Geol., vol. 25, pp. 661–666.

Berthoud, C. E. (1866) *Description of the hot springs of Soda Creek*, Acad. Nat. Sci. Philadelphia, Pr., vol. 18, pp. 342–345.

159

Bird, Junius B. (1938) *Antiquity and migrations of the early inhabitants of Patagonia*, Geog. Rev., vol. 28, pp. 250–275.

———— (1939) *Artifacts in Canadian River terraces*, Sci., n.s., vol. 89, no. 2311, pp. 340–341.

———— (1949) *See* Bennett, Wendell C., and Bird, Junius B. (1949).

Blackman, E. E. (1907) *Prehistoric man in Nebraska*. Records of the Past, vol. 6, part 3, pp. 76–79.

Blake, W. P. (1899) *The Pliocene skull of California and flint implements of Table Mountain*, Jour. Geol., vol. 7, pp. 631–637.

Blanckenhorn, M. (1911) *See* Selenka, L., and Blanckenhorn, M. (1911).

Bliss, Wesley L. (1939) *Early man in western and northwestern Canada*, Sci., n.s., vol. 89, pp. 365–366.

———— (1940a) *A chronological problem presented by Sandia Cave, New Mexico*, Am. Antiquity, vol. 5, pp. 200–201.

———— (1940b) *Sandia Cave*, Am. Antiquity, vol. 6, pp. 77–78.

Boas, Franz (1933) *Relations between north-west America and northeast Asia*, in *The American Aborigines*, 5th Pacific Sci. Cong., Univ. Toronto Press, Toronto, pp. 355–370.

Bode, F. D. (1937a) *Geology of Lake Mohave outlet channel*, in Campbell, E. W. C., and others (1937).

———— (1937b) *See* Stock, Chester, and Bode, F. D. (1937).

Bórmida, Marcelo (1950) *See* Menghin, Osvaldo F. A., and Bórmida, Marcelo (1950).

Boule, Marcellin (1923) *Fossil men: Elements of human paleontology*, transl. from French, with introduction by Jessie Elliot Ritchie and James Ritchie, Edinburgh, Oliver and Boyd.

———— (1928) *La prétendue industrie humaine, osseuse, du Pliocène du Nebraska*, L'Anthropologie, vol. 38, pp. 443–444.

Boutwell, J. M. (1911) *The Calaveras skull*, U.S. Geol. Survey Prof. Paper 73, pp. 54–55.

Bowden, A. O., and Lopatin, Ivan A. (1936) *Pleistocene man in southern California*, Sci., n.s., vol. 84, pp. 507–508.

Brand, Donald D. (1940) *Regarding Sandia Cave*, Am. Antiquity, vol. 5, p. 339.

———— (1944a) *A note on Baja California*, Soc. Mex. Antropología: Terc. Reunión Mesa Redonda, Mexico City, pp. 163–164.

———— (1944b) *A note on the pre-ceramic man in northern Mexico*, Soc. Méx. Antropología: Terc. Reunión Mesa Redonda, Mexico City, p. 164.

BIBLIOGRAPHY

Brew, John Otis (1943) *A selected bibliography of American Indian archaeology east of the Rocky Mountains,* Excavators' Club, Papers, vol. 2, no. 1, 90 pages.

Brinton, Daniel G. (1887) *On ancient human footprints from Nicaragua,* Am. Philos. Soc., vol. 24, pp. 437–444.

Broom, Robert (1937) *On Australopithecus and its affinities,* in *Early man,* International Symposium, Acad. Nat. Sci. Philadelphia, pp. 285–292.

Brown, Barnum (1928) *Recent finds relating to prehistoric man in America,* New York Acad. Medicine, Bull., 2d s., vol. 4, pp. 824–828.

——— (1929) *Folsom culture and its age* (abstract), Geol. Soc. Am., Bull., vol. 40, pp. 128–129.

——— (1932) *The buffalo drive,* Nat. Hist., vol. 32, pp. 75–82.

Browne, Jim (1940) *Projectile points,* Am. Antiquity, vol. 5, pp. 209–213.

Bryan, Frank (1930) *Archaeological remains in the Black and Grand prairies of Texas,* Texas Arch. and Paleont. Soc., Bull., vol. 2, pp. 76–84.

——— (1931) *Notes on the archaeology of central Texas,* Am. Anthrop., n.s., vol. 33, no. 1, pp. 16–31.

——— (1938) *A review of the geology of the Clovis finds reported by Howard and Cotter,* Am. Antiquity, vol. 4, pp. 113–130.

Bryan, Kirk (1929) *In* Brown, Barnum (1929), pp. 128–129.

——— (1935) *Minnesota man—a discussion of the site,* Sci., n.s., vol. 82, pp. 170–171.

——— (1937a) *Geology of the Folsom deposits in New Mexico and Colorado,* in *Early man,* Philadelphia, J. B. Lippincott Co., pp. 139–152.

——— (1937b) *Ancient man in America,* Geog. Rev., vol. 27, pp. 507–509.

——— (1938) *See* Ray, C. N., and Bryan, Kirk (1938).

——— (1939a) *Stone cultures near Cerro Pedernal, New Mexico, and their geologic antiquity,* Texas Arch. and Paleont. Soc., Bull., vol. 11, pp. 9–46.

——— (1939b) *See* Albritton, Claude C., Jr., and Bryan, Kirk (1939).

——— (1941a) *Geologic antiquity of man in America,* Sci., n.s., vol. 93, pp. 505–514.

——— (1941b) *Correlation of the deposits of Sandia Cave, New*

161

Mexico, with the glacial chronology, Smithson. Misc. Coll., vol. 99, no. 23, pp. 45–64.

———— (1941c) *Pre-Columbian agriculture in the Southwest as conditioned by periods of alluviation*, Assoc. Am. Geog., Ann., vol. 31, pp. 219–242. Printed also, slightly condensed, in 8th Am. Sci. Cong., Pr., vol. 2 (1942), pp. 57–74.

———— (1945) *Recent work on early man at the Gruta de Candonga in the Argentine Republic*, Am. Antiquity, vol. 11, pp. 58–60.

———— (1946) *Comentario e intento de correlación con la cronología glacial*, Memo. Seg. Cong. Mex. Ciencias Sociales, vol. 5, pp. 220–225.

———— (1948) *Los suelos complejos y fósiles de la altiplanicie de México, en relación a los cambios climáticos*, Soc. Geol. Mex., Bull., vol. 13, pp. 1–20.

———— (1951) *See* Moss, John H., and others (1951).

Bryan, Kirk, and Gidley, J. W. (1926) *Vertebrate fossils and their enclosing deposits from the shore of Pleistocene Lake Cochise, Arizona*, Am. Jour. Sci., 5th s., vol. 11, pp. 477–488.

Bryan, Kirk, and McCann, Franklin T. (1943) *Sand dunes and alluvium near Grants, New Mexico*, Am. Antiquity, vol. 8, pp. 281–290.

Bryan, Kirk, and MacClintock, Paul (1938) *What is implied by "disturbance" at the site of Minnesota man*, Jour. Geol., vol. 46, no. 3, pp. 279–292.

Bryan, Kirk, and Ray, C. N. (1938) *Long channelled point found in alluvium beside bones of Elephas columbi*, Texas Arch. and Paleont. Soc., Bull., vol. 10, pp. 263–268.

Bryan, Kirk, and Ray, Louis L. (1939) *Geologic antiquity of the Lindenmeier site in Colorado*, Smithson. Misc. Coll., vol. 99, no. 2, 76 pages.

Bryan, Kirk, Retzek, Henry, and McCann, Franklin T. (1938) *Discovery of Sauk Valley man of Minnesota, with an account of the geology*, Texas Arch. and Paleont. Soc., Bull., vol. 10, pp. 114–135.

Bryan, Kirk, and Toulouse, Joseph H., Jr. (1943) *The San Jose nonceramic culture and its relation to a puebloan culture in New Mexico*, Am. Antiquity, vol. 8, pp. 269–280.

Bryan, W. A. (1929) *The recent bone-cavern find at Bishop's Cap, New Mexico*, Sci., n.s., vol. 70, pp. 39–41.

Burmaster, E. R. (1932) In *Reports of archaeological field work in North America during 1931*, Am. Anthrop., n.s., vol. 34, p. 491.

Byers, Douglas S. (1942) *Fluted points from Wisconsin,* Am. Antiquity, vol. 7, p. 400.

———— (1943) *A new site,* Am. Antiquity, vol. 8, p. 300.

Calvin, Samuel (1902) *In* Chamberlin, T. C. (1902), pp. 777–778.

Campbell, E. W. C. (1936) *Archaeological problems in the southern California deserts,* Am. Antiquity, vol. 1, no. 4, pp. 295–300.

Campbell, E. W. C., and Campbell, W. H. (1935) *The Pinto Basin site,* Southwest Mus. Papers, no. 9, 51 pages.

———— (1937) *The Lake Mohave site, in* Campbell, E. W. C., and others (1937), pp. 9–44.

———— (1940) *A Folsom complex in the Great Basin,* The Masterkey, vol. 14, pp. 7–11.

Campbell, E. W. C., and others (1937) *The archeology of Pleistocene Lake Mohave,* Southwest Mus. Papers, no. 11.

Campbell, T. N. (1940a) *Notes on artifacts,* Geol. Soc. Am., Bull., vol. 51, pp. 1640–1644.

———— (1940b) *See* Kelley, J. Charles, Campbell, T. N., and Lehmer, Donald J. (1940).

———— (1942) *See* Kelley, J. Charles, and Campbell, T. N. (1942).

Campbell, W. H. (1935) *See* Campbell, E. W. C., and Campbell, W. H. (1935).

———— (1937) *See* Campbell, E. W. C., and Campbell, W. H. (1937).

———— (1940) *See* Campbell, E. W. C., and Campbell, W. H. (1940).

Carter, George F. (1951) *Man in America: A criticism of scientific thought,* Sci. Monthly, vol. 73, no. 5, pp. 297–307.

Cassell, Raymond K. (1941) *A postulated corridor of Folsom migration,* Michigan Acad. Sci., Arts, Letters, Papers, vol. 26, pp. 451–457.

Casson, Stanley (1939) *The discovery of man,* New York, Harper and Bros., 339 pages.

Castañeda, Pedro de (1896) *The narrative of the expedition of Coronado, 1540–1542, in* Winship, George Parker (1896).

Castellanos, Alfredo (1943) *Antigüedad geologica del yacimiento de los restos humanos de la Gruta de Candonga (Córdoba),* Pub. Inst. Fisiografía y Geol., Univ. Nac. Litoral, no. 14.

Castillo, Antonio del (1886) *See* Barcena, Mariano, and Castillo, Antonio del (1886).

Cathoud, A. (1937) *See* Walter, H. V., Cathoud, A., and Mattos, Anibal (1937).

Caywood, Louis R. (1948) *Yuma point from western Idaho*, Am. Antiquity, vol. 13, p. 251.

Chaffee, Robert G. (1939) *See* Colbert, Edwin H., and Chaffee, Robert G. (1939).

Chamberlin, R. T. (1917a) *Interpretation of the formations containing human bones at Vero, Florida*, Jour. Geol., vol. 25, pp. 25–39.

—————— (1917b) *Further studies at Vero, Florida*, Jour. Geol., vol. 25, pp. 667–683.

Chamberlin, T. C. (1902) *The geologic relations of the human relics of Lansing, Kansas*, Jour. Geol., vol. 10, no. 7, pp. 745–799.

Champe, John L. (1946) *Ash Hollow Cave*, Univ. Nebraska Studies, n.s., no. 1.

Chaney, Ralph W. (1935) *In* Howard, E. B. (1936h), p. 301.

Chaney, Ralph W., and Mason, Herbert L. (1936) *A Pleistocene flora from Fairbanks, Alaska*, Am. Mus. Nat. Hist., Novitates, no. 887.

Claflin, William H., Jr. (1931) *The Stalling's Island mound, Columbia County, Georgia*, Peabody Mus. Am. Arch. and Ethnol., Papers, Harvard Univ., vol. 14, no. 1.

Clapp, C. H. (1917) *Sooke and Duncan map-areas, Vancouver Island*, Geol. Survey Canada, Mem. 96, p. 348.

Claypole, E. W. (1893) *Preglacial man not improbable*, Am. Geol., vol. 11, pp. 191–194.

Coffin, R. G. (1937) *Northern Colorado's first settlers*, Colorado State College, Fort Collins, 19 pages.

Colbert, Edwin H. (1937) *The Pleistocene mammals of North America and their relations to Eurasian forms*, in *Early man*, Philadelphia, J. B. Lippincott Co., pp. 173–184.

—————— (1940) *Mammoth and man*, Nat. Hist., vol. 46, pp. 96–103.

—————— (1942a) *The association of man with extinct mammals in the Western Hemisphere*, 8th Am. Sci. Cong., Pr., vol. 2, pp. 17–29.

—————— (1942b) *The Pleistocene faunas of Asia and their relationships to early man*, New York Acad. Sci., Tr., 2d s., vol. 5, no. 1, pp. 1–10.

Colbert, Edwin H., and Chaffee, Robert G. (1939) *A study of Tetrameryx and associated fossils from Papago Spring Cave, Sonoita, Arizona*, Am. Mus. Nat. Hist., Novitates, no. 1034, 21 pages.

Collier, Donald (1947) *See* Martin, Paul S., Quimby, George I., and Collier, Donald (1947).

Collins, Henry B., Jr. (1937) *Arctic area*, Am. Antiquity, vol. 3, p. 188.

———— (1943) *Eskimo archaeology and its bearing on the problem of man's antiquity in America*, Am. Philos. Soc., Pr., vol. 86, no. 2, pp. 220–235.

Conkling, R. P. (1932) *Conkling Cavern: The discoveries in the Bone Cave at Bishop's Cap, New Mexico*, West Texas Hist. and Sci. Soc., Publ., Bull. 44, no. 4, pp. 6–19.

Connery, J. H. (1932) *Recent find of mammoth remains in the Quaternary of Florida, together with arrowhead*, Sci., n.s., vol. 75, no. 1950, p. 516.

Connolly, C. J. (1949) *The Tepexpan endocranial cast*, Viking Fund Pub. in Anthropol., no. 11, pp. 130–131.

Cook, H. J. (1911) *Note on a skull with imbedded arrowhead*, Records of the Past, vol. 10, part 4, pp. 339–341.

———— (1922) *In* Osborn, H. F. (1922a), pp. 1–2.

———— (1925) *Definite evidence of human artifacts in the American Pleistocene*, Sci., n.s., vol. 62, no. 1612, pp. 459–460.

———— (1926) *The antiquity of man in America*, Sci. Am., vol. 135, pp. 334–336.

———— (1927a) *New geological and paleontological evidence bearing on the antiquity of mankind in America*, Nat. Hist., vol. 7, no. 3, pp. 240–247.

———— (1927b) *New trails of ancient man*, Sci. Am., vol. 137, pp. 114–117.

———— (1927c) *Notes on recently discovered American Pleistocene artifacts*, New York Acad. Sci., Tr., vol. 29.

———— (1928a) *Further evidence concerning man's antiquity at Frederick, Oklahoma*, Sci., n.s., vol. 67, no. 1736, pp. 371–373.

———— (1928b) *Glacial-age man in New Mexico*, Sci. Am., vol. 139, no. 1, pp. 38–40.

———— (1928c) *See* Hay, O. P., and Cook, H. J. (1928).

———— (1930) *See* Hay, O. P., and Cook, H. J. (1930).

———— (1931a) *More evidence of the "Folsom culture" race*, Sci. Am., vol. 144, pp. 102–103.

———— (1931b) *The antiquity of man as indicated at Frederick, Oklahoma: A reply*, Washington Acad. Sci., Jour., vol. 21, no. 8, pp. 161–166.

Cooke, C. W. (1926) *Fossil man and Pleistocene vertebrates in Florida*, Am. Jour. Sci., 5th s., vol. 12, pp. 441–452.

165

—— (1928) *The stratigraphy and age of the Pleistocene deposits in Florida from which human bones have been reported*, Washington Acad. Sci., Jour., vol. 18, no. 15, pp. 414–421.

—— (1945) *Geology of Florida*, Florida Geol. Survey, Bull. 29, 339 pages.

Cooke, C. W., and Mossom, Stuart (1929) *Geology of Florida*, Florida Geol. Survey, 20th Ann. Rept., pp. 29–227.

Cope, E. D. (1878) *Pliocene man* (unsigned editorial), Am. Nat., vol. 12, pp. 125–126.

—— (1879) *The cave bear of California*, Am. Nat., vol. 13, p. 791.

—— (1889) *The Silver Lake of Oregon and its region*, Am. Nat., vol. 23, no. 275, pp. 970–982.

—— (1891) *The California cave bear*, Am. Nat., vol. 25, pp. 997–999.

—— (1895) *The antiquity of man in North America*, Am. Nat., vol. 29, pp. 593–599.

Cordero, Julio Febres G. (1944) *Nuestras oleadas de migracion arcaica*, Acta Am., vol. 2, nos. 1, 2, pp. 51–57.

Cotter, J. L. (1937a) *The occurrence of flints and extinct animals in pluvial deposits near Clovis, New Mexico, part 4, Report on excavation at the gravel pit, 1936*, Acad. Nat. Sci. Philadelphia, Pr., vol. 89, pp. 1–16.

—— (1937b) *The significance of Folsom and Yuma artifact occurrences in the light of typology and distribution*, Philadelphia Anthropol. Soc., 25th Anniv. Studies, vol. 1, pp. 27–35.

—— (1938) *The occurrence of flints and extinct animals in pluvial deposits near Clovis, New Mexico, part 6, Report on field season of 1937*, Acad. Nat. Sci. Philadelphia, Pr., vol. 90, pp. 113–117.

Cressman, Luther Sheeleigh (1937) *The Wikiup damsite no. 1 knives*, Am. Antiquity, vol. 3, pp. 53–67.

—— (1939) *Early man and culture in the northern Great Basin region of south-central Oregon*, Carnegie Inst. Washington, Year Book, no. 38, pp. 314–317.

—— (1940a) *Early man and culture in south-central Oregon*, Am. Philos. Soc., Year Book, 1939, pp. 194–196.

—— (1940b) *Studies on early man in south-central Oregon*, Carnegie Inst. Washington, Year Book, no. 39, pp. 300–306.

—— (1940c) *Early man and culture in the northern Great Basin region of south-central Oregon. Preliminary report*, Univ. Oregon Mon., Stud. in Anthropol., no. 3, pp. 1–15.

———— (1941) *Early man in the northern Great Basin region of south-central Oregon*, 6th Pacific Sci. Cong., Pr., vol. 4, pp. 169–175.

———— (1942) *Archaeological researches in the northern Great Basin* (with collaboration of Frank C. Baker, Henry P. Hansen, Paul S. Conger, and Robert F. Heizer), Carnegie Inst. Washington, Pub. 538, 158 pages.

———— (1943) *Results of recent archaeological research in the northern Great Basin region of south-central Oregon*, Am. Philos. Soc., Pr., vol. 86, no. 2, pp. 236–246.

———— (1944a) *Reply to A. D. Krieger's review of L. S. Cressman's archaeological researches in the northern Great Basin*, Am. Antiquity, vol. 10, pp. 206–211.

———— (1944b) *New information on south-central Oregon atlatls*, The Masterkey, vol. 18, pp. 169–179.

———— (1945) *A case of probable osteomyelitis in an Indian skeleton*, Western Jour. Surgery, Obstetrics, Gynecology, vol. 53, pp. 332–335.

———— (1946) *Early man in Oregon: Stratigraphic evidence*, Sci. Mo., vol. 62, pp. 43–51.

———— (1947) *Further information on projectile points from Oregon*, Am. Antiquity, vol. 13, pp. 177–179.

———— (1948) *Odell Lake site, a new Paleo-Indian camp site in Oregon*, Am. Antiquity, vol. 14, pp. 57–58.

Cressman, Luther Sheeleigh, and Krieger, Alex D. (1940) *Atlatls and associated artifacts from south-central Oregon*, Univ. Oregon Mon., Stud. in Anthropol., no. 3, pp. 16–52.

Cressman, Luther Sheeleigh, and Laughlin, W. S. (1941) *A probable association of mammoth and artifacts in the Willamette Valley, Oregon*, Am. Antiquity, vol. 6, pp. 339–342.

Cressman, Luther Sheeleigh, and Williams, Howel (1940) *Early man in south-central Oregon: Evidence from stratified sites*, Univ. Oregon Mon., Stud. in Anthropol., no. 3, pp. 53–78.

Cresson, H. T. (1890) *In* Wright, G. F. (1890), p. 555.

———— (1892) *Paleolithic man in the southern portion of the Delaware Valley*, Sci., 2d s., vol. 20, p. 304.

Cummings, Byron (1927) *Cochise's yesterday*, The Tombstone Epitaph, vol. 49, no. 4, pp. 12–25.

———— (1928) *Cochise of yesterday*, Arizona, Old and New, vol. 1, no. 4, pp. 9–10, 26–28.

Dana, J. D. (1875) *On Dr. Koch's evidence with regard to the contemporaneity of man and the mastodon in Missouri*, Am. Jour. Sci., 3d s., vol. 9, pp. 335–346, 398.

Deevey, Edward S., Jr. (1951) *See* Flint, Richard Foster, and Deevey, Edward S., Jr. (1951).

DeLaguna, Frederica (1947) *The prehistory of northern North America as seen from the Yukon*, Memoirs of the Soc. for Am. Arch., no. 3. Supplement to Am. Antiquity, vol. 12, no. 3, part 2.

DeTerra, Helmut (1946a) *Discovery of an Upper Pleistocene human fossil at Tepexpam, Valley of Mexico*, Rev. Mex. Estudios Antropol., vol. 8, pp. 287–288.

———— (1946b) *New evidence for the antiquity of early man in Mexico*, Rev. Mex. Estudios Antropol., vol. 8, pp. 69–88.

———— (1946c) *Stones and bones*, Time, vol. 47, March 25, pp. 92, 95.

———— (1947) *Preliminary note on the discovery of fossil man at Tepexpan in the Valley of Mexico*, Am. Antiquity, vol. 13, pp. 40–44.

———— (1949) *Early man in Mexico*, Viking Fund Pub. in Anthropol., no. 11, pp. 11–86.

Dickeson, M. W. (1846) *Fossils from Natchez, Mississippi*, Acad. Nat. Sci. Philadelphia, Pr., vol. 3, pp. 106–107.

Dorsey, G. A. (1902) *In* Holmes, W. H. (1902a), pp. 744–745.

Drake, D. (1850) *Human remains from alluvial deposits at New Orleans*, in *A systematic treatise on the principal diseases of the interior valley of North America* . . . , Cincinnati, pp. 76–77.

Dubois, Eugene (1894) *Pithecanthropus erectus, eine menschenäehnliche Übergangsform aus Java*, Jaarboek van het Mijnwezen, vol. 24, pp. 5–77.

———— (1896) *On Pithecanthropus erectus: A transitional form between man and the apes*, Royal Dublin Soc., Scien. Tr., 2d ser., vol. 6, pp. 1–18.

Dunning, J. R. (1946) *See* Reid, A. F., and others (1946).

Eddy, Samuel, and Jenks, A. E. (1935) *A kitchen midden with bones of extinct animals in the upper lakes area*, Sci., n.s., vol. 81, no. 2109, p. 535.

Edwards, William E. (1951) *The stratified Paleo-Indian Anderson site of central-eastern Florida* (MS).

Eiseley, L. C. (1935) *See* Schultz, C. B., and Eiseley, L. C. (1935).

———— (1936) *See* Schultz, C. B., and Eiseley, L. C. (1936a) and (1936b).

BIBLIOGRAPHY

—————— (1937) *Index mollusca and their bearing on certain problems of prehistory: A critique*, Philadelphia Anthropol. Soc., vol. 1, 25th Anniv. Studies, pp. 77–93.

—————— (1939a) *Evidences of a pre-ceramic cultural horizon in Smith County, Kansas*, Sci., n.s., vol. 89, p. 221.

—————— (1939b) *Pollen analysis and its bearing on American prehistory: A critique*, Am. Antiquity, vol. 5, no. 2.

—————— (1941) *Review of E. H. Sellards: Early man in America, index to localities and selected bibliography*, Am. Antiquity, vol. 7, pp. 84–85.

—————— (1942a) *Post-glacial climatic amelioration and the extinction of Bison taylori*, Sci., n.s., vol. 95, pp. 646–647.

—————— (1942b) *The Folsom mystery*, Sci. Am., vol. 167, pp. 260–261.

—————— (1942c) *Review of Frank C. Hibben: Evidences of early occupation in Sandia Cave, New Mexico, and other sites in the Sandia Manzano region*, Am. Antiquity, vol. 7, pp. 415–417.

—————— (1943a) *Archaeological observations on the problem of post-glacial extinction*, Am. Antiquity, vol. 8, pp. 209–217.

—————— (1943b) *Pseudo-fossil man*, Sci. Am., vol. 168, pp. 118–119.

—————— (1943c) *Did the Folsom bison survive in Canada?*, Sci. Mo., vol. 56, pp. 468–472.

—————— (1943d) *Review of Raymond W. Murray: Man's unknown ancestors*, Am. Jour. Phys. Anthropol., n.s., vol. 1, pp. 428–429; Am. Anthropol., n.s., vol. 46 (1944), pp. 255–256.

—————— (1944) *Review of Morris F. Skinner: The fauna of Papago Springs Cave, Arizona, and a study of Stockoceros; with three new Antilocaprines from Nebraska and Arizona*, Am. Antiquity, vol. 9, pp. 460–461.

—————— (1945a) *Indian mythology and extinct fossil vertebrates*, Am. Anthropol., n.s., vol. 47, pp. 318–320.

—————— (1945b) *The mastodon and early man in America*, Sci., n.s., vol. 102, pp. 108–110.

—————— (1945c) *Myth and mammoth in archaeology*, Am. Antiquity, vol. 11, pp. 84–87.

—————— (1946a) *The fire-drive and the extinction of the terminal Pleistocene fauna*, Am. Anthropol., n.s., vol. 48, pp. 54–59.

—————— (1946b) *Men, mastodons and myth*, Sci. Mo., vol. 62, pp. 517–524.

169

———— (1946c) *Review of F. E. Zeuner: The Pleistocene period,* Am. Jour. Phys. Anthropol., n.s., vol. 4, pp. 107–108.

———— (1947) *The fire and the fauna,* Am. Anthropol, n.s., vol. 49, no. 4, part 1, pp. 678–680.

Evans, Glen L. (1940) *Notes on terrace deposits,* Geol. Soc. Am., Bull., vol. 51, pp. 1644–1649.

———— (1947) *See* Sellards, E. H., and others (1947).

———— (1951) *Prehistoric wells in eastern New Mexico,* Am. Antiquity, vol. 17, no. 1, part 1, pp. 1–9.

Evans, Glen L., and Meade, Grayson E. (1945) *Quaternary of the Texas High Plains,* Univ. Texas, Pub. 4401, pp. 485–507.

Evans, O. F. (1930) *The antiquity of man as shown at Frederick, Oklahoma: A criticism,* Washington Acad. Sci., Jour., vol. 20, no. 19, pp. 475–479.

Fastlicht, Samuel (1949) *The jaws of the Tepexpan skeleton,* Viking Fund Pub. in Anthropol., vol. 11, pp. 127–129.

Fenenga, Franklin (1940) *A reply to "Folsom and Nepesta points,"* Am. Antiquity, vol. 6, pp. 78–79.

Fenner, C. N. (1912) *See* Hrdlicka, Ales (1912).

Figgins, J. D. (1927) *The antiquity of man in America,* Nat. Hist., vol. 27, no. 3, pp. 229–239.

———— (1931) *An additional discovery of the association of a "Folsom" artifact and fossil mammal remains,* Colorado Mus. Nat. Hist., Pr., vol. 10, no. 4, pp. 23–24.

———— (1933a) *A further contribution to the antiquity of man in America,* Colorado Mus. Nat. Hist., Pr., vol. 12, no. 2, pp. 4–8.

———— (1933b) *The bison of the western area of the Mississippi basin,* Colorado Mus. Nat. Hist., Pr., vol. 12, no. 4, pp. 16–33.

———— (1934) *Folsom and Yuma artifacts,* Colorado Mus. Nat. Hist., Pr., vol. 13, no. 2, pp. 1–6.

———— (1935a) *New world man,* Colorado Mus. Nat. Hist., Pr., vol. 14, no. 1, pp. 1–5.

———— (1935b) *Folsom and Yuma artifacts,* part 2, Colorado Mus. Nat. Hist., Pr., vol. 14, no. 2, pp. 1–7.

———— (1935c) *In* Roberts, F. H. H., Jr. (1935a), p. 32.

Fischel, H. E. (1939) *Folsom and Yuma culture finds,* Am. Antiquity, vol. 4, pp. 232–264.

———— (1941) *Supplementary data on early man in America,* Am. Antiquity, vol. 6, pp. 346–348.

Flint, Richard Foster (1947) *Glacial geology and the Pleistocene epoch*, New York, John Wiley and Sons.

Flint, Richard Foster, and Deevey, Edward S., Jr. (1951) *Radiocarbon dating of late-Pleistocene events*, Am. Jour. Sci., vol. 249, pp. 257–300.

Ford, James H., and Willey, Gordon R. (1941) *An interpretation of the prehistory of the eastern United States*, Am. Anthropol., n.s., vol. 43, no. 3, pp. 325–363.

Foster, J. W. (1874) *Pre-historic races of the United States of America*, 3d ed., Chicago, S. C. Griggs and Co.

Frankforter, W. D. (1948a) *See* Schultz, C. B., and Frankforter, W. D. (1948).

———— (1948b) *See* Schultz, C. B., Lueninghoener, Gilbert S., and Frankforter, W. D. (1948).

———— (1951) *See* Moss, John H., and others (1951).

Free, E. E. (1916) *An ancient lake basin on the Mohave River*, Carnegie Inst. Washington, Year Book, no. 15, pp. 90–91.

Frick, Childs (1930) *Alaska's frozen fauna*, Nat. Hist., vol. 30, pp. 71–80.

Furlong, E. L. (1904a) *An account of the preliminary excavations in a recently explored Quaternary cave in Shasta County, California*, Sci., n.s., vol. 20, pp. 53–55.

———— (1904b) *See* Sinclair, W. J., and Furlong, E. L. (1904).

Garretson, Martin S. (1938) *The American bison*, New York Zool. Soc., 254 pages.

Gazin, C. L. (1936) *In* Roberts, F. H. H., Jr. (1936a), p. 17.

Giddings, J. L., Jr. (1938) *Buried wood from Fairbanks, Alaska*, Tree Ring Bull., vol. 4, no. 4, Tucson, Arizona, pp. 3–8.

———— (1948) *Diagonal flaking from Kotzebue, Alaska*, Am. Antiquity, vol. 14, no. 2, p. 127.

———— (1949) *Early flint horizons on the north Bering Sea coast*, Washington Acad. Sci., Jour., vol. 39, no. 3, pp. 85–90.

———— (1950) *Traces of early man on the north Bering Sea coast*, Univ. Pennsylvania Mus., Bull., vol. 14, no. 4, pp. 3–13.

———— (1951) *The Denbigh flint complex*, Am. Antiquity, vol. 16, no. 3, pp. 193–203.

Gidley, J. W. (1906) *See* Matthew, W. D., and Gidley, J. W. (1906).

———— (1912) *Paleontological evidence bearing on the problem of the origin of the American aborigines*, Am. Anthropol., n.s., vol. 14, pp. 18–23.

171

———— (1926a) *Fossil man in Florida* (abstract), Geol. Soc. Am., Bull., vol. 37, no. 1, pp. 239–240.

———— (1926b) *Investigation of evidences of early man at Melbourne and Vero, Florida,* Smithson. Misc. Coll., vol. 78, no. 1, pp. 23–26.

———— (1926c) *Fossil man associated with mammoth in Florida,* Washington Acad. Sci., Jour., vol. 16, no. 11, p. 310.

———— (1926d) *See* Bryan, Kirk, and Gidley, J. W. (1926).

———— (1927) *Investigating evidence of early man in Florida,* Smithson. Misc. Coll., vol. 78, no. 7, pp. 168–174.

———— (1929a) *Ancient man in Florida: Further investigations,* Geol. Soc. Am., Bull., vol. 40, no. 2, pp. 491–501; abstract, Pan-Am. Geol., vol. 51, no. 3, p. 236.

———— (1929b) *Further study of the problem of early man in Florida,* Smithson. Inst., Explor. and Field Work in 1928, pp. 13–20.

———— (1930) *Investigation of early man in Florida,* Smithson. Inst., Explor. and Field Work in 1929, pp. 37–38.

———— (1931) *Further investigations on evidences of early man in Florida,* Smithson. Inst., Explor. and Field Work in 1930, pp. 41–44.

Gidley, J. W., and Loomis, F. B. (1926) *Fossil man in Florida,* Am. Jour. Sci., 5th s., vol. 12, pp. 254–264.

Gilbert, G. K. (1887) *On a prehistoric hearth under the Quaternary deposits in western New York,* Sci. Am. Suppl., vol. 23, no. 577, p. 9221.

———— (1889) *In* McGee, W. J. (1889b), p. 312.

Gilder, R. F. (1907a) *The Nebraska loess man,* Records of the Past, vol. 6, part 2, pp. 35–39.

———— (1907b) *A primitive human type in America: The finding of the "Nebraska man,"* Putnam's Monthly, vol. 1, pp. 407–409.

———— (1911) *Scientific "inaccuracies" in reports against probability of geological antiquity of remains of Nebraska loess man considered by its discoverer,* Records of the Past, vol. 10, part 3, pp. 157–169.

Gillette, J. M. (1943) *Ancestorless man: The anthropological dilemma,* Sci. Mo., vol. 57, pp. 533–545.

Gliddon, G. R. (1854) *See* Nott, J. C., and Gliddon, G. R. (1854).

Goddard, P. E. (1926) *The antiquity of man in America,* Nat. Hist. vol. 26, pp. 257–259.

172

———— (1927) *Facts and theories concerning Pleistocene man in America*, Am. Anthropol., n.s., vol. 29, pp. 262–266.

Goggin, John M. (1950) *An early lithic complex from central Florida*, Am. Antiquity, vol. 16, no. 1, pp. 46–49.

Gould, C. N. (1929a) *The fossil glyptodon in the Frederick gravel beds*, Oklahoma Acad. Sci., Pr., vol. 8, pp. 148–150.

———— (1929b) *On the recent finding of another flint arrowhead in the Pleistocene at Frederick, Oklahoma*, Washington Acad. Sci., Jour., vol. 19, pp. 66–68.

Graffham, Allen (1944) *Notes on basalt artifacts found in the Pleistocene gravels of Kansas*, Kansas Acad. Sci., Tr., vol. 47, pp. 259–260.

Greenman, Emerson F., and Stanley, George M. (1941) *Two post-Nipissing sites near Killarney, Ontario*, Am. Antiquity, vol. 6, pp. 305–313.

———— (1942) *The archeology and geology of two early sites near Killarney, Ontario*, Michigan Acad. Sci., Arts, Letters, Papers, vol. 28, pp. 505–530.

Gregory, W. K. (1927) *Hesperopithecus apparently not an ape nor a man*, Sci., n.s., vol. 66, no. 1720, pp. 579–581.

Gregory, W. K., and Hellman, Milo (1923a) *Notes on the type of Hesperopithecus haroldcooki Osborn*, Am. Mus. Nat. Hist., Novitates, no. 53, 16 pages.

———— (1923b) *Further notes on the molars of Hesperopithecus and of Pithecanthropus*, Am. Mus. Nat. Hist., Bull., vol. 48, pp. 509–526.

Gross, Hugo (1951) *Mastodons, mammoths, and man in America*, Texas Arch. and Paleont. Soc., Bull., vol. 22, pp. 101–131.

Grosse, A. V. (1946) *See* Reid, A. F., and others (1946).

Haag, William G. (1942) *Early horizons in the Southeast*, Am. Antiquity, vol. 7, pp. 209–222.

Hack, John T. (1942) *The changing physical environment of the Hopi Indians*, Peabody Mus. Am. Arch. and Ethnol., Papers, Harvard Univ., vol. 35, no. 1.

———— (1943) *Antiquity of the Finley site*, Am. Antiquity, vol. 8, pp. 235–241.

Hansen, Henry P. (1946) *Early man in Oregon: Pollen analysis and post-glacial climate and chronology*, Sci. Mo., pp. 52–62.

———— (1951) *See* Moss, John H., and others (1951).

Harrington, M. R. (1921) *Cuba before Columbus*, Indian Notes and

Monographs, Mus. Am. Indian, Heye Foundation, New York, pp. 165, 199.

———— (1930) *The mystery of Gypsum Cave*, Sci. Am., vol. 143, pp. 34–36.

———— (1933) *Gypsum Cave, Nevada*, Southwest Mus. Papers, no. 8, 197 pages.

———— (1934a) *A camel-hunter's camp in Nevada*, The Masterkey, vol. 8, no. 1, pp. 22–24.

———— (1943b) *Explorations in Nevada*, Carnegie Inst. Washington, Year Book, no. 33, p. 306.

———— (1934c) *The meaning of Gypsum Cave*, Texas Arch. and Paleont. Soc., Bull., vol. 6, pp. 58–69.

———— (1938a) *Folsom man in California*, The Masterkey, vol. 12, no. 4, pp. 133–137.

———— (1938b) *Pre-Folsom man in California*, The Masterkey, vol. 12, no. 5, pp. 173–175.

———— (1939a) *Trailing early Californians*, The Masterkey, vol. 13, pp. 163–166.

———— (1939b) *The age of the Borax Lake finds*, The Masterkey, vol. 13, pp. 208–209.

———— (1942) *Return to Borax Lake*, The Masterkey, vol. 16, pp. 214–215.

———— (1945) *Farewell to Borax Lake*, The Masterkey, vol. 19, pp. 181–184.

———— (1946) *New Work at Borax Lake*, The Masterkey, vol. 20, no. 6, pp. 189–190.

———— (1948) *An ancient site at Borax Lake, California*, Southwest Mus. Papers, no. 16.

Haury, Emil W. (1943) *The stratigraphy of Ventana Cave, Arizona*, Am. Antiquity, vol. 8, pp. 218–223.

Haury, Emil W., and others (1950) *The stratigraphy and archaeology of Ventana Cave, Arizona*, Univ. of Arizona and Univ. of New Mexico.

Hay, O. P. (1917a) *The Quaternary deposits at Vero, Florida, and the vertebrate remains contained therein*, Jour. Geol., vol. 25, no. 1, pp. 52–55.

———— (1917b) *On the finding of supposed Pleistocene human remains at Vero, Florida*, Washington Acad. Sci., Jour., vol. 7, pp. 358–360.

——— (1917c) *Vertebrata mostly from stratum no. 3, at Vero, Florida, together with description of new species,* Florida Geol. Survey, 9th Ann. Rept., pp. 43–68.

——— (1918a) *Further consideration of the occurrence of human remains in the Pleistocene deposits at Vero, Florida,* Am. Anthropol., n.s., vol. 20, no. 1, pp. 1–36.

——— (1918b) *A review of some papers on fossil man at Vero, Florida,* Sci., n.s., vol. 47, pp. 370–371.

——— (1918c) *Doctor Ales Hrdlicka and the Vero man,* Sci., n.s., vol. 48, no. 1245, pp. 459–462.

——— (1919a) *Descriptions of some mammalian and fish remains from Florida of probably Pleistocene age,* U.S. Nat. Mus., Pr., vol. 56, pp. 103–112.

——— (1919b) *On Pleistocene man at Trenton, New Jersey,* Anthropol. Scraps, no. 2, pp. 5–8.

——— (1920) *Bureau of American Ethnology, Bulletin 60* (review), Anthropol. Scraps, no. 3, pp. 9–12.

——— (1923) *The Pleistocene of North America and its vertebrated animals from the states east of the Mississippi River and from the Canadian provinces east of longitude 95 degrees,* Carnegie Inst. Washington, Pub. 322, pp. 38–39, 122–123, 159–160, 163–199, 208, 222, 233, 263, 373, 379.

——— (1926) *On the geological age of Pleistocene vertebrates found at Vero and Melbourne, Florida,* Washington Acad. Sci., Jour., vol. 16, pp. 387–392.

——— (1927a) *A review of recent reports on the investigations made in Florida on Pleistocene geology and paleontology,* Washington Acad. Sci., Jour., vol. 17, pp. 277–283.

——— (1927b) *The Pleistocene of the western region of North America and its vertebrated animals,* Carnegie Inst. Washington, Pub. 322-B, 346 pages.

——— (1928a) *On the antiquity of the relics of man at Frederick, Oklahoma,* Sci., n.s., vol. 67, pp. 442–444.

——— (1928b) *Pleistocene man in Europe and in America,* New York Herald-Tribune, July 1; also reprinted as a separate with slight changes, 8 pages.

——— (1928c) *Again on Pleistocene man at Vero, Florida,* Washington Acad. Sci., Jour., vol. 18, pp. 233–241.

——— (1929a) *On the recent discovery of a flint arrowhead in early*

Pleistocene deposits at Frederick, Oklahoma, Washington Acad. Sci., Jour., vol. 19, pp. 93–98.

———— (1929b) *On some recent excursions into Pleistocene geology and paleontology,* Washington Acad. Sci., Jour., vol. 19, pp. 463–469.

Hay, O. P., and Cook, H. J. (1928) *Preliminary descriptions of fossil mammals recently discovered in Oklahoma, Texas, and New Mexico,* Colorado Mus. Nat. Hist., Pr., vol. 8, no. 2, part 1, p. 33.

———— (1930) *Fossil vertebrates collected near, or in association with, human artifacts at localities near Colorado, Texas; Frederick, Oklahoma; and Folsom, New Mexico,* Colorado Mus. Nat. Hist., Pr., vol. 9, no. 2, pp. 4–40.

Haynes, H. W. (1883) *The argillite implements found in the gravels of the Delaware River at Trenton, New Jersey, compared with the paleolithic implements of Europe,* Boston Soc. Nat. Hist., Pr., pp. 132–137.

———— (1890) *In* Wright, G. F. (1890), pp. 509–512.

Heilprin, Angelo (1887) *Exploration on the west coast of Florida,* Wagner Free Inst. Sci., Tr., vol. 1, pp. 14–15.

Heizer, Robert F. (1938) *A complete atlatl dart from Pershing County, Nevada,* New Mexico Anthropol., vol. 2, pp. 68, 70–71.

———— (1940a) *A note on Folsom and Nepesta points,* Am. Antiquity, vol. 6, no. 1, pp. 79–80.

———— (1940b) *The archaeology of central California: I, The early horizon,* Anthropol. Records, vol. 12, no. 1, Univ. of California Press.

———— (1951) *Preliminary report on the Leonard rockshelter site, Pershing County, Nevada,* Am. Antiquity, vol. 17, no. 2, pp. 89–98.

Heizer, Robert F., and Cook, S. F. (1951) *Fluorine and other chemical tests of some North American human and animal bones* (MS).

Hellman, Milo (1923) *See* Gregory, W. K., and Hellman, Milo (1923a) and (1923b).

———— (1925) *See* Sullivan, L. R., and Hellman, Milo (1925).

Hewes, Gordon W. (1943) *Camel, horse, and bison associated with human burials and artifacts near Fresno, California,* Sci., vol. 97, no. 2519, pp. 328–329.

———— (1946) *Early man in California and the Tranquillity site,* Am. Antiquity, vol. 11, no. 4, pp. 209–215.

Hibben, F. C. (1937) *Association of man with Pleistocene mammals in the Sandia Mountains, New Mexico,* Am. Antiquity, vol. 2, no. 4, pp. 260–263.

———— (1940) *Sandia man,* Sci. Am., vol. 163, pp. 14–15.

———— (1941a) *Evidences of early occupation in Sandia Cave, New Mexico, and other sites in the Sandia-Manzano region* (with appendix on correlation of the deposits of Sandia Cave, New Mexico: glacial chronology by Kirk Bryan), Smithson. Misc. Coll., vol. 99, no. 23, pp. i–vi, 1–44.

———— (1941b) *Sandia Cave,* Am. Antiquity, vol. 6, p. 266.

———— (1941c) *Archaeological aspects of the Alaska muck deposits,* New Mexico Anthropol., vol. 5, no. 4, pp. 151–157.

———— (1942) *Pleistocene stratification in the Sandia Cave, New Mexico,* 8th Am. Sci. Cong., Pr., vol. 2, pp. 45–48.

———— (1943) *Evidences of early man in Alaska,* Am. Antiquity, vol. 8, pp. 254–259.

———— (1944) *Our search for the earliest Americans,* Harper's Magazine, vol. 189, July, pp. 139–147.

———— (1946) *The first thirty-eight Sandia points,* Am. Antiquity, vol. 11, no. 4, pp. 257–258.

Holder, Preston, and Wike, Joyce (1949) *The frontier culture complex, a preliminary report on a pre-historic hunters' camp in southwestern Nebraska,* Am. Antiquity, vol. 14, no. 4, part 1, pp. 260–266.

Hollick, A. (1898) *In* Mercer, H. C. (1898), pp. 378–380.

Holmes, G. William (1951) *See* Moss, John H., and others (1951).

Holmes, W. H. (1892) *Modern quarry refuse and palaeolithic theory,* Sci., 2d s., vol. 20, pp. 295–297.

———— (1893a) *Are there traces of glacial man in the Trenton gravels?,* Jour. Geol., vol. 1, pp. 15–37.

———— (1893b) *Traces of glacial man in Ohio,* Jour. Geol., vol. 1, pp. 147–163.

———— (1893c) *Vestiges of early man in Minnesota,* Am. Geol., vol. 11, pp. 219–240.

———— (1898) *Primitive man in the Delaware Valley,* Am. Assoc. Adv. Sci., Pr., vol. 46, pp. 364–370.

———— (1899) *Preliminary revision of the evidence relating to auriferous gravel man in California* (first paper), Am. Anthropol., n.s., vol. 1, pp. 107–121; *idem* (second paper), pp. 614–645.

———— (1901) *Review of the evidence relating to auriferous gravel man in California,* Smithson. Inst., Ann. Rept. 1899, pp. 419–472.

—— (1902a) *Fossil human remains found near Lansing, Kansas,* Am. Anthropol., n.s., vol. 4, pp. 743–752.

—— (1902b) *Flint implements and fossil remains from a sulphur spring at Afton, Indian Territory,* Am. Anthropol., n.s., vol. 4, pp. 108–129.

—— (1912) *See* Hrdlicka, Ales, and others (1912).

—— (1918a) *On the antiquity of man in America,* Sci., n.s., vol. 47, no. 1223, pp. 561–562.

—— (1918b) *In* Hrdlicka, Ales (1918), p. 64.

—— (1919) *Handbook of aboriginal American antiquities,* Bur. Am. Ethnol., Bull. 60, pp. 51–94.

Hooton, Earnest Albert (1933) *Notes on five Texas crania,* Texas Arch. and Paleont. Soc., Bull., vol. 5, pp. 25–39.

—— (1937a) *Biology and fossil man,* in *Apes, men and morons,* New York, G. P. Putnam's Sons.

—— (1937b) *In* Roberts, F. H. H., Jr. (1937a), pp. 174–175.

Hopwood, A. T. (1935) *Fossil elephants and man,* Geologists' Assn., Pr., vol. 46, pp. 46–60.

Hornaday, W. T. (1889) *The extermination of the American bison,* Smithson. Inst., Rept. of the Nat. Mus.

Howard, E. B. (1930) *Archaeological research in the Guadalupe Mountains,* Univ. Pennsylvania Mus., Jour., vol. 21, nos. 3, 4, pp. 189–202.

—— (1931) *Field work in the Southwest,* Univ. Pennsylvania Mus., Bull., vol. 3, no. 1, pp. 11–14.

—— (1932) *Caves along the slopes of the Guadalupe Mountains,* Texas Arch. and Paleont. Soc., Bull., vol. 4, pp. 7–19.

—— (1933) *Association of artifacts with mammoth and bison in eastern New Mexico* (abstract), Sci., n.s., vol. 78, p. 524.

—— (1934) *Grooved spearpoints,* Pennsylvania Archeol., Bull., vol. 3, no. 6, pp. 1–15.

—— (1935) *Evidence of early man in North America, based on geological and archaeological work in New Mexico,* Univ. Pennsylvania Mus., Jour., vol. 24, nos. 2, 3, pp. 55–171.

—— (1936a) *Early man in America,* Am. Philos. Soc., vol. 76, no. 3, pp. 327–333.

—— (1936b) *An outline of the problem of man's antiquity in North America,* Am. Anthropol., n.s., vol. 38, pp. 394–413.

—— (1936c) *The antiquity of man in America,* Sci. Mo., vol. 43, pp. 367–371.

178

———— (1936d) *Studies of early man*, Carnegie Inst. Washington, Year Book, no. 35, p. 323.

———— (1936e) *Early man in America with particular reference to the southwestern United States*, Am. Nat., vol. 70, p. 313.

———— (1936f) *The association of human culture with an extinct fauna in New Mexico*, Am. Nat., vol. 70, pp. 314–323.

———— (1936g) *Early human remains in the southwestern United States*, 16th Intern. Geol. Cong., Rept., vol. 2, Washington, pp. 1325–1333.

———— (1936h) *The occurrence of flints and extinct animals in pluvial deposits near Clovis, New Mexico*, part 1, *Introduction*, Acad. Nat. Sci. Philadelphia, Pr., vol. 87, pp. 299–303.

———— (1936i) *See* Schultz, C. B., and Howard, E. B. (1936).

———— (1937a) *The emergence of a general Folsom pattern*, Philadelphia Anthropol. Soc., vol. 1, 25th Anniv. Studies, pp. 111–115.

———— (1937b) *The Folsom problem in North America*, Zeitschr. für Rassenkunde, vol. 6, no. 3, pp. 331–336.

———— (1937c) *Bone point in association with elephant*, Sci. News Letter, March 20.

———— (1939a) *Folsom and Yuma points from Saskatchewan*, Am. Antiquity, vol. 4, pp. 277–279.

———— (1939b) *The Clovis finds are not two million years old*, Am. Antiquity, vol. 5, no. 1, pp. 43–51.

———— (1940) *Studies bearing upon the problem of early man in Florida*, Carnegie Inst. Washington, Year Book, no. 39, pp. 309–312.

———— (1943a) *Folsom and Yuma problems*, Am. Philos. Soc., Pr., vol. 86, pp. 255–259.

———— (1943b) *The Finley site: Discovery of Yuma points, in situ, near Eden, Wyoming*, Am. Antiquity, vol. 8, pp. 224–234.

Howard, E. B., and Antevs, Ernst (1934) *Studies on antiquity of man in America*, Carnegie Inst. Washington, Year Book, no. 33, pp. 309–311.

Howard, E. B., Satterthwaite, Linton, Jr., and Bache, Charles (1941) *Preliminary report on a buried Yuma site in Wyoming*, Am. Antiquity, vol. 7, pp. 70–74.

Howard, Hildegarde (1931) *A new species of road-runner from Quaternary cave deposits in New Mexico*, Condor, vol. 33, pp. 206–209.

179

Howells, W. W. (1938) *Crania from Wyoming resembling "Minnesota Man,"* Am. Antiquity, vol. 3, no. 4, pp. 318–326.

—— (1947) *Review of Weidenreich, Franz: Apes, giants, and man,* Am. Antiquity, vol. 12, no. 4, p. 277.

Hrdlicka, Ales (1902) *The crania of Trenton, New Jersey,* Am. Mus. Nat. Hist., Bull., vol. 16, pp. 23–62.

—— (1903) *The Lansing skeleton,* Am. Anthropol., n.s., vol. 5, pp. 323–330.

—— (1907) *Skeletal remains suggesting or attributed to early man in North America,* Bur. Am. Ethnol., Bull. 33, 113 pages.

—— (1917) *Preliminary report on finds of supposedly ancient human remains at Vero, Florida,* Jour. Geol., vol. 25, no. 1, pp. 43–51.

—— (1918) *Recent discoveries attributed to early man in America,* Bur. Am. Ethnol., Bull. 66, 67 pages.

—— (1919) *Examination of ancient human remains in Florida,* Smithson. Inst., Ann. Rept. 1917, pp. 10–12.

—— (1937a) *In* Roberts, F. H. H., Jr. (1937a), p. 174.

—— (1937b) *The Minnesota "Man,"* Am. Jour. Phys. Anthropol., vol. 22, no. 2, pp. 175–199.

—— (1937c) *Early man in America: What have the bones to say?,* in *Early man,* Philadelphia, J. B. Lippincott Co., pp. 93–104.

—— (1940) *Review of Stanley Casson: Discovery of man,* Am. Jour. Phys. Anthropol., vol. 27, p. 168.

—— (1942) *The problem of man's antiquity in America,* 8th Am. Sci. Cong., Pr., vol. 2, pp. 53–55.

§ Hrdlicka, Ales, Holmes, W. H., Willis, Bailey, Wright, F. E., and Fenner, C. N. (1912) *Early man in South America,* Bur. Am. Ethnol., Bull. 52.

Huffington, Roy M., and Albritton, Claude C., Jr. (1941) *Quaternary sands on the southern High Plains of western Texas,* Am. Jour. Sci., vol. 239, pp. 325–338.

Hughes, Jack T. (1949) *Investigations in western South Dakota and northeastern Wyoming,* Am. Antiquity, vol. 14, no. 4, part 1, pp. 270–277.

Hurley, Patrick M. (1950) *Progress report on age measurements,* Trans. Am. Geophys. Union, vol. 31, no. 1, pp. 142–144.

Hurst, C. T. (1937) *Early man in Colorado,* El Palacio, vol. 43, nos. 22–26.

———— (1941) *A Folsom locality in the San Luis Valley, Colorado*, Southwestern Lore, vol. 7, no. 2.

———— (1943) *A Folsom site in a mountain valley of Colorado*, Am. Antiquity, vol. 8, pp. 250–253.

Hurt, Wesley R., Jr. (1942) *Folsom and Yuma points from the Estancia Valley, New Mexico*, Am. Antiquity, vol. 7, pp. 400–402.

———— (1949) *Resemblances between the pre-ceramic horizons of the Southeast and Southwest*, paper read at 14th Ann. Meeting of the Soc. for Am. Arch., Bloomington, Ind., May 13.

Imbelloni, José (1943) *The peopling of America*, Acta Am., vol. 1, pp. 309–330.

Inghram, M. G. (1946) *See* Norris, L. D., and Inghram, M. G. (1946).

Jameson, J. Franklin (1907) *Spanish explorers in the southern United States, 1528–1543*.

Jenks, A. E. (1932a) *Pleistocene man in Minnesota*, Sci., n.s., vol. 75, pp. 607–608.

———— (1932b) *The problem of the culture from the Arvilla gravel pit*, Am. Anthropol., n.s., vol. 34, pp. 455–466.

———— (1933) *Minnesota Pleistocene "Homo"—an interim communication*, Nat. Acad. Sci., Pr., vol. 19, no. 1, pp. 1–6.

———— (1934) *The discovery of an ancient Minnesota maker of Yuma and Folsom flints*, Sci., n.s., vol. 80, p. 205.

———— (1935a) *Recent discoveries in Minnesota prehistory*, Minnesota Hist., vol. 16, pp. 1–21.

———— (1935b) *See* Eddy, Samuel, and Jenks, A. E. (1935).

———— (1936) *Pleistocene man in Minnesota*, Univ. Minnesota Press, Minneapolis, 197 pages.

———— (1937) *Minnesota's Browns Valley man and associated burial artifacts*, Am. Anthrop. Assoc., Mem. 49, 49 pages.

———— (1938) *Minnesota man: A reply to a review by Dr. Ales Hrdlicka*, Am. Anthropol., n.s., vol. 40, pp. 328–336.

Jenks, A. E., and Simpson, Mrs. H. H., Sr. (1941) *Beveled artifacts in Florida of the same type as artifacts found near Clovis, New Mexico*, Am. Antiquity, vol. 6, pp. 314–319.

Jenks, A. E., and Wilford, L. A. (1938) *Sauk Valley skeleton*, Texas Arch. and Paleont. Soc., Bull., vol. 10, pp. 136–168.

Johnson, Frederick, and others (1942) *The Boylston street fishweir*, Robert S. Peabody Foundation for Archaeology, Papers, vol. 2, 212 pages.

———— (1951) *Radiocarbon dating*, Am. Antiquity, vol. 17, no. 1, part 2, Soc. for Am. Arch., Memoirs, no. 8, 65 pages.

Johnson, Leonard G. (1947) *Some ancient dart points of New Mexico*, Chicago Nat. Hist. Mus., Bull. 9.

Johnston, W. A. (1933) *Quaternary geology of North America in relation to the migration of man*, in *The American aborigines*, Univ. Toronto Press, Toronto, p. 41.

Johnston, W. D. (1901) *The High Plains and their utilization*, U.S. Geol. Survey, 21st Ann. Rept., part 4, pp. 601–741.

Joor, J. F. (1895) *Notes on a collection of archeological and geological specimens collected in a trip to Avery's Island*, Am. Nat., vol. 29, pp. 394–398.

Kay, G. F. (1939) *Pleistocene history and early man in America*, Geol. Soc. Am., Bull., vol. 50, pp. 453–464.

Kay, G. F., and Leighton, M. M. (1938) *Geological notes on the occurrence of "Minnesota Man,"* Jour. Geol., vol. 46, pp. 268–278.

Keith, Sir Arthur (1925) *The antiquity of man*, 2d ed., London, Williams and Norgate, Ltd.

———— (1929) *The antiquity of man*, 2d ed., 7th impression, London, Williams and Norgate, Ltd., pp. 458–476.

———— (1931) *New discoveries relating to the antiquity of man*, New York, W. W. Norton and Co.

Kelley, J. Charles, and Campbell, T. N. (1942) *What are the burnt rock mounds of Texas?*, Am. Antiquity, vol. 7, pp. 319–322.

Kelley, J. Charles, and Lehmer, Donald J. (1940) *The association of archaeological materials with geological deposits in the Big Bend region of Texas*, Sul Ross State Teachers College, Bull., vol. 21, no. 3, pp. 11–173. (Also listed as West Texas Hist. and Sci. Soc. Pub., no. 10.)

Kelly, A. R. (1938) *A preliminary report on archaeological explorations at Macon, Georgia*, Bur. Am. Ethnol., Anthropol., Papers, no. 1, Bull. 119, 68 pages, 12 plates.

Kidd, Kenneth E. (1951) *Fluted points in Ontario*, Am. Antiquity, vol. 16, no. 3, p. 260.

Kidder, A. V. (1924) *An introduction to the study of southwestern archaeology*, New Haven, Connecticut, Yale Univ. Press, pp. 18, 31.

———— (1938) *Arrowheads or dart points*, Am. Antiquity, vol. 4, no. 2, pp. 156–157.

BIBLIOGRAPHY

Knapp, G. N. (1898) *On the implement-bearing sand deposits at Trenton*, Am. Assoc. Adv. Sci., Pr., vol. 46, p. 350.

Knopf, Adolph (1933) *Summary of principal results* and *The age of the ocean*, in *Physics of the Earth*, part 4, *The age of the Earth*, Nat. Res. Council, Com. on Physics of the Earth, Washington, pp. 3–9, 65–72.

———— (1949) *The geologic records of time*, Time and Its Mysteries, 3d s., New York.

Knox, Arthur S. (1942) *The pollen analysis of silt and the tentative dating of the deposits*, *in* Johnson, Frederick, and others (1942), pp. 105–129.

Koch, A. K. (1839a) *Evidences of the contemporaneous existence of man with mastodon in Missouri*, Philadelphia Presbyterian, Jan. 12, 1839; reprinted in Am. Jour. Sci., vol. 36 (1839), pp. 198–200, and in *idem*, 3d s., vol. 9 (1875), pp. 338–339.

———— (1839b) *Remains of mastodon in Missouri*, St. Louis Com. Bull., June 25; quoted in Philadelphia North American, July 11; reprinted in Am. Jour. Sci. Arts, vol. 37, pp. 191–192.

———— (1843) *Description of the Missourium theristocaulodon (Koch), or Missouri leviathan (Leviathan missouriensis)*, *in* Dana, J. D. (1875), pp. 339–340.

———— (1857) *Mastodon remains, in the State of Missouri, together with evidence of the existence of man contemporaneously with the mastodon*, Acad. Sci. St. Louis, Tr., vol. 1, pp. 61–64.

Koenigswald, G. H. R. von (1935) *Eine fossile saugetierfauna mit Simia aus Sudchina*, Proc. K. Akad. Wetansch. Amsterdam, vol. 38, part 2, pp. 872–879.

———— (1939) *The relationship between the fossil mammalian faunae of Java and China, with special reference to early man*, Peking Nat. Hist. Bull., vol. 13, pp. 293–298.

Kollmann, J. (1884) *Höhes alter der Menschenrassen*, Zeitschr. für Ethnol., vol. 16, pp. 191–193.

Kovarik, Alois F. (1931) *Calculating the age of minerals from radioactivity data and principles*, Nat. Res. Council, Bull. 80, part 3, pp. 73–123.

Krieger, Alex D. (1940) *See* Cressman, Luther Sheeleigh, and Krieger, Alex D. (1940).

———— (1944) *Review of L. S. Cressman and collaborators: Archaeological researches in the northern Great Basin*, Am. Antiquity, vol. 9, pp. 351–359.

———— (1947a) *Certain projectile points of the early American hunters*, Texas Arch. and Paleont. Soc., Bull., vol. 18, pp. 7–27.

———— (1947b) *See* Sellards, E. H., and others (1947).

———— (1950) *A suggested general sequence of North American projectile points*, Univ. Utah, Dept. of Anthropol., Anthropol. Papers, no. 11.

———— (1951) *Review of DeTerra and others: Tepexpan man*, Am. Antiquity, vol. 15, no. 4, part 1, pp. 343–349.

Kroeber, A. L. (1940) *Conclusions: The present status of Americanistic problems*, in *The Maya and their neighbors*, chap. 34, pp. 460–487.

Kümmel, H. B. (1898) *The age of the artifact-bearing sand at Trenton*, Am. Assoc. Adv. Sci., Pr., vol. 46, pp. 348–350.

Laughlin, W. S. (1941) *See* Cressman, Luther Sheeleigh, and Laughlin, W. S. (1941).

———— (1949) *Preliminary tests for presence of blood group substance in Tepexpan man*, Viking Fund Pub. in Anthropol., no. 11, pp. 132–135.

Leechman, Douglas (1950) *An implement of elephant bone from Manitoba*, Am. Antiquity, vol. 16, pp. 157–160.

Lehmer, Donald J. (1940) *See* Kelley, J. Charles, Campbell, T. N., and Lehmer, Donald J. (1940).

Leidy, Joseph (1889) *Notice of some fossil human bones*, Wagner Free Inst. Sci., Tr., vol. 2, pp. 9–12.

Leighton, M. M. (1936) *Geological aspects of the findings of primitive man, near Abilene, Texas*, Medallion Papers, no. 24, 44 pages.

———— (1937) *The significance of profiles of weathering in stratigraphic archaeology*, in *Early man*, Philadelphia, J. B. Lippincott Co., pp. 163–172.

———— (1938) *See* Kay, G. F., and Leighton, M. M. (1938).

Leverett, Frank (1893) *Supposed glacial man in southwestern Ohio*, Am. Geol., vol. 11, pp. 186–189.

———— (1931) *The Pensacola terrace and associated beaches and bars in Florida*, Florida Geol. Survey, Bull. 7, pp. 33–37.

Lewis, H. C. (1880) *The Trenton gravel and its relation to the antiquity of man*, Acad. Nat. Sci. Philadelphia, Pr., pp. 296–309.

———— (1881) *The antiquity of man in eastern America, geologically considered* (abstract), Am. Assoc. Adv. Sci., Pr., vol. 29, pp. 706–709.

BIBLIOGRAPHY

Libby, W. F. (1946) *Atmospheric helium three and radiocarbon from cosmic radiation*, Physical Review, 2d s., vol. 69, pp. 671–672.

—— (1950) *See* Arnold, J. R., and Libby, W. F. (1950).

Lindgren, Waldemar (1911) *Fossils of the Tertiary auriferous gravels*, in *The Tertiary gravels of the Sierra Nevada of California*, U.S. Geol. Survey Prof. Paper 73, pp. 51–53.

Loomis, F. B. (1924) *Artifacts associated with the remains of a Columbian elephant at Melbourne, Florida*, Am. Jour. Sci., 5th s., vol. 8, no. 48, pp. 503–508.

—— (1926a) *Early man in Florida*, Nat. Hist., vol. 26, pp. 260–262.

—— (1926b) *See* Gidley, J. W., and Loomis, F. B. (1926).

Lopatin, Ivan A. (1939) *Fossil man in the vicinity of Los Angeles, California*, 6th Pac. Sci. Cong., Pr., vol. 4, pp. 177–181.

—— (1936) *See* Bowden, A. O., and Lopatin, Ivan A. (1936).

Lothrop, Samuel Kirkland (1926) *Pottery of Costa Rica and Nicaragua*, Mus. Am. Indian, Heye Foundation, New York, vol. 1, pp. 101–104.

Lotrich, Victor F. (1938) *Comparison of a blade with two Folsom fragments*, Colorado Mag., vol. 15, no. 1, pp. 15–17.

Lucas, F. A. (1899) *The fossil bison of North America*, U.S. Nat. Mus., Pr., vol. 21, p. 758.

Lueninghoener, Gilbert C. (1948) *See* Schultz, C. B., and others (1948).

Lugn, A. L. (1934) *Outline of Pleistocene geology of Nebraska*, Nebraska State Mus., Bull., vol. 1, no. 41, pp. 319–356.

—— (1935) *The Pleistocene geology of Nebraska*, Nebraska Geol. Survey, Bull. 10, 2d s., pp. 103–100, 197.

—— (1936) *See* MacClintock, Paul, and others, (1936).

Lull, R. S. (1921) *Fauna of the Dallas sand pits*, Am. Jour. Sci., 5th s., vol. 2, pp. 159–176.

Lyell, Sir Charles (1849) *A second visit to the United States of America*, 2d ed., vol. 2, John Murray, London, pp. 195–198.

—— (1863) *The geological evidences of the antiquity of man*, 2d Am. ed., George W. Childs, Philadelphia, pp. 43–44, 200–205.

McAdams, William (1881) *A stone implement from a well in Illinois*, Am. Assoc. Adv. Sci., Pr., vol. 29, pp. 720–721.

McCann, F. T. (1938) *See* Bryan, Kirk, Retzek, Henry, and McCann, Franklin T. (1938).

185

———— (1943) *See* Bryan, Kirk, and McCann, Franklin T. (1943).

McCary, B. C. (1947) *A survey and study of Folsom-like points found in Virginia,* Arch. Soc. Virginia, Quart. Bull., vol. 2, no. 1.

———— (1948) *A report on Folsom-like points found in Granville County, North Carolina,* Arch. Soc. Virginia, Quart. Bull., vol. 3, no. 1.

———— (1951) *A workshop site of early man in Dinwiddie County, Virginia,* Am. Antiquity, vol. 17, no. 1, part 1, pp. 9–17.

MacClintock, Paul (1938) *See* Bryan, Kirk, and MacClintock, Paul (1938).

MacClintock, Paul, Barbour, E. H., Schultz, C. B., and Lugn, A. L. (1936) *A Pleistocene lake in White River Valley,* Am. Nat., vol. 70, pp. 346–360.

McClung, C. E. (1908) *Restoration of the skeleton of Bison occidentalis,* Kansas Univ., Sci. Bull., vol. 4, pp. 249–252.

McCown, Theodore D. (1941) *The antiquity of man in the New World,* Am. Antiquity, vol. 6, pp. 203–213.

MacCurdy, G. G. (1917a) *Archaeological evidences of man's antiquity at Vero, Florida,* Jour. Geol., vol. 25, no. 1, pp. 56–62.

———— (1917b) *The problem of man's antiquity at Vero, Florida,* Am. Anthropol., n.s., vol. 19, no. 2, pp. 252–261.

————, ed. (1937) *Early man,* Philadelphia, J. B. Lippincott Co.

McGee, W. J. (1887) *On the finding of a spear head in the Quaternary beds of Nevada,* Sci. Am. Suppl., vol. 23, no. 577, pp. 9221–9222.

———— (1888) *Paleolithic man in America: His antiquity and his environment,* Popular Sci. Monthly, vol. 34, pp. 20–36.

———— (1889a) *The geologic antecedents of man in the Potomac Valley,* Am. Anthropol., vol. 2, pp. 227–234.

———— (1889b) *An obsidian implement from Pleistocene deposit in Nevada,* Am. Anthropol., vol. 2, pp. 301–312.

———— (1893) *Man and the glacial period,* Am. Anthropol., vol. 6, pp. 85–95.

MacGowan, Kenneth (1950) *Early man in the new world,* New York, The Macmillan Co.

MacLean, J. P. (1875) *A manual of the antiquity of man,* New York, published for the author, pp. 114–122.

Maldonado Koerdell, Manuel (1947) *Nota preliminar sobre una fauna subfósil de pequeños vertebrados en un aniguo delta de la región de Zumpango, México,* Rev. Soc. Mex. Hist. Nat., vol. 8, nos. 1–4, pp. 243–250.

———— (1948) *Los vertebrados fósiles del Cuaternario en México,* Rev. Soc. Mex. Hist. Nat., vol. 9, nos. 1, 2, pp. 1–35.

———— (1949) *Las industrias prehistóricas de México,* Inst. Nac. Antropol., Hist., vol. 3, pp. 9–16.

———— and Aveleyra-Arroyo de Anda, Luis (1949) *Nota preliminar sobre dos artefactos del Pleistoceno superior hallados en la región de Tequixquiac, México,* El México Antiguo, vol. 7, pp. 154–161.

Martin, H. T. (1902) *In* Williston, S. W. (1902a), pp. 313–315.

———— (1918) *Letter relating to artifact found near Russell Springs, Kansas, in* Sellards (1940a) p. 387.

Martin, Paul S., Quimby, George I., and Collier, Donald (1947) *Indians before Columbus: Twenty thousand years of North American history revealed by archeology,* Univ. of Chicago Press.

Martin, Paul S., Rinaldo, John B., and Antevs, Ernst (1949) *Cochise and Mogollon sites, Pine Lawn Valley, western New Mexico,* Fieldiana Anthropol., vol. 38, no. 1, Chicago Nat. Hist. Mus.

Martínez del Río, Pablo (1947) *El hombre fósil de Tepexpam,* Cuadernos Americanos, vol. 34, no. 4, pp. 139–150.

———— (1952) *El mamut de Santa Isabel Iztapan,* Cuadernos Americanos, vol. 64, no. 4, pp. 149–170.

Mason, Herbert L. (1936) *See* Chaney, Ralph W., and Mason, Herbert L. (1936).

Matthew, W. D., and Gidley, J. W. (1906) *In* Putnam, F. W. (1906), pp. 231–232.

Mattos, Anibal (1937) *See* Walter, H. V., Cathoud, A., and Mattos, Anibal (1937).

Meade, Grayson E. (1945) *See* Evans, Glen L., and Meade, Grayson E. (1945).

———— (1947) *See* Sellards, E. H., and others (1947).

Melton, Frank A. (1940) *A tentative classification of sand dunes; its application to dune history in the southern High Plains,* Jour. Geol., vol. 48, pp. 113–174; Jour. Geomorphol., vol. 3, no. 4, pp. 359–361.

Menghin, Osvaldo F. A., and Bórmida, Marcelo (1950) *Investigaciones prehistóricas en cuevas de Tandilia (Prov. de Buenos Aires),* Archivo Para las Ciencias del Hombre, vol. 3, pp. 5–36.

Mercer, H. C. (1898) *A new investigation of man's antiquity at Trenton, N. J.,* Am. Assoc. Adv. Sci., Pr., vol. 46, pp. 370–380.

———— (1914) *Preliminary report on the discovery of human remains in an asphalt deposit at Rancho La Brea*, Sci., n.s., vol. 40, no. 1023, pp. 198–203.

———— (1924) *Present status of investigations concerning the antiquity of man in California*, Sci., n.s., vol. 60, no. 1540, pp. 1–2.

———— (1933) *Present status of the problem of the antiquity of man in North America* (abstract), Sci., n.s., vol. 78, no. 2032, p. 524.

———— (1935) *A review of evidence relating to the status of the problem of antiquity of man in Florida*, Sci., n.s., vol. 82, no. 2118, p. 103.

———— (1936) *Present status of knowledge relating to antiquity of man in America*, 16th Intern. Geol. Cong., Rept., vol. 2, Washington, pp. 1313–1323.

———— (1937) *Introductory remarks*, in *Early man*, Philadelphia, J. B. Lippincott Co., pp. 19–22.

Merrill, Robert S. (1948) *A progress report on the dating of archaeological sites by means of radioactive elements*, Am. Antiquity, vol. 13, no. 4, pp. 281–286.

Mertie, J. B., Jr. (1937) *The Yukon-Tanana region, Alaska*, U.S. Geol. Survey, Bull. 872.

Meserve, F. G., and Barbour, E. H. (1932) *Association of an arrow point with Bison occidentalis in Nebraska*, Nebraska State Mus., Bull., vol. 1, pp. 239–242.

Miller, Carl F. (1950) *Early cultural horizons in the southeastern United States*, Am. Antiquity, vol. 15, no. 4, p. 273.

Montagu, M. F. Ashley (1942) *The earliest account of the association of human artifacts with fossil mammals in North America*, Sci., n.s., vol. 95, pp. 380–381.

Montagu, M. F. Ashley, and Peterson, C. Bernard (1944) *The earliest account of the association of human artifacts with fossil mammals in North America*, Am. Philos. Soc., Pr., vol. 87, no. 5, pp. 407–419.

Moss, John H., and others (1951) *Early man in the Eden valley*, Museum Monographs, Univ. Mus., Univ. of Pennsylvania, Philadelphia, 124 pages.

Mossom, Stuart (1929) *See* Cooke, C. W., and Mossom, Stuart (1929).

Movius, Hallam L., Jr. (1944) *Early man and Pleistocene stratigraphy in southern and eastern Asia*, Peabody Mus. Am. Arch. and Ethnol., Papers, Harvard Univ., vol. 19, no. 3.

BIBLIOGRAPHY

Murray, Raymond W. (1943) *Man's unknown ancestors*, Milwaukee, Wisconsin, Bruce Pub. Co.

Nelson, N. C. (1918a) *Additional studies in the Pleistocene at Vero, Florida* (review), Sci., n.s., vol. 47, pp. 394–395.

―――― (1918b) *Chronology in Florida*, Am. Mus. Nat. Hist., Anthropol. Papers, vol. 22, part 2, pp. 77–103.

―――― (1928) *Pseudo-artifacts from the Pliocene of Nebraska*, Sci., n.s., vol. 67, no. 1734, pp. 316–317.

―――― (1933) *The antiquity of man in America in the light of archaeology*, in *The American aborigines*, Univ. Toronto Press, pp. 85–130.

―――― (1935) *Early migration of man to America*, Nat. Hist., vol. 35, no. 4, p. 356.

―――― (1937a) *Data for Gobi-Alaska relationship*, Nat. Hist., vol. 39, pp. 70–71.

―――― (1937b) *Notes on cultural relations between Asia and America*, Am. Antiquity, vol. 2, no. 4, pp. 267–272.

Newberry, J. S. (1886) *Carta al editor de La Tribuna*, La Naturaleza, vol. 18, pp. 284–285.

Norris, L. D., and Inghram, M. G. (1946) *Half-life determination of carbon (14) with a mass spectrometer and low absorption counter*, Physical Review, vol. 70, p. 772.

Nott, J. C., and Gliddon, G. R. (1854) *Types of mankind*, Philadelphia, Lippincott, Grambo and Co.

Osborn, H. F. (1907a) *Discovery of a supposed primitive race of men in Nebraska*, Century Mag., n.s., vol. 73, no. 3, pp. 371–375.

―――― (1907b) *In* Hrdlicka, Ales (1907), p. 71.

―――― (1910) *The age of mammals in Europe, Asia and North America*, New York, The Macmillan Co.

―――― (1922a) *Hesperopithecus, the first anthropoid primate found in America*, Am. Mus. Nat. Hist., Novitates, no. 37, 5 pages.

―――― (1922b) *Hesperopithecus, the anthropoid primate of western Nebraska*, Nature, vol. 110, no. 2756, pp. 281–283.

―――― (1927) *Recent discoveries relating to the origin and antiquity of man*, Sci., n.s., vol. 65, pp. 481–488.

―――― (1932) *The "Elephas meridionalis" stage arrives in America*, Colorado Mus. Nat. Hist., Pr., vol. 11, no. 1, pp. 1–3.

―――― (1936) *Proboscidea*, vol. 1, Am. Mus. Press, New York, 802 pages.

Owen, L. A. (1903) *More concerning the Lansing skeleton*, Bibliotheca Sacra, July, pp. 572–578.

Pattillo, L. Gray, Jr. (1940) *See* Albritton, Claude C., Jr., and Pattillo, L. Gray, Jr. (1940).

Pei, W. C. (1929) *An account of the discovery of an adult Sinanthropus skull in the Chou Kou Tien deposit*, Geol. Soc. China, Bull., vol. 8, pp. 203–205.

Peterson, C. Bernard (1944) *See* Montagu, M. F. Ashley, and Peterson, C. Bernard (1944).

Pickle, R. W. (1946) *Discovery of Folsom-like arrowpoint and artifacts of mastodon bone in southwest Virginia*, Tennessee Arch., Tennessee Arch. Soc., vol. 3, no. 1, p. 3.

Powell, J. W. (1893) *Are there evidences of man in the glacial gravels?*, Popular Sci. Monthly, vol. 43, pp. 316–326.

Price, W. Armstrong (1944) *The Clovis site: Regional physiography and geology*, Am. Antiquity, vol. 9, no. 4, pp. 401–407.

Putnam, F. W. (1885) *Man and the mastodon*, Sci., 2d s., vol. 6, no. 143, pp. 375–376.

———— (1898) *Early man in the Delaware Valley*, Am. Assoc. Adv. Sci., Pr., vol. 46, p. 344.

———— (1901) *A problem in American anthropology*, Smithson. Inst., Ann. Rept. 1899, pp. 473–486.

———— (1906) *Evidence of the work of man on objects from Quaternary caves in California*, Am. Anthropol., n.s., vol. 8, pp. 229–235.

Quimby, George I. (1947) *See* Martin, Paul S., Quimby, George I., and Collier, Donald (1947).

Rainey, Froelich G. (1937) *Arctic area*, Am. Antiquity, vol. 3, p. 188.

———— (1939) *Archaeology in central Alaska*, Am. Mus. Nat. Hist., Anthropol. Papers, vol. 36, part 4, pp. 351–405.

———— (1940) *Archaeological investigations in central Alaska*, Am. Antiquity, vol. 5, pp. 299–308.

Ray, C. N. (1929) *A differentiation of the prehistoric cultures of the Abilene section*, Texas Arch. and Paleont. Soc., Bull., vol. 1, pp. 7–22.

———— (1938a) *New evidences of ancient man in Texas, found during Prof. Kirk Bryan's visit* (editorial), Texas Arch. and Paleont. Soc., Bull., vol. 10, pp. 269–273.

———— (1938b) *See* Bryan, Kirk, and Ray, C. N. (1938).

———— (1940a) *Was the American mano and metate an invention made during Pleistocene time?*, Sci., n.s., vol. 91, pp. 190–191.

——— (1940b) *The deeply buried Gibson site,* Texas Arch. and Paleont. Soc., Bull., vol. 12, pp. 223–237.

——— (1942) *Ancient artifacts and mammoth's teeth of the McLean site,* Texas Arch. and Paleont. Soc., Bull., vol. 14, pp. 137–138.

——— (1943a) *A Texas skeleton,* Sci., n.s., vol. 98, p. 344.

——— (1943b) *Human burial covered by twenty-one feet of silt,* Texas Arch. and Paleont. Soc., Bull., vol. 15, pp. 110–116.

——— (1945) *Stream bank silts of the Abilene region,* Texas Arch. and Paleont. Soc., Bull., vol. 16, pp. 117–147.

——— (1948) *The facts concerning the Clear Fork culture,* Am. Antiquity, vol. 13, pp. 320–322.

Ray, C. N., and Bryan, Kirk (1938) *Folsomoid point found in alluvium beside a mammoth's bones,* Sci., n.s., vol. 88, pp. 257–258.

Ray, C. N., and Sayles, E. B. (1941) *An agreement on Abilene region terminology,* Texas Arch. and Paleont. Soc., Bull., vol. 13, pp. 175–176.

Ray, Louis L. (1939) *See* Bryan, Kirk, and Ray, Louis L. (1939).

——— (1940) *Glacial chronology of the southern Rocky Mountains,* Geol. Soc. Am., Bull., vol. 51, pp. 1851–1918.

——— (1942) *Symposium on Folsom-Yuma problems,* Sci., n.s., vol. 95, pp. 22–23.

Reid, A. F., Dunning, J. R., Weinhouse, S., and Grosse, A. V. (1946) *Half-life of C 14,* Physical Review, vol. 70, p. 431.

Renaud, E. B. (1928) *L'antiquité de l'homme dans l'Amérique du Nord,* L'Anthropologie, vol. 38, pp. 23–49.

——— (1931) *Prehistoric flaked points from Colorado and neighboring districts,* Colorado Mus. Nat. Hist., Pr., vol. 10, no. 2, pp. 6–21.

——— (1932a) *Archaeological survey of eastern Colorado,* 2d Rept., Univ. Denver, Dept. Anthropol., pp. 27–28.

——— (1932b) *Yuma and Folsom artifacts (new material),* Colorado Mus. Nat. Hist., Pr., vol. 11, no. 2, pp. 5–18.

——— (1934a) *Archaeological survey of western Nebraska,* Univ. Denver, Dept. Anthropol., pp. 12–20.

——— (1934b) *The first thousand Yuma-Folsom artifacts,* Univ. Denver, Dept. Anthropol., mimeo., 13 pages.

Retzek, Henry (1938) *See* Bryan, Kirk, and others (1938).

Richards, H. G. (1936) *Mollusks associated with early man in the Southwest,* Am. Nat., vol. 70, pp. 369–371.

——— (1937) *Marine Pleistocene mollusks as indicators of time and*

191

ecological conditions, in *Early man*, Philadelphia, J. B. Lippincott Co., pp. 75–84.

——— (1939) *Reconsideration of the dating of the Abbot farm site at Trenton, New Jersey*, Am. Jour. Sci., vol. 237, pp. 345–354.

Richardson, F. B. (1941) *Nicaragua*, Carnegie Inst. Washington, Year Book, no. 40, pp. 300–302.

Richardson, F. B., and Ruppert, K. (1942) *Nicaragua*, Carnegie Inst. Washington, Year Book, no. 41, pp. 269–271.

Rinaldo, John B. (1949) *See* Martin, Paul S., Rinaldo, John B., and Antevs, Ernst (1949).

Roberts, Frank H. H., Jr. (1935a) *A Folsom complex. Preliminary report on investigations at the Lindenmeier site in northern Colorado*, Smithson. Misc. Coll., vol. 94, no. 4, Pub. 3333, 35 pages.

——— (1935b) *A Folsom camp site and workshop*, Smithson. Inst., Explor. and Field Work in 1934, pp. 61–64.

——— (1936a) *Additional information on the Folsom complex; report on the second season's investigations at the Lindenmeier site in northern Colorado*, Smithson. Misc. Coll., vol. 95, no. 10, Pub. 3390, 38 pages.

——— (1936b) *Recent discoveries of the material culture of Folsom man*, Am. Nat., vol. 70, pp. 337–345.

——— (1937a) *New world man*, Am. Antiquity, vol. 2, no. 3, pp. 172–177.

——— (1937b) *The Folsom problem in American archaeology*, in *Early man*, Philadelphia, J. B. Lippincott Co., pp. 153–162.

——— (1937c) *New developments in the problem of the Folsom complex*, Smithson. Inst., Explor. and Field Work in 1936, pp. 67–74.

——— (1938) *The Lindenmeier site in northern Colorado contributes additional data on the Folsom complex*, Smithson. Inst., Explor. and Field Work in 1937, pp. 115–118.

——— (1939a) *On the trail of ancient hunters in the western United States and Canada*, Smithson. Inst., Explor. and Field Work in 1938, pp. 103–110.

——— (1939b) *The Folsom problem in American archaeology*, Smithson. Inst., Ann. Rept. 1938, pp. 531–546.

——— (1940a) *Pre-pottery horizon of the Anasazi and Mexico*, in *The Maya and their neighbors*, chap. 24, pp. 331–340.

——— (1940b) *Developments in the problem of the North American Paleo-Indian*, Smithson. Misc. Coll., vol. 100, pp. 51–116.

———— (1942a) *Archaeological and geological investigations in the San Jon District, eastern New Mexico*, Smithson. Misc. Coll., vol. 103, no. 4, 30 pages.

———— (1942b) *Recent evidence relating to an early Indian occupation in North America*, 8th Am. Sci. Cong., Pr., vol. 2, pp. 31–38.

———— (1943a) *Evidence for a Paleo-Indian in the New World*, Acta Am., vol. 1, no. 2, pp. 171–201.

———— (1943b) *A new site*, Am. Antiquity, vol. 8, p. 300.

———— (1944) *Etna Cave, Nevada*, Sci. Mo., vol. 59, no. 2, pp. 153–155.

———— (1945a) *The New World Paleo-Indian*, Smithson. Inst., Ann. Rept. 1944, pp. 403–433.

———— (1945b) *A deep burial on the Clear Fork of the Brazos River, Texas* Arch. and Paleont. Soc., Bull., vol. 16, pp. 9–30.

———— (1951a) *The early Americans*, Sci. Am., vol. 184, no. 2, pp. 15–19.

———— (1951b) *Radiocarbon dates and early man*, Am. Antiquity, vol. 17, no. 1, part 2, Soc. for Am. Arch., Memoirs, no. 8, pp. 20–22.

Rogers, David Banks (1929) *Prehistoric man of the Santa Barbara Coast*, Santa Barbara Mus. Nat. Hist.

Romer, A. S. (1933) *Pleistocene vertebrates and their bearing on the problem of human antiquity in North America*, in *The American aborigines*, Univ. Toronto Press, pp. 49–84.

Romero, Javier (1949) *The physical aspects of Tepexpan man*, Viking Fund Pub. in Anthropol., no. 11, pp. 87–117.

Rouse, Irving (1950) *Vero and Melbourne man: A cultural and chronological interpretation*, New York Acad. Sci., Tr., 2d s., vol. 12, no. 7, pp. 220–224.

———— (1951) *A survey of Indian River archaeology, Florida*, New Haven, Connecticut, Yale Univ. Press, Yale University Publications in Anthropology, no. 44, 263 pages.

Ruppert, K. (1942) *See* Richardson, F. B., and Ruppert, K. (1942).

Russell, Frank (1899) *Human remains from the Trenton gravels*, Am. Nat., vol. 33, no. 386, pp. 143–153.

Russell, I. C. (1885) *Geological history of Lake Lahontan*, U.S. Geol. Survey Mono. 11, 288 pages.

Rutherford, Sir Ernest (1937) *Radioactivity*, Encyclopaedia Britannica, vol. 18, pp. 886–897.

Salisbury, R. D. (1898) *On the origin and age of the relic-bearing* sands at Trenton, N. J., Am. Assoc. Adv. Sci., Pr., vol. 46, pp. 350–355.

—— (1902) In Chamberlin, T. C. (1902), pp. 778–779.

Sardeson, F. W. (1938) Saint Anthony Falls and Minnesota man, Pan-Am. Geol., vol. 69, pp. 92–100.

Satterthwaite, Linton, Jr. (1941) See Howard, Edgar B., Satterthwaite, Linton, Jr., and Bache, Charles (1941).

—— (1951) See Moss, John H., and others (1951).

Sauer, Carl O. (1944) A geographic sketch of early man in America, Geog. Rev., vol. 34, pp. 529–573.

Sayles, E. B. (1936) In Leighton, M. M. (1936), pp. v–viii.

—— (1945) The San Simon branch, excavations at Cave Creek and in the San Simon Valley, I, Material culture, Medallion Papers, no. 34.

Sayles, E. B., and Antevs, Ernst (1941) The Cochise culture, Medallion Papers, no. 29, 81 pages.

Scharf, David (1935) The Quaternary history of the Pinto Basin, Southwest Mus. Papers, no. 9, pp. 11–20.

Schmidt, Emil (1872) Zur Urgeschichte Nordamerikas, Archiv für Anthrop., vol. 5, pp. 153–172, 233–259.

Schultz, C. B. (1932a) Association of artifacts and extinct mammals in Nebraska, Nebraska State Mus., Bull., vol. 1, no. 33, pp. 271–282.

—— (1932b) See Barbour, E. H., and Schultz, C. B. (1932a) and (1932b).

—— (1934) The Pleistocene mammals of Nebraska, Nebraska State Mus., Bull., vol. 1, no. 41, pp. 357–392.

—— (1936a) See Barbour, E. H., and Schultz, C. B. (1936a) and (1936b).

—— (1936b) See MacClintock, Paul, and others (1936).

—— (1937) See Barbour, E. H., and Schultz, C. B. (1937).

—— (1938) The first Americans, Nat. Hist., vol. 42, no. 5, pp. 346–356, 378.

—— (1941a) See Barbour, E. H., and Schultz, C. B. (1941).

—— (1941b) Early man in the Great Plains, Compass, vol. 21, pp. 28–38.

—— (1943) Some artifact sites of early man in the Great Plains and adjacent areas, Am. Antiquity, vol. 8, pp. 242–249.

—— (1951) See Moss, John H., and others (1951).

Schultz, C. B., and Eiseley, L. C. (1935) Paleontological evidence for

BIBLIOGRAPHY

the antiquity of the Scottsbluff bison quarry and its associated artifacts, Am. Anthropol., n.s., vol. 37, no. 2, pp. 306–319.

———— (1936a) An added note on the Scottsbluff quarry, Am. Anthropol., n.s., vol. 38, no. 3, pp. 521–524.

———— (1936b) Did glacial man inhabit Nebraska?, Nebraska Alumnus.

Schultz, C. B., and Frankforter, W. D. (1948) Preliminary report on the Lime Creek sites; new evidence of early man in southwestern Nebraska, Nebraska State Mus., Bull., vol. 3, no. 4, part 2, pp. 43–62.

Schultz, C. B., and Howard, E. B. (1936) The fauna of Burnet Cave, Guadalupe Mountains, New Mexico, Acad. Nat. Sci. Philadelphia, Pr., vol. 87, pp. 273–298.

Schultz, C. B., Lueninghoener, Gilbert C., and Frankforter, W. D. (1948) Preliminary geomorphological studies of the Lime Creek area, Nebraska State Mus., Bull., vol. 3, no. 4, part 1, pp. 31–42.

Schultz, C. B., and Stout, Thompson M. (1945) Pleistocene loess deposits of Nebraska, Am. Jour. Sci., vol. 243, pp. 231–244.

Scoggin, Charles (1940) Folsom and Nepesta points, Am. Antiquity, vol. 5, pp. 290–298.

Selenka, L., and Blanckenhorn, M. (1911) Die Pithecanthropus-Schlichten auf Java. Geologische und Palaeontologische Ergebnisse der Trinil-Expedition (1907–1908), Leipzig, W. Engelmann.

Sellards, E. H. (1916a) On the discovery of fossil human remains in Florida in association with extinct vertebrates, Am. Jour. Sci., 4th s., vol. 42, no. 247, pp. 1–18.

———— (1916b) Human remains from the Pleistocene of Florida, Sci., n.s., vol. 44, no. 1139, pp. 615–617.

———— (1916c) Human remains and associated fossils from the Pleistocene of Florida, Florida Geol. Survey, 8th Ann. Rept., pp. 123–160.

———— (1917a) On the association of human remains and extinct vertebrates at Vero, Florida, Jour. Geol., vol. 25, no. 1, pp. 4–24.

———— (1917b) Further notes on human remains from Vero, Florida, Am. Anthropol., n.s., vol. 19, no. 2, pp. 239–251.

———— (1917c) Note on the deposits containing human remains and artifacts at Vero, Florida, Jour. Geol., vol. 25, pp. 659–660.

———— (1917d) Review of the evidence on which the human remains found at Vero, Florida, are referred to the Pleistocene, Florida Geol. Survey, 9th Ann. Rept., pp. 69–84.

──── (1918) *The skull of a Pleistocene tapir including description of a new species and a note on the associated fauna and flora,* Florida Geol. Survey, 10th Ann. Rept., pp. 57–70.

──── (1919) *Literature relating to human remains and artifacts at Vero, Florida,* Am. Jour. Sci., 4th s., vol. 47, pp. 358–360.

──── (1930) *Malakoff image* (abstract), Geol. Soc. Am., Bull., vol. 41, no. 1, p. 207.

──── (1932) *Geologic relations of deposits reported to contain artifacts at Frederick, Oklahoma,* Geol. Soc. Am., Bull., vol. 43, pp. 783–796.

──── (1935) *Discoveries at Round Rock, Texas,* Sci. News Letter, vol. 27, p. 67.

──── (1936) *Recent studies of early man in the southwestern part of the United States,* Am. Nat., vol. 70, pp. 361–369.

──── (1937) *The Vero finds in the light of present knowledge,* in *Early man,* Philadelphia, J. B. Lippincott Co., pp. 193–210.

──── (1938) *Artifacts associated with fossil elephant,* Geol. Soc. Am., Bull., vol. 49, pp. 999–1009.

──── (1940a) *Early man in America, index to localities and selected bibliography,* Geol. Soc. Am., Bull., vol. 51, pp. 373–431.

──── (1940b) *Pleistocene artifacts and associated fossils from Bee County, Texas,* Geol. Soc. Am., Bull., vol. 51, pp. 1627–1657.

──── (1941) *Stone images from Henderson County, Texas,* Am. Antiquity, vol. 7, pp. 29–38.

──── (1945) *Fossil bison and associated artifacts from Texas* (abstract), Geol. Soc. Am., Bull., vol. 56, pp. 1196–1197.

──── (1947) *Early Man in America, index to localities and selected bibliography, 1940–1945,* Geol. Soc. Am., Bull., vol. 58, pp. 955–978.

Sellards, E. H., Evans, Glen L., and Meade, Grayson E. (1947) *Fossil bison and associated artifacts from Plainview, Texas* (with description of artifacts by Alex D. Krieger), Geol. Soc. Am., Bull., vol. 58, pp. 927–954.

Shaler, N. S. (1880) *On the age of the Delaware gravel beds containing chipped pebbles,* Peabody Mus. Am. Arch. and Ethnol., Rept., Harvard Univ., vol. 2, pp. 44–47.

──── (1889) *The geology of Nantucket,* U.S. Geol. Survey, Bull. 53, pp. 24–25.

──── (1893) *Antiquity of man in eastern North America,* Am. Geol., vol. 11, pp. 180–184.

Shapiro, H. L. (1937) *In* Roberts, F. H. H., Jr. (1937a), p. 176.

Shetrone, Henry C. (1936) *The Folsom phenomena as seen from Ohio*, Ohio State Arch. and Hist. Quart., vol. 45, no. 3, pp. 240–256.

Shimek, B. (1903) *Loess and the Lansing man*, Am. Geol., vol. 32, pp. 353–369.

———— (1908) *Nebraska "loess man*," Geol. Soc. Am., Bull., vol. 19, pp. 243–254.

———— (1917) *The loess and the antiquity of man*, Iowa Acad. Sci., Pr., vol. 24, pp. 93–98.

Shippee, J. M. (1948) *Nebo Hill, a lithic complex in western Missouri*, Am. Antiquity, vol. 14, no. 1, pp. 29–32.

Shufeldt, R. W. (1917) *Fossil birds found at Vero, Florida*, Florida Geol. Survey, 9th Ann. Rept., pp. 35–42.

Shuler, E. W. (1923) *Occurrence of human remains with Pleistocene fossils, Lagow sand pit, Dallas, Texas*, Sci., n.s., vol. 57, no. 1472, pp. 333–334.

———— (1934) *Collecting fossil elephants at Dallas, Texas*, Texas Arch. and Paleont. Soc., Bull., vol. 3, pp. 24–29.

Simpson, G. G. (1929) *The extinct land mammals of Florida*, Florida Geol. Survey, 20th Ann. Rept., p. 268.

———— (1930a) *Pleistocene mammalian fauna of the Seminole field, Pinellas County, Florida*, Am. Mus. Nat. Hist., Bull., vol. 56, pp. 569–572.

———— (1930b) *Additions to the Pleistocene of Florida*, Am. Mus. Nat. Hist., Novitates, no. 406, 14 pages.

———— (1931) *Origin of mammalian faunas as illustrated by that of Florida*, Am. Nat., vol. 65, pp. 258–270.

———— (1933) *A Nevada fauna of Pleistocene type and its probable association with man*, Am. Mus. Nat. Hist., Novitates, no. 667, 10 pages.

———— (1940) *Review of the mammal-bearing Tertiary of South America*, Am. Philos. Soc., Pr., vol. 83, pp. 649–709.

Simpson, Mrs. H. H., Sr. (1941) *See* Jenks, A. E., and Simpson, Mrs. H. H., Sr. (1941).

Simpson, J. Clarence (1948) *Folsom-like points from Florida*, The Florida Anthropol., vol. 1, pp. 11–15.

Simpson, Ruth D. (1946) *The seal was broken*, The Masterkey, vol. 20, pp. 154–156.

—— (1947a) *Missouri mysteries*, The Masterkey, vol. 21, pp. 199–201.

—— (1947b) *A classic Folsom from Lake Mohave*, The Masterkey, vol. 21, pp. 24–25.

Sinclair, W. J. (1904) *The exploration of the Potter Creek Cave*, Univ. California Pub., Am. Arch. and Ethnol., vol. 2, no. 1, pp. 1–27.

—— (1908) *Recent investigations bearing on the question of the occurrence of Neocene man in the auriferous gravels of the Sierra Nevada*, Univ. California Pub., Am. Arch. and Ethnol., vol. 7, no. 2, pp. 107–131.

Sinclair, W. J., and Furlong, E. L. (1904) *Euceratherium, a new ungulate from the Quaternary caves of California*, Univ. California Pub., Dept. Geol., Bull. 3, pp. 411–418.

Skinner, Morris F. (1942) *The fauna of Papago Springs Cave, Arizona, and a study of Stockoceros; with three new Antilocaprines from Nebraska and Arizona*, Am. Mus. Nat. Hist., Bull., vol. 80, pp. 143–220.

Skinner, Morris F., and Kaisen, Ove C. (1947) *The fossil Bison of Alaska and preliminary revision of the genus*, Am. Mus. Nat. Hist., Bull., vol. 89, pp. 123–256.

Smith, Arthur George (1951) *Fluted points from Milan, Ohio*, Southwestern Lore, vol. 17, no. 1.

Smith, Elmer R. (1941) *Archaeology of Deadman Cave, Utah*, Univ. Utah, Bull., vol. 32, no. 4.

Smith, H. I. (1910) *An unknown field in American archaeology*, Am. Geog. Soc., Bull., vol. 42, no. 7, pp. 511–521.

Smith, H. T. U. (1938) *Geomorphic evidence relating to the antiquity of man in north-central Kansas* (abstract), Geol. Soc. Am., Bull., vol. 49, p. 1901.

Solecki, Ralph (1951) *How man came to North America*, Sci. Am., vol. 184, no. 1, pp. 11–15.

Spier, Leslie (1916)˙*New data on the Trenton argillite culture*, Am. Anthropol., n.s., vol. 18, no. 2, pp. 181–189.

—— (1918) *The Trenton argillite culture*, Am. Mus. Nat. Hist., Anthropol. Papers, vol. 22, pp. 167–226.

—— (1928a) *Concerning man's antiquity at Frederick, Oklahoma*, Sci., n.s., vol. 67, no. 1728, pp. 160–161.

—— (1928b) *A note on reputed ancient artifacts from Frederick, Oklahoma*, Sci., n.s., vol. 68, no. 1756, p. 184.

BIBLIOGRAPHY

—— (1929) *In* Hay, O. P. (1929a), p. 94

Spillman, Franz (1936) *In* Osborn, H. F. (1936), pp. 571–574.

Spinden, H. J. (1937) *First peopling of America as a chronological problem*, in *Early man*, Philadelphia, J. B. Lippincott Co., pp. 105–114.

Stanley, George M. (1941) *See* Greenman, Emerson F., and Stanley, George M. (1941) and (1942).

Sterling, Matthew (1943) *On Folsom finds, El Norte de México y el Sur de los Estados Unidos*, Soc. Mex. de Anthropol., p. 165.

Sterns, F. H. (1918) *The Pleistocene man of Vero, Florida, a summary of the evidence of man's antiquity in the new world*, Sci. Am. Suppl., vol. 85, no. 2214, pp. 354–355.

—— (1919) *The Pleistocene man of Vero, Florida, a review of the latest evidence and theories*, Sci. Am. Suppl., vol. 87, no. 2251, pp. 118–119.

Stewart, Alban (1897) *Notes on the osteology of Bison antiquus Leidy*, Kansas Univ. Quart., vol. 6, pp. 127–135.

Stewart, T. D. (1945) *Report on the J. C. Putnam skeleton from Texas*, Texas Arch. and Paleont. Soc., Bull., vol. 16, pp. 31–39.

—— (1946) *A reexamination of the fossil human skeletal remains from Melbourne, Florida, with further data on the Vero skull*, Smithson. Misc. Coll., vol. 106, no. 10, 28 pages.

—— (1949a) *Initial impressions regarding the Tepexpan skeleton*, Viking Fund Pub. in Anthropol., no. 11, pp. 125–126.

—— (1949b) *Comparisons between Tepexpan man and other early Americans*, Viking Fund Pub. in Anthropol., vol. 11, pp. 137–145.

—— (1951) *Antiquity of man in America demonstrated by the fluorine test*, Sci., vol. 113, no. 2936, pp. 391–392.

Stock, Chester (1924) *A recent discovery of ancient human remains in Los Angeles, California*, Sci., n.s., vol. 60, no. 1540, pp. 2–5.

—— (1930a) *Rancho La Brea: A record of Pleistocene life in California*, Los Angeles Mus., Pub. 1, Sci. Series 1, pp. 28–30.

—— (1930b) *Quaternary antelope remains from a second cave deposit in the Organ Mountains, New Mexico*, Los Angeles Mus., Pub. 2, Sci. Series 2, 18 pages.

—— (1931) *Problems of antiquity presented in Gypsum Cave, Nevada*, Sci. Mo., vol. 32, pp. 22–32.

—— (1932) *A further study of the Quaternary antelopes of Shelter*

199

Cave, New Mexico, Los Angeles Mus., Pub. 3, Sci. Series 3, 45 pages.

———— (1936) *The succession of mammalian forms within the period in which human remains are known to occur in America*, Am. Nat., vol. 70, pp. 324–331.

Stock, Chester, and Bode, F. D. (1937) *The occurrence of flints and extinct animals in pluvial deposits near Clovis, New Mexico*, part 3, *Geology and vertebrate paleontology of the late Quaternary near Clovis, New Mexico*, Acad. Nat. Sci. Philadelphia, Pr., vol. 88, pp. 219–241.

Stout, Thompson M. (1945) *See* Schultz, C. B., and Stout, Thompson M. (1945).

Strong, W. D. (1932a) *An archeological reconnaissance in the Missouri Valley*, Smithson. Inst., Explor. and Field Work in 1931, Pub. 3134, pp. 151–158.

———— (1932b) *Recent discoveries of human artifacts associated with extinct animals in Nebraska*, Sci. Serv. Res. Ann., no. 130, 8 pages.

———— (1933) *Signal Butte, a prehistoric narrative in the High Plains*, Smithson. Inst., Explor. and Field Work in 1932, pp. 69–72.

———— (1935) *An introduction to Nebraska archeology*, Smithson. Misc. Coll., vol. 93, no. 10, pp. 220–239, 269–271, 278–280.

———— (1940) *From history to pre-history in the northern Great Plains*, Smithson. Misc. Coll., vol. 100, pp. 353–394.

Studer, Floyd (1935) *Folsom point with fossil mammals*, Sci. News Letter, vol. 27, p. 92.

Sullivan, L. R., and Hellman, Milo (1925) *The Punin calvarium*, Am. Mus. Nat. Hist., Anthropol. Papers, vol. 23, pp. 313–317.

Thiel, G. A. (1936) *The Pleistocene geology of the Prairie Lake region*, in *Pleistocene man in Minnesota*, Univ. Minnesota Press, Minneapolis, pp. 17–33.

Thomas, Edward S. (1952) *The Orleton farms mastodon*, Ohio Jour. Sci., vol. 52, no. 1, pp. 1–5.

Thompson, Raymond M. (1948) *Notes on the archaeology of the Utukok River, northwestern Alaska*, Am. Antiquity, vol. 14, pp. 62–65.

Thone, Frank (1929) *Did earliest Americans hunt sloth?*, Sci. News Letter, vol. 16, no. 445, pp. 237–239.

Todd, J. E. (1903) *In* Winchell, N. H. (1903), pp. 291–294.

Toulouse, Joseph H., Jr. (1943) *See* Bryan, Kirk, and Toulouse, Joseph H., Jr. (1943).

Tyrell, J. B. (1890) *Post-Tertiary deposits of Manitoba and the adjoining territories of northwestern Canada*, Geol. Soc. Am., Bull., vol. 1, pp. 395–410.

Uhle, Max (1936) *In* Osborn, H. F. (1936), p. 574.

Upham, Warren (1884) *Glacial geology of Little Falls, Minnesota, area*, in *Vestiges of early man in Minnesota*, Am. Nat., vol. 18, pp. 706–708.

———— (1888) *The recession of the ice-sheet in Minnesota and its relation to the gravel deposits overlying the quartz implements found by Miss Babbitt at Little Falls, Minnesota*, Boston Soc. Nat. Hist., Pr., vol. 23, pp. 436–447.

———— (1893) *Man and the glacial period*, Am. Geol., vol. 11, pp. 189–191.

———— (1902a) *Man in the ice age at Lansing, Kansas, and Little Falls, Minnesota*, Am. Geol., vol. 30, pp. 135–150.

———— (1902b) *Man in Kansas during the Iowan stage of the glacial period*, Sci., n.s., vol. 16, pp. 355–356.

———— (1902c) *Primitive man and his stone implements in the North American loess*, Am. Antiq. and Oriental Jour., vol. 24, pp. 413–420.

———— (1902d) *Glacial man in Kansas*, Am. Anthropol., n.s., vol. 4, pp. 566–568.

Usher, W. (1854) *In* Nott, J. C., and Gliddon, G. R. (1854), pp. 327–372.

Van Royen, William (1933) *See* Bell, E. H., and Van Royen, William (1933).

———— (1934) *See* Bell, E. H., and Van Royen, William (1934a) and (1934b).

Vaughan, T. W. (1907) *In* Hrdlicka, Ales (1907), pp. 64–66.

———— (1917) *On reported Pleistocene human remains at Vero, Florida*, Jour. Geol., vol. 25, no. 1, pp. 40–42.

Vigfusson, Vladimar Alfred (1940) *A carved stone from D'Arcy, Saskatchewan*, Am. Antiquity, vol. 5, pp. 334–335.

Volk, Ernest (1911) *The archaeology of the Delaware Valley*, Peabody Mus. Am. Arch. and Ethnol., Papers, Harvard Univ., vol. 5, 258 pages.

Walker, Edwin F. (1945) *America's Indian background*, Southwest Mus. Leaflets, no. 18.

Wallace, Alfred Russell (1887) *The antiquity of man in North America*, Nineteenth Century, vol. 22, pp. 667, 679.

201

Walter, H. V., Cathoud, A., and Mattos, Anibal (1937) *The Confins man—A contribution to the study of early man in South America,* in *Early man,* Philadelphia, J. B. Lippincott Co., pp. 341–348.

Ward, H. B. (1906) *See* Barbour, E. H., and Ward, H. B. (1906a) and (1906b).

——— (1907) *Peculiarities of the "Nebraska Man,"* Putnam's Monthly, vol. 1, p. 410–413.

Wauchope, Robert (1939) *Fluted points from South Carolina,* Am. Antiquity, vol. 4, pp. 344–346.

Webb, C. H. (1948) *Evidences of pre-pottery cultures in Louisiana,* Am. Antiquity, vol. 13, pp. 227–231.

Webb, J. G. (1907) *In* Hrdlicka, Ales (1907), pp. 53, 55–56.

Wedel, Waldo R. (1940) *Culture sequences in the central Great Plains,* Smithson. Misc. Coll., vol. 100, pp. 291–352.

——— (1941) *Archeological investigations at Buena Vista Lake, Kern County, California,* Bur. Am. Ethnol., Bull. 130.

——— (1947) *Culture chronology in the central Great Plains,* Am. Antiquity, vol. 12, no. 3, part 1, pp. 148–155.

Weidenreich, Franz (1939) *On the earliest representatives of modern mankind recovered on the soil of East Asia,* Peking Nat. Hist. Bull., vol. 13, pp. 161–171.

——— (1940) *Some problems dealing with ancient man,* Am. Anthropol., n.s., vol. 42, pp. 375–383.

——— (1941) *The site and technique of the excavations of fossil man in Choukoutien, China,* New York Acad. Sci., Tr., 2d s., vol. 4, pp. 23–31.

——— (1943) *The skull of Sinanthropus pekinensis: A comparative study on a primitive hominid skull,* Palaeont. Sinica, n.s. D, no. 10, whole s. no. 127, pp. 1–484.

——— (1945) *Giant early man from Java and South China,* Am. Mus. Nat. Hist., Anthropol. Papers, vol. 40, part 1.

——— (1949) *Preliminary report on the anatomical character of the human skeleton from Tepexpan,* Viking Fund Pub. in Anthropol., no. 11, pp. 123–124.

Weinhouse, S. (1946) *See* Reid, A. F., and others (1946).

Wheeler, S. M. (1942) *Archaeology of Etna Cave,* Nevada State Park Comm.

Whitney, J. D. (1880) *Auriferous gravels of the Sierra Nevada of California,* Mus. Comp. Zool., Harvard College, Mem. 6, no. 1, pp. 288–321.

BIBLIOGRAPHY

Wickham, H. F. (1919) *Fossil beetles from Vero, Florida*, Florida Geol. Survey, 12th Ann. Rept., pp. 5–7; also Am. Jour. Sci., 4th s., vol. 47, no. 281, pp. 355–357.

Wieland, G. R. (1918) *The Vero man and the sabre tooth*, Sci., n.s., vol. 48, no. 1230, pp. 93–94.

Wike, Joyce (1949) *See* Holder, Preston, and Wike, Joyce (1949).

Wilder, H. H. (1923) *Prehistory of the two Americas*, in *Man's prehistoric past*, New York, The Macmillan Co., pp. 283–383.

———— (1926) *Ancient skulls and skeletons in America*, in *The pedigree of the human race*, New York, Henry Holt and Co., p. 164.

Wilford, L. A. (1938) *See* Jenks, A. E., and Wilford, L. A. (1938).

Willey, Gordon R. (1941) *See* Ford, James H., and Willey, Gordon R. (1941).

Williams, Howel (1940) *See* Cressman, Luther Sheeleigh, and Williams, Howel (1940).

Willis, Bailey (1912) *See* Hrdlicka, Ales, and others (1912).

Williston, S. W. (1897) *Homo sapiens*, in *Pleistocene of Kansas*, Kansas Geol. Survey, Bull., vol. 2, p. 301.

———— (1898) *The Pleistocene of Kansas*, Kansas Acad. Sci., Tr., vol. 15, p. 91.

———— (1902a) *An arrow-head found with bones of Bison occidentalis Lucas, in western Kansas*, Am. Geol., vol. 30, pp. 313–315.

———— (1902b) *A fossil man from Kansas*, Sci., n.s., vol. 16, pp. 195–196.

———— (1903) *In* Winchell, N. H. (1903), p. 291.

———— (1905a) *On the occurrence of an arrow-head with bones of an extinct bison*, Intern. Cong. Americanists, Pr , 13th sess., pp. 336–337.

———— (1905b) *On the Lansing man*, Am. Geol., vol. 35, pp. 342–346; also in Intern. Cong. Americanists, Pr., 13th sess., pp. 85–89.

Wilson, M. Thomas (1895) *On the presence of fluorine as a test for the fossilization of animal bones*, Am. Nat., vol. 29, pp. 301–317, 439–456, 719–725.

———— (1898) *Investigation in the sand pits of the Lalor field, near Trenton, N. J.*, Am. Assoc. Adv. Sci., vol. 46, pp. 381–383.

———— (1901) *La haute ancienneté de l'homme dans l'Amérique du Nord*, L'Anthropologie, vol. 12, pp. 297–339.

Winchell, N. H. (1902) *The Lansing skeleton*, Am. Geol., vol. 30, pp. 189–194.

203

—————— (1903) *The Pleistocene geology of the Concannon farm, near Lansing, Kansas*, Am. Geol., vol. 31, pp. 263–308.

—————— (1911) *The aborigines of Minnesota*, Minnesota Hist. Soc., 761 pages.

—————— (1913) *The weathering of aboriginal stone artifacts*, Minnesota Hist. Soc., Coll., vol. 16, part 1, 186 pages.

—————— (1917) *The antiquity of man in America compared with Europe*, Minnesota Acad. Sci., Bull., vol. 5, no. 3, pp. 121–151.

Winship, George Parker (1896) *The Coronado expedition, 1540–1542*, U.S. Bur. Am. Ethnol., 14th Ann. Rept., pp. 329–613.

Wissler, Clark (1916) *The present status of the antiquity of man in North America*, Sci. Mo., vol. 2, pp. 234–238.

Witte, Adolph H. (1942) *Channelled points from Clear Fork sites in North Texas*, Texas Arch. and Paleont. Soc., Bull., vol. 14, pp. 27–31.

Witter, F. M. (1892) *Arrow points from the loess* (abstract), Sci., n.s., vol. 19, p. 22.

Woodbury, George (1937) *In* Roberts, F. H. H., Jr. (1937a), pp. 175–176.

Woodward, Arthur (1922) *A supposed ancestral man in North America*, Nature, vol. 109, no. 2745, p. 750.

—————— (1935) *Recent progress in the study of early man*, Sci., n.s., vol. 82, no. 2131, pp. 399–407.

—————— (1937) *Atlatl dart foreshafts from the La Brea pits*, Southern California Acad. Sci., Bull., vol. 36, pp. 41–60.

Wormington, H. M. (1948) *A proposed revision of Yuma point terminology*, Colorado Mus. Nat. Hist., Pr., vol. 18, no. 2.

—————— (1949) *Ancient man in North America*, Denver Mus. Nat. Hist., Popular Series, no. 4, 3d ed., 198 pages.

Wright, A. A. (1893) *Older drift in the Delaware Valley*, Am. Geol., vol. 11, pp. 184–186.

Wright, F. E. (1912) *See* Hrdlicka, Ales, and others (1912).

Wright, G. F. (1883) *An attempt to estimate the age of the palaeolithic-bearing gravels in Trenton, New Jersey*, Boston Soc. Nat. Hist., Pr., vol. 21, pp. 137–147.

—————— (1888a) *On the age of the Ohio gravel beds*, Boston Soc. Nat. Hist., Pr., vol. 23, pp. 427–436.

—————— (1888b) *Pre-glacial man in Ohio*, Ohio Arch. and Hist. Soc., Pub., vol. 1, pp. 257–259.

BIBLIOGRAPHY

———— (1890) *The ice age in North America and its bearings upon the antiquity of man*, 2d ed., New York, D. Appleton and Co., pp. 506–571.

———— (1892) *Man and the glacial period*, in Intern. Sci. Series, vol. 69, New York, D. Appleton and Co., pp. 242–301.

———— (1893) *Evidences of glacial men in Ohio*, Popular Sci. Monthly, vol. 43, pp. 29–39.

———— (1898) *Special explorations in the implement-bearing deposits on the Lalor farm, Trenton, N. J.*, Am. Assoc. Adv. Sci., Pr., vol. 46, pp. 355–364.

———— (1903) *In* Winchell, N. H. (1903), pp. 294–295.

———— (1911) *Glacial man at Trenton, N. J.*, Records of the Past, vol. 10, pp. 273–282.

Index

211